Theological Soundings 2

Other volumes of *Theological Soundings*
available in English:

God and Man

Edward Schillebeeckx OP

*translated by Edward Fitzgerald
and Peter Tomlinson*

Sheed and Ward · London and Sydney

First published 1969
Sheed and Ward Ltd, 33 Maiden Lane, London WC2, and
Sheed and Ward Pty Ltd, 204 Clarence Street, Sydney NSW 2000

© Sheed and Ward Ltd 1969

Nihil obstat: Leo J. Steady PhD STD *Censor*
Imprimatur: +Robert F. Joyce *Bishop of Burlington*
April 14 1969

SBN 7220 0592 X

Made and printed in Great Britain by
William Clowes and Sons Ltd, London and Beccles

Preface

There is a more and more clearly growing conviction nowadays that man's salvation comes about within his daily life "in the world," in his relationship with the strictly "secular." The negative aspect of this conviction makes itself felt in a growing resistance to any "unworldly" faith; for example, a Christianity which exists *beside* and *above* ordinary everyday life with its joys and sufferings, its fears and its hopes.

The attitude to which objection is taken—and it is one which is only gradually being overcome—is that which regarded the religious life as something cut off from ordinary human affairs in the world as though by an iron curtain. Religious people seemed to "practise" their religion in church only, or in a few prayers which they said with closed eyes, as though deliberately to exclude "the world." Only in this connection was there any talk of atonement and salvation, of the Crucifixion and the Resurrection—truths which, incidentally, the religious man really believed in this way. But apart from the extent to which it provided occasion for the making of sacrifices and the practice of virtue, "secular life," ordinary human relationships, remained outside this world of faith. There was no feeling for the world as such, no sensing of its problems. The result, perhaps not deliberate, was that earthly matters were left in the hands of those who proclaim themselves unbelievers. And if they did have to turn their attention to this earth, this practical, tangible world of mankind, religious people tended primarily to see only its alienation from God—war, hatred, envy, tension, sensuality, the abuse of power, broken human lives and social evils.

As a reaction to this basic attitude there is a tendency nowadays—and with what vehemence it is sometimes expressed!—to insist that religion is not an ideological superstructure based on our human and worldly relationships, and that at the same time it is not a hothouse plant which can flourish only if it is protected against the frosts of this world. The wall built around religion as an isolated sphere is now being razed on all sides. This resistance to segregation and to a Christianity and Catholicism isolated from the rest of the world is becoming increasingly typical of contemporary religious feeling. Christians are sincerely striving to include ordinary human affairs and secular matters in the orbit of their religion; for example, the growing unity of the world, the emancipation of the emergent countries, world peace, and the organization of a worthwhile society for all men. The modern religious man regards all these things as the material which allows him to give tangible form to his faith, in which he can express it in as natural and sincere a fashion as possible.

This new religious attitude to the world also expresses itself in an objection to the use of any specifically religious. language, and a particular point is made of using ordinary, everyday, "profane" language in order to express religious feelings in words derived from profound human experience. Many people are looking for a Christianity which is no longer specifically ecclesial, or even Christian, but which makes itself felt, unobtrusively perhaps but effectively all the same, in all spheres of human life.

Naturally this tendency involves a difficulty in coming to terms with the Church and matters relating to the Church insofar as they actually come into contact with them. Sociological inquiries have shown that even among the many who are no longer "practising" Christians there is still a belief in God's existence as the basis of human existence, and even in the man Jesus as an expression of the love of God for mankind. However, such people find it impossible to allow any place in their lives for the Church as it is in the concrete. They reject "the Church" unless the word "Church" is taken to mean a community amongst men; unless, in other words, it is merely the religious form for what human solidarity and brotherhood amongst men should mean in the world. There is thus unquestionably a strong tendency towards a form of Christianity without a "Church" and a threat that it will be replaced by the idea of human solidarity.

Thus when we examine the present situation from two aspects we can observe two related tendencies: in the Church of Christ there is a move towards secularization, while in mankind and in the world there is a counter-"ecclesial" tendency. In the next three, closely related, parts of the series entitled "Theological Soundings" we propose to present a number of already published articles relating to this twofold tendency.

In a first book we deal in particular with the relationship between God and man. In a second book we propose to deal with the relationship between religion in general and the Christian religion in particular. In a third book we shall deal with the fundamental principles of "Christian secularism" and certain of its practical applications.

In the present book, *God and Man,* we propose to clarify the fundamental principles which, in the opinion of the author, govern the practical problems involved.

E. SCHILLEBEECKX, O.P.

Nijmegen

Abbreviations

AAS	*Acta Apostolicae Sedis,* Rome 1909ff.
Bijd.	*Bijdragen,* Maastricht
DS	H. Denzinger, *Enchiridion Symbolorum,* ed. Adolf Schönmetzer, Freiburg 1965[33]
DV	*Dieu Vivant,* Paris 1945ff.
LV	*Lumière et Vie,* Lyons 1951ff.
NRT	*Nouvelle Revue Théologique,* Louvain 1925ff.
NTT	*Ned. Theol. Tijdschrift*
PL	*Patrologiae Cursus completus, Series Graeca,* ed. J. P. Migne, Paris 1844f.
Schol.	*Scholastik,* Freiburg 1926ff.
ST	St. Thomas Aquinas, *Summa Theologiae*
TGL	*Tijdschrift voor Geestelijk Leven*
TP	*Tijdschrift voor Philosophie,* Louvain 1929ff.
TT	*Tijdschrift voor Theologie*
VS	*La Vie Spirituelle*

Contents

Contents

GOD AND MAN

1 God in Dry Dock

I am well aware that the title I have chosen for this first
chapter is blasphemous. To be in "dry dock" is an expression
originally used of a ship which needed such extensive repairs
that it had to be withdrawn from service and put in a position
in which its underwater parts could be examined at leisure;
by extension it came to apply to anything that had become
problematical and thus needed to be set aside for examina-
tion, and perhaps revision. The justification for using the
expression here with regard to God is that it suggests precisely what a lot of people are thinking. If the title chosen
had been "The Idea of God in Dry Dock," it would have
reflected the present-day situation even more accurately. But
modern man is not greatly enamoured of ideas. He prefers
realities, and it is just these realities which represent his
problem. Well, what is the situation where modern man is
concerned?

1. For one thing, modern man is more aware than were
any of his ancestors of his secular task in this world, and in
striving to accomplish it he feels independent and very much
on his own; hence he is often inclined to feel that religion is
a specious hypothesis, and in any case a useless one. In fact
we even hear it suggested that religion is a hypothesis which
is becoming more and more clearly untenable as time goes
on. Surely, the argument runs, as man obtains a more and
more profound understanding of life and the world around
him, the ideological religious background fades away in a

3

constantly diminishing perspective, so that ultimately it will reach vanishing point and disappear into thin air. Our scientifically slanted age seems to encourage this presumed disappearance of a religion whose shortcomings have been so exposed. In the natural sciences—sociology, psychology, depth psychology, and, finally, philosophy—and, indeed, in all other spheres, the spirit of man has gradually advanced into those formerly hidden domains whose obscure inaccessibility for the human mind was once regarded as identical with the mystery in which God came into tangible contact with the world. But nowadays, for every step forward man takes, God has to take a step backwards.[1]

The whole process began, of course, in ancient times. Primitive man knew nothing at all about the direct causes of thunder and lightning, of fertility in the Nile valley, of inundations, of sulphur springs—or of life, sickness and death. Because he was ignorant of the causes of these things he believed that good or evil spirits were directly at work in the background in all such matters. In consequence it became what one might call lifemanship on his part to establish a favourable relationship between himself and these higher and more powerful beings. But in the course of time man gradually came into possession of the secrets behind these enigmas, and after that he was inclined to thank the spirits for services rendered and dismiss them for good. This was only a first farewell, however; the process was to go on in human history until the Great Spirit himself was compelled to beat a step-by-step retreat. Again and again "he" was seen to lose ground, first in one sphere and then in another.

However, it then turned out (and this has happened again and again) that there was still some point, somewhere or other in the world, which confronted the mind of man with mystery, so that scope was left for the continued existence of the Great Spirit.

[1] See the next chapter, "The Search for the Living God."

But our own day has ended even this—at least, that is what very many people seem to think. Modern man is observing the phenomenon of a constantly retreating God, and the shouts of exultation which go up from the unbelievers exceed in volume even that first triumphant shout that went up in the nineteenth century, recording the death of God. Some people here and there still believe, of course, but the trumpet has already sounded and it has given forth no uncertain note —fundamentally the retreat of God on all fronts is an accomplished fact. For example, the passage of the first Sputnik through space was reported in the Russian press as a sort of gleeful demonstration of God's complete débâcle and the official certificate of his definitive death. The fact that some people nevertheless persist in believing in God is put down to their inability to realize that the historical process of expansion in man's knowledge and experience is identical with the gradual shrinking of God's domain. Such people rely on the many problems of life and matter which still remain mysterious and reassure themselves with the thought that there is obviously still room in the world for God, that there is still a place in which his house stands foursquare. It is conceived as a sort of final line of defence; his domicile into which no human hand or eye, no human mind, can ever penetrate, however precise and accurate the scientific apparatus at its disposal. At world exhibitions dedicated to the humanity of man one still finds a "pavilion of God." The unbeliever looks down commiseratingly on such anachronistic ideas and deplores the backwardness and ignorance of people who fail to recognize the continuing dynamic of scientific progress and make themselves a God to fill the gaps in their knowledge. They are like the peasants who believed in God and got their priest to flourish the holy-water sprinkler over the fields to ensure a good harvest. Don't they really know that "since the invention of artificial fertilizers" peasants no longer need the holy-water sprinkler and have therefore lost any sense of the

Church? And the harvests still arrive on time as usual. Let's be reasonable: those problems which are admittedly still unsolved in the world will, in principle, find their solution as science progresses still further, developing all its practical possibilities for the creation and management of a secular order which will be truly human, intellectually and physically. God has already vacated the fields, and things are improving on their own. Social welfare is now in the hands of science, and in a few years scientific planning and technological achievements have done more for the sick, the poor and the aged than "religious works of charity" managed to do in centuries. Where zealous missionaries bumble around—and have done so for ages—trying to improve the lives of backward peoples, scientific institutions under the aegis of governments work wonders in a very short space of time. God has therefore become a useless hypothesis. The world is really and truly in the hands of man—it is his field of action. No God is necessary to improve the scientific apparatus man has at his disposal.

Fine, but what about man himself? Where does he come from? Does he perhaps come from God after all? At this point atheistic philosophy proposes to demolish the last refuge of the believer: It is true that I am alive without having asked to be born; that I am living in a world for whose existence I bear no responsibility. But at least I am living in it as a free man, and this freedom may give life in this world a meaning and make it worthy of human beings. We must create the values which alone can make such a worthwhile human existence possible. It all depends on human freedom, and on that alone. It may well be that this secular mission will never be quite satisfactorily accomplished; that it is, in fact, a Sisyphean task. No matter. In that case it is the duty of man to accept this risk courageously, with his eyes open to all that it involves. Even when it cannot see beyond the horizon, human freedom must dare to tackle even what is preposterous and apparently hopeless. Where man is too fainthearted to accept this worldly task freely and gladly, along with all its sometimes heartbreaking consequences, he is betraying his own nature as man—that is to say, as a free man in an uncertain world. To postulate a divine providence which must in the last resort eliminate all risk and lead everything to a good conclusion for those who love God is to seek a cowardly solution. Belief in the supernatural and in the suprahistorical is the final remnant of a certain attitude towards life in which man does not dare to tackle life for himself and therefore projects a solution of the historical mystery into the hereafter—into eternity—since he lacks the courage to accept its significance and face the fact that its problems defy solution.

Following on the above arguments the idea of God has been declared an offence to human dignity, an excuse for clinging to the past and for tolerating economic, social and political anarchy.[2] And indeed we must ask ourselves seriously whether the alleged "cultural inertia"[3] on the part of believers is not an evident fact among us today. Isn't it a fact that "the reactionaries" are found chiefly among religious people? And hasn't atheism perhaps got a point when it calls on the evidence of history to show that believers use their beliefs as an excuse for their own sloth and timidity and their refusal to face the urgent problems of the day courageously?

[2] For a searching inquiry from the existentialist point of view in which the cowardice involved in religious flight from the world is opposed to the courage found in atheism, see the following: Simone de Beauvoir, "Pour une morale de l'ambiguité," in *Les Temps Modernes* 2 (1946), 193–211, and 3 (1947), 846–874; also "L'existentialisme et la sagesse des nations," *ibid.* 1 (1945), 385–404. F. Jeanson, *Le problème moral et la pensée de Sartre* (Coll. Pensée et Civilisation), Paris 1947, and "Athéisme et liberté," in *LV* 13 (1954), 85–96. M. Merleau-Ponty, *Sense and Non-Sense,* trans. Hubert L. Dreyfus and Patricia Allen Dreyfus, Evanston, Ill., Northwestern University Press, 1964.

[3] See also L. J. Rogier, *Het verschijnsel der culturele inertie bij de Nederlandse katholieken,* Amsterdam 1958. See also note 6.

Aren't we constantly being reminded of the fact that, with
all due respect to one or two minor pioneering attempts, the
others were always ahead of us when it came to doing something practical—relieving, for example, the wretched condition of working people in the nineteenth century? And
wasn't it only when we were shamed into action by their
efforts that we believers finally and hesitantly made some
attempt to join in? In addition, of course, the reproaches
about Galileo are still with us. Even nowadays it still looks as
though religious people are nervously fearful of anything
that looks like progress in scientific, psychological, economic,
social and political affairs.

2. For our part we must seriously ask ourselves whether
it wasn't the believers themselves who brought atheism into
being—not by their beliefs, of course, but by their distorted
interpretation of those beliefs. And there we have it: it was
through their erroneous ideas about God that believers gave
atheism its real chance. However, we should not overlook the
implication of this: that atheism is nothing other than a rejection of those erroneous ideas about God and a condemna-
tion of a Christianity which is not being systematically lived
and experienced. In short, the real atheists are probably not
always to be found where we think we have encountered
them. Because of all this it has frequently been pointed out
that perhaps present-day atheism is, after all, a merciful dispensation, a new chance for salvation offered us by God, a
chance to purify our beliefs of all the human dross and all
the selfish distortions inevitably involved in any attempt to
ensure ourselves a quiet life.

The fact that man was created by the living God means
that he is constantly receiving himself from God; that he is
real in himself, firmly fixed in his own inviolable independence, and nevertheless wholly from, in and of God both in his
thought and his will and his essential existence in this world.
I find myself in this mysterious state and I am unable to

extricate myself from it: on the one hand I am really and truly myself; I stand freely and courageously in this world and take my life in my own hands, arranging it according to what I in my freedom choose to set as my aim in life, thus becoming more and more myself. On the other hand, in this whole being I am at the same time, and into the finest warp and woof of my being, wholly from God, from whom I derive myself and by whom I am constantly given to myself. In this dependence on God I am nevertheless myself; that is to say, a being who possesses the power of taking his life freely into his own hands. Our whole life is lived within the vast sphere of the personal God who embraces us. It is therefore pointless to seek him in isolation *somewhere* in this world.

The world is *in* him. "In him we live, move and have our being." We have been inclined to seek an understandable and a tangible God with a resting place somewhere in this world as one of the many amongst the finite things around us. In consequence, when we found ourselves faced with an insoluble riddle we were inclined to suppose that we had come near to God's dwelling place. Or we sought after a God who would dry human tears, a God who would eliminate the risks attendant on our exposed existence in this world, alleviate our gloomy expectations and remove our insecurity. We have seen this sort of thing happening in our immediate environment only too often. Haven't believers "enlightened" by "the Fatima prophecy"—or, rather, misled by a distorted interpretation of it—relied supinely on what was going to happen in the mysterious year 1960, which was to bring such wonders to the world? They fail to realize that the only surprises are those which result from human free will in the world and its power to bring events about, or perhaps from natural forces not yet fully under man's control. The fact that believers put their trust in God is not what brings grist to the atheist mill, but that in the meantime they neglect their secular duty and their worldly tasks. They sit back and

wait for the year 1960, which seems so full of promise. And
nothing happens but the events which result from their own
slothful neglect. No, the real mystery of God lies in the fact
that with his world man lives *in* God—in a godly or an un-
godly fashion. The trouble is that man keeps on looking for
a God who will provide him with insurance against the in-
justices of this world, a God who, bypassing man's free will,
would be prepared to intervene in the affairs of this world
to ensure man's personal safety. We forget that our freedom
to bring about events in this world is the revelation of God's
action, and that this revelation is a charge imposed on our
free will. We constantly seek God where he is not to be
found, and for this reason unbelievers hold that believers
themselves provide proof that God does not exist. But our
belief in the existence of God should be a conviction, a divine
certainty that our free, responsible and resolute behaviour in
this world is secure in him who is Life. When scientific progress closes all the ways along which we thought we could
come into contact with God somewhere in this world, in
much the same fashion as we come into contact with the
world itself, then all it is doing is to close off the approaches
to a finite God, a non-God.

It is the paths which in any case lead into a blind alley
which are thus being closed; and then, on the basis of an
existence for which we bear no responsibility and in the
midst of a limitless and problematical world, we suddenly
realize that what we experience as deathly emptiness is only
the breadth and depth of God's immeasurable inwardness.
The fact that we can lose God in everything means equally
that we can find him in everything too. The way to God leads
straight through our ordinary everyday life and work. Our
darkness, the chill darkness of our human loneliness in a
world to which we—and we alone—must in our freedom give
significance, is nothing but God's presence in unobtrusive
activity. If we have the impression that this world and our

human existence in it is in itself already sufficiently enlightened and needs no divine light, this merely comes from the
fact that we, with our world, are living *in* God, whose approach casts no shadows. We stand in his light. Our being
in this world is his light. The blind alley in which we live
is itself the limitlessness of God, and therefore to search for
ways in which we can find him *somewhere* will lead us away
from him, since he is already with us. And yet again and
again we feel this desire to seek him elsewhere, but when we
try our hands grasp only the empty air and we hear behind
us the loud laughter of the atheist. The air we grasp is empty
because God is omnipresent.

Perhaps the prompt retreat of God each time man makes a
step forward in his history really shows us that it is only a
pseudo-God which fades away, and not the living God under
whose protection man has just made this very step forward.
Again and again he walks one step further with us; and together, God and ourselves, we dislodge the pseudo-God.

3. But does this mean that the living God is then only
an immeasurable and incomprehensible God? Can we never
point our finger at him in this world and say confidently:
"There is God"?

When the children cluster round the Crib at Christmas
and exclaim in delighted amazement: "Look, there's the don-
key!" "And there's the star!" "And that's one of the Three
Kings with a present!" "See the camel?" "And look, there's
Jesus!"—then the believer bows his head. . . . "And there is
God." He, the living God, knows that his immeasurable, all-
embracing, matter-of-course presence is impenetrable obscurity for his creatures, and that man therefore longs to meet
him somewhere along the way, so that he can point his finger
and hear a whisper "cold" or "warm" like children at their
games when the seeker gets nearer or goes farther away from
the place where the thing he is seeking is to be found. God
knows the human heart. The infinite and the immeasurable

have become finite in Christ Jesus. God now stands in our midst in a tangible manifestation, in a form in which we can truly bump into him. He really is there—in the house of the astute accountant Zaccheus, at Jacob's well, or up there on the mountain-top. Why, yesterday he even passed this way, but he went on to Jerusalem. He is in the temple. Or he has gone to the open country to the south of the town. He is there—on the Cross. We can fully grasp the limitlessness of God only when it draws near to us in our own limited time, when it is visible to us as a man's face is visible to us, when it is at our side in our earthly life, when it is demonstrable: as a man, but such a man as has never been seen before.

Actually the mystery of God still remains. What Christ showed us was not so much God himself, though he did this too. What he showed us above all was what a *man* is like who has declared himself to be fully committed to God, the invisible Father. He showed us the practical form of religious worship, the face of the truly religious man. And so, in a roundabout way so to speak, he also showed us what God is. His witness to God is a visible support for us. His visible, living relationship to the invisible God reveals the mystery of the true God to us. Through him we know that the Father is with him *in all things,* even in loneliness and worldly oppression—and in that loneliness which can now be the expression of an unobtrusive presence. From him we learn that regardless of the extent to which the world is governed by natural and historical laws and the free will of men, all its events are in the fatherly hands of God, so that no sparrow falls outside his wise dispensation—even the hairs on our heads are numbered. The world in which we live and the tasks our freedom in it imposes on us thus become a dialogue with the living God, an invitation challenging us to face the world in a freedom secure by its unity with him. In this man Jesus we can see how a dialogue relationship is possible between God and man, and that this prayer represents the profoundest meaning of life. In this way we can become aware of the finger of God in all the happenings of life, and there is even room in life for the demonstrable miracle.

But in Christ we can also see that the world has been entrusted to the hands of man, that man himself must see to it that this world is put into good order. We can also see that if this is to be done it is not enough for us to put on our Sunday clothes and pray like the Pharisees while injustice goes unchecked in the world. Christ laid the basis for a new attitude towards life. Man's dialogue with the world can attain its full significance only in his dialogue with God. Life in the world (how very much inclined we are to call it "profane" life) then becomes an *aspect* of the integral religious attitude. The recognition of secular reality becomes a subordinate part of this integral religious attitude, because the *Creator* of the universe and of man in the world is God and the Father of our Lord Jesus Christ. With this the cultural inertia of believers is condemned in principle as a lack of consistent Christianity. From this point of view what has been called "laicization," or secularization, is actually very much at home in Christianity and in the Church; it is an event within the life of God's people. In themselves these words are ambiguous, but their Christian significance lies in the obligation imposed on the faithful, consciously secure in God, to arrive within their dialogue with God at an honest view of the world and a recognition of their task in it. Objectively speaking, the exclusively profane or atheistic laicization is merely a *hairesis,* a separation of secular reality from the whole to which it belongs: namely, the faithful existential relationship to the living God. It is only outside this relationship that the secular becomes "profaned."[4] Thus a belief in God is no longer an excuse for indifference to man's earthly dwelling place and a lack of

[4] This matter is investigated more fully in Chapter 4, "Life in God and Life in the World."

interest in the building up of a society worthy of humanity.
On the other hand, this belief does not provide us with "instant" solutions. Solutions are not there for the taking just
because we are believers—not even in relation to the problems of good and evil. Seeking and striving, and living in
contact with God's holiness in his Church, the Christian must
work for the good and the true through the historicity of his
own earthly life. Solutions will not fall into our laps.[5] Moral
standards are the fruit of laborious reconnaissance expedi-
tions. They have not been inscribed clearly on a tablet for
man as in Cecil de Mille's film, *The Ten Commandments*.
The believer has to seek for solutions of world problems
amidst all kinds of doubts and in constantly changing historical situations. Competence and courage are no less necessary
for the believer than they are for the unbeliever. However,
the believer's efforts are not made in isolation; he has heard:
"I am never alone. The Father is always with me." These
words of Christ represent the deepest meaning of man's sincere seeking and concern in life, and here indeed his faith
and his love open up perspectives for him. But only study,
knowledge and a real dialogue with the world will provide
him with the practical solutions which the earthly life of
humanity demands. But, granting all this, it is the Spirit of
Christ who will suggest to his "saints in the world" which
amongst the various practical possibilities is the best that can
be adopted in the here and now. In practical matters the

[5] By our mistaken ideas of Christian morality we have only too often laid
ourselves open to reproach from atheists: "If God exists, then perfection has
already been achieved outside this world; since perfection cannot be increased,
there is, strictly speaking, nothing to do" (M. Merleau-Ponty, *Sense and
Non-Sense*, trans. Hubert L. Dreyfus and Patricia Allen Dreyfus, Evanston,
Ill., Northwestern University Press, 1964, p. 74); or they compare a resolute
seeking with a false possession: "Ce qui définit tout humanisme, c'est que le
monde moral n'est pas *un monde donné*, étranger à l'homme et auquel
celui-ci devrait s'efforcer d'accéder du dehors; c'est le monde voulu par
l'homme. . . ." (Simone de Beauvoir, "Pour une morale de l'ambiguité,"
art. cit., p. 199).

attitude of the saints in this world will always include something which tradition calls "charisma"—the divine impulsion towards whatever is necessary at a given moment. And in this core of their attitude is the secret of the inner dialogue with God.

It looks as if this holiness of the genuinely human man in the midst of the world were going to become the great charisma of the future, ushering in a period of lay sanctity. The responsibility of the layman for this world must be the source of a new kind of holiness lighting up the darkness. Our world needs such latter-day saints: saints who carry the dogma of creation into practice instead of leaving the ordering of secular affairs in the hands of unbelievers, abandoning it to the profane atheistic world. The affairs of the Church are not merely matters which interest the ecclesiastical hierarchy exclusively. They also embrace whatever emerges from God's faithful people as the fruit of their eucharistic community of grace with Christ: the visible presence of grace. This holiness, the holiness of the Church as man's salvation in a visible historical form, must be present in this world in and through the Catholic laity too. The faithful laity are part of "the sign which is set up amongst the nations" through which the world can see that there is something worthwhile about this community which calls itself the Church of Christ. Man's worldly task must have its place in the affairs of the Church, and not be merely the result of some chance proficiency or personal predilection. The laity are in the world as part of God's wide creation, part of the creation of the living God, the God of our salvation. As Rahner, Guardini and others have repeatedly pointed out, good intentions alone are not enough here. Objective accuracy, competence and the scientific approach, the dialogue with the world—everything, in fact, which the nature of our task in the present world demands of us—must be included in this religious "good intention." All this is the secular form of the Christian good intention. This is the only way in which the Christian dogma of creation can be taken in its full seriousness.

4. But this Christian "secularity" merges into the mystery of faith, and that is always a gift of God—even its object. All things become important in intimacy with God, including the common task; and, in the preservation of goodness, this remains important. However, this does not mean that we see how this is so. Although we cannot see its ultimate significance, we keep resolutely on. At least, atheists cannot charge us with desertion here. We too are working in the dark, and this means that lay holiness must be sustained by an inner realization of the gratuity—the character as grace—of this religious secular task too. This further presupposes that within this same Church there must be a vital organ to bear witness to this holiness in a form which will make its transcendence to this world clearly visible: namely, the life of the evangelical counsels. The existence of these two Christian forms of life in the Church as two specialized aspects of the *one* Christian life will ensure on the one hand that the Christian task in the world shall not be distorted into a pseudo-religious world optimism, and on the other that the eschatological way of life of the "state of perfection" shall remain the expression of a transcendental appraisal of secular values.

5. We may conclude that the secularization of the world and the phenomenon of the churchless masses which goes with it represent, in some cases at least, an unmistakable sliding towards atheism. We are faced with a "truth gone astray," and at the moment the world is bemused by it. But today's churchlessness might easily be a preliminary phase leading to a purged and renewed Church of the future.[6] In

6 Quite a number of voices have been raised in recent years to point out that churchlessness should not simply be equated with Godlessness, that it might well be a transitional stage leading to a new vision of the Church. See I. Rosier, *I Looked for God's Absence*, New York, Sheed and Ward, 1959; I. Gadourek, *Cultuuraan-vaarding en cultuurontwijking*, Groningen 1958, and P. Smits, *Op zoek naar nihilisme*, Assen 1959.

any case, we must not blind ourselves by staring too hard
at the dangers of the new social reality in which we are living, wholly genuine though they are. The new possibilities
which the situation opens up are equally worthy of our attention. We may well find that the "laicization" of our modern world, in which God is regarded as a useless hypothesis,
will serve to clear the ground, and that then, thanks to the
leaven of true Christianity, the ancient and apparently dying
belief in God can reawaken in a purified form and arrive at
the shape of the future, which will always belong to God.

2 The Search for the Living God

Theology, which claims God himself as its subject, has every reason to be modest nowadays, since everywhere his non-existence is proclaimed as an almost existential experience.[1] As a result we are compelled to circumscribe more exactly the area in which theology, as faith which has become science, establishes contact with the reality of God.

At one time there was a naive assumption that the unknown was equivalent to this reality. Whenever science came up against a barrier and found its advance halted by something incomprehensible people were immediately inclined to bring in the name of God. Because the natural sciences and man's knowledge of his own psyche were not particularly far advanced this sort of thing happened frequently; and as

[1] From the copious literature on this subject we refer the reader to the following books and articles: L. Casserley, *De ontkerstening van de moderne wereld*, Bruges 1954; H. Urs von Balthasar, *De moderne mens op zoek naar God*, Bruges 1957; K. Rahner, *Christendom en Kerk in onze tijd*, Bruges 1955, and *Wissenschaft als "Konfession"?* in *Schriften zur Theologie III*, Einsiedeln 1956, pp. 455–472. Also to be consulted, on atheism: F. Jeanson, "Athéisme et liberté," in *LV* 13 (1954), 85–96; J. Lacroix, "Sens et valeur de l'athéisme actuel," in *Esprit* 22 (1954), 167–191; M. Merleau-Ponty, *In Praise of Philosophy*, Evanston, Ill., 1963; G. Siegmund, *Der Kampf um Gott*, Berlin 1957; P. Rostenne, *La foi des athées*, Paris 1953; A. Etcheverry, *Le conflit actuel des humanismes*, Paris 1955; R. Jolivet, "Le problème de l'Absolu dans la philosophie de M. Merleau-Ponty," in *TP* 19 (1957), 53–100; J. Maritain, *La signification de l'athéisme contemporain*, Paris-Bruges 1949; A. Dondeyne, *Foi chrétienne et pensée contemporaine*, Leuven 1951; H. de Lubac, *The Drama of Atheist Humanism*, New York 1950; *Monde moderne et sens de Dieu* (Semaine des intellectuels catholiques 1953), Paris 1954.

the unknown was equated with God—though perhaps not primarily by the scientists themselves—in accordance with the custom of the time God was very much in the center of man's thought. But with the great progress of science and technology in our own day what was formerly put down to God is now more and more ascribed to mundane causes. A well-known humanist, Doctor J. P. van Praag, has observed— not particularly felicitously perhaps, and even somewhat un-academically—that unchurchedness has increased "since the invention of artificial fertilizers."[2]

Now this perspective of the coming of age of science un-doubtedly explains the decrease of a certain need for God, even if it is not in itself sufficient to invalidate the need itself. This laicization of science may be regarded as a good thing for religion, since by definition God is a reality which evades the exact sciences. Even the unknown in science can never be equated with God.

Moreover, formerly God was quite often regarded as a function of our human life. Man was not regarded as stand-ing in a religious relationship to God, but the other way round. God, in fact, was reduced to the status of an idol in the service of man. God and his Church were expected to provide what science and technology are now in a position to provide abundantly: a more comfortable and materially happier life on this earth, and a society worthy of human be-ings. Nowadays the world can provide itself with all this, thanks to its own technological progress, and quite obviously it can do so far more generously than the prayers of former times ever could. It is therefore not surprising that there are many people who feel that we no longer need God. Despite this, the process of laicization is a good thing. To take the domain of psychology, where, for example, the mentally de-

[2] This is a lecture given at the Nederlands Gesprek Centrum in Oosterbeek, February 7th and 8th, 1958. (A short account of the proceedings is in *De Tijd*, February 10, 1958, p. 4.)

ranged can be helped more effectively by the psychiatrist than
they can by the priest, this particular form of laicization helps
to remove the clutter from the real sphere in which the
search for God must be situated.

And this is not all. Looking back in history, we can find
repeated examples of how a measure of humanitarianism
originally due to religion, and arising in the first place from
religious conviction, is transferred to the world, and there,
naturally, laicized. An obvious example: when his consciousness was still young and vestigial man did not sense that a
sick person had a right to be looked after and cared for by
society. This sensitivity arose out of religion; evangelical love
took pity on the weak. The evangelical spirit compensated
for the lack of moral human insight. Nowadays the situation
is altogether different: people regard it as a matter of course
that society and its state should concern themselves with such
matters. In other words, we have arrived at a stage in which
Christian charity has been secularized; and in its laicized
form it has now struck deep roots into human consciousness
—so much so that social welfare takes on the form of an inalienable human right. What formerly sprang from Christian
charity as a work of benevolence has become such an everyday affair in our own time that people regard it as a normal
human right. In its secularized form this part of what was
formerly Christian charity is now known as "social justice."
Thus what was done at one time by the religious man out of
his religious philanthropy is being progressively translated to
the profane, the human sphere, where, laicized and humanized, it continues to exist under a new and more worldly
name.

This particular form of laicization edges religion out of a
certain essentially worldly sphere, but this is not necessarily
a bad thing, or in itself a loss. On the contrary, we can even
regard it as a definite gain, as a fruit of the redemption. This

translation of values means no more than that this or that profoundly human outlook, or way of life, which was at one time necessarily the fruit of a religious belief in God, has now grown beyond the sphere of the Church and has become a generally acknowledged human achievement. Redeeming grace, the theme of Christianity, has become a secular reality in Christ and his Church; it has spread, and is still spreading, in all directions. It has influenced Western thought and behaviour for centuries. The specific consequences of the evangelical spirit which appeared miraculous and unparalleled twenty centuries ago have been so thoroughly socialized, so interiorized in the secular world-outlook of mankind, that the profoundly humane pronouncements of the staunchest modern atheist concerning love and justice towards his fellow human beings would be unthinkable without the historical premise of Christianity—on which, in the meantime, man is turning his back. Secularized it remains a boon for humanity, even for Christianity as such. For this secularization means only that the core of religiousness lies *elsewhere*, although it will always be expressed in our worldly life. This suggests also that when we believers acknowledge the requirements of social justice, in our present situation this does not yet mean that we are exercising Christian charity. The more intensively this secularization is carried out, the stronger the evangelical demands on our lives will become and the more radiant the true face of Christian holiness, because the religious background against which formerly these supplementary functions became understandable cannot itself be secularized. What the world assimilates from the religious life, and then often carries out in a secularized form better and more efficiently than religion could formerly, when modern technical means were simply not available, is in the last resort something that secular mankind ought to have found out for itself, but which, because of the very slow and gradual development of its consciousness, and above all because of its naturally unregenerate nature, it actually reached only in the light of religious experience.

In all this, secularization, and in this sense the absence of God, represents a plus rather than a minus factor. It does no more than indicate the worldly maturity of modern man, who has taken the ordering of this secular sphere into his own hands. When the supplementary functions of religion in the world gradually fall away altogether (though there is a certain element of utopianism about this perspective since mankind clearly chooses to remain in an unregenerate condition) the proper soil of religion in the heart of man will necessarily reveal itself even more significantly. Then it will clearly be seen that in its primary intention religion is superior to all secular affairs, and that from a secular technological standpoint God is, indeed, a useless hypothesis. Man does not need God in order to find his way about in this world, and it is therefore a sphere in which modern man no longer misses God.

Even human history does not show us God. Precisely because he demonstrates his effective presence in this world in his own way, he seems to be absent. He is, after all, totally different from all experienced reality. On the natural level, we experience him precisely as the one who exceeds all experience. Man can thus reach out to God only as to someone who is absent from the normal totality of created things. The transcendent significance he gives to history is beyond any of our conceptions of human finality and purpose precisely because of its transcendence. Indeed, history strikes us as lacking sense in any human understanding of the word. This is, in fact, so much the case that history looks to us like a motley collection of arrant nonsense complicated by abrasive suffering. Thus all appearances speak against the existence of God. Our human insight finds it impossible to justify his providence. In consequence some people regard the idea of divine providence as the utmost absurdity, more absurd certainly than a flagrant denial of his existence. Where man is concerned God is powerless precisely because of the divinity of his existence, which can manifest itself only in absence. It is precisely the divine nature of his presence and his activity that makes him seem absent from us.

Whenever we try to grasp and take hold of God as an object we find ourselves still in this finite world and never in the presence of God. However, there are forms of presence which draw our attention only as the result of a certain orientation of a conscious ignorance. We are concerned with a purely personal presence which can nevertheless not be situated amongst all those other things that manifest themselves to us directly by their presence. The impossibility of our accounting for our existence ourselves, and the fundamental experience of our wholly contingent presence in this world, brings us face to face with the invisible but real mystery of a personal Giver whose heart is greater than his gifts which surround us and of which we ourselves form part. Divine liberality forms the intangible background of our inner and outer world whose reality and contingency constantly betrays its vital source, but which always stands in the gap between him and us. Only when man shows sufficient courage to see himself and the world truthfully, as a fact, as a reality thrown at his feet, as a presence in itself unexplainable, can he begin to regard this tangible presence as the evidence of a very different Presence manifesting itself in an indirect fashion therein. Only when we face the world in our simple quality as human beings—as neither *homo faber* nor *homo oeconomicus*—and approach these realities in their simple, artless truth, can we realize our secure existence in a deeper mystery of a personal absolute freedom. But to this end we must first accept the fact that truth is something more than man's eager grasp on tangible data. The natural affirmation of God's existence is no more than a critically confirmed affirmation on the basis of this world of our secure existence in the personal mystery of God, a mystery, however, that we cannot encounter on that same basis. Any arrogant attempt to seize God's presence merely confines us still more definitely in the isolation of our life in this world since it deprives us of that interiority which is secured only when we become conscious of ourselves within the security of the divine creative mystery. When God reveals his presence to us only through the act in which he founds our existence, whilst remaining transcendent even in this act,[3] this means that he is there not *because* we exist, although it is only through our own existence that we have come to realize his divine existence; it means that we are there only as a function of him. Thus the natural affirmation of God's existence is completed only in the willing surrender to the divine mystery which lies at the accepted origin of what we experience in this world. In this sense the existential experience of God's absence, combined with our own profound interest in the inner problematics of man's own existence and that of the world, represents the "experience" of our secure being in an all-embracing mystery of transcendental but personal love. In this love we would willingly take a personal part, but in the nature of things we cannot, although on the basis of the creative act through which God draws our attention, as an essential requirement of our existence, to his presence as a loving person, we already have an inner consciousness of his *appeal to surrender*.

The direct personal relationship with the divine mystery of life, and in consequence the actual religiousness in which the presence of God develops into mutuality and encounter, becomes possible, however, only when God, acting from beyond the cloud of that mystery in which we already consciously exist, completes what he began in his creative act,

3 D. De Petter, *Werkelijkheid en begrip*, Hilversum-Antwerp 1964, pp. 150–167.

and begins talking to us as one person speaks to and treats another. In the natural affirmation of God man has already come to realize that although in free relationship to the world he is not, in the last resort, of this world, though he is not on his own able to give a *personal* significance to this free relationship which transcends the world. Regarded as the absolute bedrock of human and objectively unlimited freedom, God necessarily eludes all merely human attempts at understanding. But God himself now personally accomplishes this miracle, since it is precisely at that point where man faces the world in free subjectivity that he is directly approached by the living God in order that he may rise above himself, step outside himself, and live in personal intimacy with God. This supramundane personal loneliness of human freedom is just the point at which the question of personal communion with God arises, because it is there, at the summit of his transcendence over his worldly relationship, that on the basis of God's creation, and precisely because of his freedom, man is directly attuned to the mystery of the living God, even though he is incapable of reaching it by his own resources. By its very nature, therefore, religion is a personal act of human freedom which abandons its lonely outlook and lets itself be taken up by grace into the mutuality of God's presence, and thus into the intimacy of the divine life.

But from this personal communion with the living God we must now retrace the way we have already come, since as a result of this personal communion everything now takes on a much more profound dimension. Thanks to this personal living relationship with God enabling man to step outside himself and outside his earthly relationships towards a personal God, these earthly relationships themselves are given a divine significance. They develop into signs of a closer divine presence, of a presence that develops in mutuality into a personal encounter. For the *religious* man the world of nature and history becomes a passage in his dialogue with

God. At the same time it develops into God's instructions to man, and the visible form of God's answer to human prayers.

However, the fact that the world of man's history-creative freedom is now taken into personal living relationship with God also means that within this religious relationship man makes history into salvation or into judgment. Since human freedom is the factor which gives significance to history, intramundane relationships are thus directed and determined by the intimacy in which God and man have found each other, or by the rupture which is brought about when man in his freedom denies his God. In consequence, therefore, the whole of man's profane history is transformed either by the worship of God or by the denial of his existence, since even in his apostasy man remains subject to the living God by a personal transmundane relationship to him.

Thus because it is part and parcel of the divine dialogue man's existence in this world also becomes an anonymous medium of revelation and at the same time a sphere in which religious significances are established. Everywhere, history becomes either salvation or judgment. Despite, or rather *in*, its earthly nature, it also becomes an empirical manifestation of the religious relationship to God in faith or apostasy.

Against this anonymous human religious background the particular solicitude of the living God is seen to manifest itself in the history of a certain people, the people of Israel, as a means through which to prepare his definitive coming in and through the man Jesus, and to develop its significance in the history of man. What from a mundane point of view can be regarded as a merely secular event is something quite different when it is seen from the standpoint of Israel's consciousness of salvation, and therefore as an experience of God's people—then it turns out to be the historic unfolding of a divine ordinance in which God and man appear as partners in a dialogue, since it is from this personal relationship with the living God that the Jewish people, positively or

negatively, makes its own history. From God's standpoint, on
the other hand, his creative world ordinance becomes a thematic factor of his personal call to his people for their salvation. Thus God's saving action is made manifest precisely as
an intervention in human history. God's saving action itself
is revelation—it reveals itself by becoming history, and it
shapes history by revealing itself. Here God's saving grace
exercises an absolute priority over man's freedom to shape
his own history. But at the same time active divine transcendency, which is also creative in its saving intervention,
independently embraces man's freedom to make his own
history in its providential revelation. Thus in its own specific
character, and in its earthly nature, the history of man becomes, so to speak, the material in which and through which
God prepares our salvation. In this way revelation implicitly
involves the action and reaction of the Jewish people with or
against its God. In consequence God's revelation is not a
divine monologue only to be listened to, something which,
so to speak, could be tape-recorded. The significance of
revelation comes to us only from the dialogue between God
and his people. By its nature, therefore, revelation as it un-
folds itself is something which is both invitation and reply;
it is the history of the Jewish people in a covenant relationship with God.

But it follows from this that although revelation lies primarily in the saving action of God and thus in the history of
the Jewish people, this history attains the full significance of
spoken revelation only as it is experienced in Israel's consciousness of salvation. Only on the basis of this consciousness
—namely, the knowledge that the people of Israel are God's
people—does Israel understand and interpret its history as
the action of God in the lives of its people. Revelation by
action and revelation by word are inseparable in God's providential revelation. The divine dialogue in action, which
makes history into saving or damning history, is clarified in

the words of the prophet, in whom the divine dialogue finds
its clearest reflection. The Word reveals the presence and the
significance of the saving action of God to his people. Because
it is submerged in earthly history this divine saving action
even inherently demands the complementary Word. Therefore it is only in the prophetic word, in the word of him who
hears and understands the inner voice of God in historical
events, that divine revelation comes to full consciousness
amongst the chosen people. God does not merely announce
the salvation that the Jewish people must represent for themselves and for the rest of the world; he brings it about in
history, whose significance moreover he himself must clarify
and interpret in the prophetic word. In this sense saving
history is a secular event *interpreted* in the light of the divine
dialogue.

We can no longer one-sidedly interpret, say, a breach of
the dykes on the coast of Holland simply as a judgment of
God on us. The fact is that from the data available about the
condition of the dykes, the direction of the storm wind, and
the strength of the tide we can very accurately calculate the
earthly causes of what happened and discover why it happened. By the time the engineers have finished their calcula-
tions there is no gap anywhere which God might fill to
execute his judgment on us. However, for man's freedom
before the living God this event demands an explanation,
and those who experienced it must now integrate it meaningfully into their lives. Such an integration is not brought
about by the mere enumeration of earthly causes, for they
merely describe the occurrence in itself, which was only the
occasion of the *human* problem. Within the framework of a
dialogue with the living God this situation is merely a *theme*,
and at the same time a *means,* through which God invites
man to transcend himself. Seen in a broader perspective,
history made by nature and by man according to their own
laws becomes something which is offered to man by the living

God in order that, actively and creatively, man may give it a religious significance. It is precisely by thus giving significance to their history that the Jewish people as the people of God gave shape to the Old Testament revelation.[4]

Although this Old Testament revelation has a certain independent value as a form of religious experience, nevertheless in the last resort it must be regarded as the pre-history of the Christian revelation, a historical development towards the mystery of Christ, which is itself the centre and *telos* of the whole revelation. The Old Testament story is wholly directed towards this final stage. On the historical plane it prepared the way for the coming mystery of the New Testament, since it was along the basic lines of the Old Testament revelation in dialectical relationship with the history of the Jewish people that the living God gradually made known the fundamental meaning of his providential ordinance: "I will be *your* God, and you shall be *my*

4 Here we have only touched in a schematic way on the theology of revelation, which is based, among other things, on the way in which God has revealed salvation to man: we cannot enter into its details. We must keep in mind, however, that the prophetic word is capable of interpreting not only past events (such, for example, as the Exodus) but future worldly events of which signs are already discernible. The prophetic word seizes the event and interprets it in its religious significance. So, it seems, Deutero-Isaiah as the contemporary of Cyrus has understood the latter's policy of allowing the exiles to return home, interpreting this future event as a saving intervention of Jahweh, delivering his people; hence the return home became a religious event. In this sense the prophetic word is itself history-making. It can also happen that a future fact really is foretold, so that the factual occurrence in itself can be genuinely experienced as a religious event. Furthermore it is not improbable that the word can "project" history: that is, a religious idea can be externalized in a mythical narrative. The "facts" involved are in that case not historical in the secular sense; rather, they are *themata* ("themes"), religious projections in history. They are nonetheless religious realities. (It is possible that Christ's temptations in the desert can be interpreted in this way and likewise other accounts in Holy Scripture.) Moreover, a later history (e.g. the theocratic idea of monarchy after the exile) can be projected into an earlier history (e.g. the monarchy of David). Hence the "theme" of projected religious meaning seems to me to be an important element in the construction of a "theology of revelation."

people."[5] Salvation as a typical religious category is ultimately the actual encounter between God and man in mutual trust, because man's freedom to make history his salvation comes about only in historicity. The covenant as mutual trust between God and his‑people therefore had to be translated in and through the history of that people into actually experienced reality. God's demand to his people was their unwavering trust in all circumstances. Standing in the presence of the God of the covenant, God's people had to interpret the so-called inevitabilities of life with all its ordinary but sometimes painful vicissitudes as the limits within which the living God circumscribed their duty of religious faith from day to day and from moment to moment, calling lovingly on his people in and through all this to confirm their unwavering trust in him, the God of Israel, and thus—with complete confidence in his good guidance—to do what God gave them the inner power to do, without being anxious about either the ultimate outcome or the ultimate sense of it all. They are thus called upon to surrender to the mystery of God as part of their trustful personal community with him. The Old Testament revelation as a whole is the sum of historical events arising out of divine trust on the one hand and the repeated faithlessness of Israel on the other—faithlessness relieved by a number of more favourable phases.

On the historical plane this history is, thanks to the inner power of the covenant, the beginning, so to speak, of the story of the man Jesus, since what Israel as a people failed to do is about to be brought to a definitively good end in him on whom in the messianic sense the fate of the whole of

[5] Lev. 26:11–12. *The Holy Bible, Revised Standard Version,* New York, Nelson 1946, 1952. All scriptural quotations in this book are from this version copyrighted 1946 and 1952 by the Division of Christian Education of the National Council of Churches. Cf. also Jer. 7:23; 11:4; 24:7; 31:33; Ez. 11:20; 14:11; 37:27; Hos. 1:9.

humanity now depends. God, who calls for mutual trust in
the covenant, now comes personally in the historical shape
of a man to take upon himself the answering trust of humanity in the covenant. The dialogue between God and man
which has repeatedly ground to a halt in man now finds a
human sounding board in history. The divine invitation to
trust in the covenant and the answering human trust both
take shape in one and the same person, who stands as a man
in our history; and they take shape in such a way that both
the divine invitation and the answering human trust constitute themselves fulfilled divine revelation. Thus revelation
does not come about one-sidedly even in Christ. Jesus is
essentially a dialogue with the Father, a dialogue which ena-
bles him to give significance to his human situation. In and
through his loving death as a consequence of his filial attachment to the Father, and in messianic love, this man, rising
above himself in sacrifice, dedicated his human life throughout to the Father. The specific significance of the divine
ordinance is historically fulfilled in the final story of the man
Jesus, and it is only the beginning of a new saving history
based on the mystery of Christ glorified. It is in the life of
this man that we find the alpha and omega of God's revelation and of all religiousness: it was in a visible human shape
that Christ experienced his filial relationship to God in and
through this world. The incorporation of man's intramundane relationships into the personal transmundane existence
of a child of the living God attains its utmost, so to speak its
prototypical, realization here. Thus the man Jesus is the
ultimate point of reference for all revelation, for the presence
of God, and at the same time for all religiousness, for the
mutuality of this presence. In Christ Jesus God is personally
amongst us in the full sense of the word. For us Christ is the
revelation and the presence of God; and for God the Father
he is, by the power of the Spirit, at the same time the man

in whom the presence of God develops into mutuality, to our salvation. The Church is the present-day sacrament of this reality amongst us.[6]

Thus we have now briefly indicated the various factors which combine to determine our religious orientation towards the presence of the living God. In this complex unity it is the natural experience of God's presence which forms the basis of the religious presence in mutual intimacy. In view of the mission of theology, which seeks to throw light upon this saving reality, allow me now to point out two important conclusions.

Not in spite of, but to a large extent because of and thanks to, present-day laicization and the emancipation of man's outlook we believers are discovering more clearly than ever before the true dimensions of religion and the security of our human existence in the living God, and rightly so. For the realization that we cannot make direct contact with God either in nature or in ordinary human history is not an argument in favour of atheism, but in a certain respect an expression of reverence towards God; namely, a growing recognition of the fact that God transcends this world; that God is really God, that he is wholly other than the world, and that whenever we come clearly and definitely into contact with something, this reality cannot ever be God himself. All that is there is once again the world.

But there is all the same a certain ambiguity present, since it still remains to be seen whether, when we have once fully circumscribed man's horizon within earthly limits, there can still be room for a religious attitude towards God. Unless it can already be seen from this natural, human standpoint that man, although existing in a relationship with the world, is in his real core, which is called freedom, nevertheless not of this world and cannot therefore be described simply as an

[6] We only touch upon the ecclesial aspect of the presence of God here, although it is an important one.

earthly being, then the supranatural religious orientation of man towards a God revealing himself becomes a priori utterly untenable. In other words, unless there is one, all-embracing dimension of human existence (that can nevertheless not yet be called *grace*) in which the full transcendent being, or the divine reality, is visible at the very source of human experience, then the ground is cut from under the feet of religion in life. And if we nevertheless continue to regard religion as the profoundest truth of our human existence, then by the nature of things religion will find itself in stultifying competition with human life in and of this world. Modern atheist thought recognizes this perhaps more clearly than some Christians do.[7]

It strikes me that in our present-day world of religious apostasy and atheism, which undermine the religious beliefs of both Catholic and non-Catholic Christians, the appeal to independent philosophic thought on the part of the *believer* is a matter of considerable importance for theology. If this is not taken into account, theological thought, which has so manifestly renewed itself in recent years, increasing its profundity both amongst Catholics and Protestants to the great benefit of those within the Churches, will ultimately find it-

[7] With regard to a somewhat facile pronouncement of Jacques Maritain, who tends to minimize the difficulties, M. Merleau-Ponty comments: "Indeed Maritain finally comes to justify the continuous criticism of idols as essential to Christianity. The saint, he says, is a 'complete atheist' with respect to a God who would be only the guarantor of the natural order, who would consecrate not only all the world's goodness but all the world's evil as well, who would justify slavery, injustice, the tears of children, the agony of the innocent by sacred necessities, who would finally sacrifice man to the cosmos as 'the absurd Emperor of the world.' The Christian God who redeems the world and is accessible to prayer, according to Maritain, is the active negation of all this. Here, indeed, we are close to the essence of Christianity. The philosopher will only ask himself if the natural and rational concept of God as necessary being is not inevitably that of the Emperor of the world, if without this concept, the Christian God would not cease to be the author of the world. . . ." *In Praise of Philosophy,* Evanston, Ill., Northwestern University Press, 1963, p. 47.

self ignoring that part of humanity which is drifting away
from Christianity in such numbers. And the longer this process goes on, the more practising Christians will be drawn into
it. Granted that in recent years theological enthusiasm for
saving history has renewed the religious life of believers,
nevertheless in the present situation theology would re-
nounce its apostolic mission if it were not at the same time
capable of more philosophic thought. The two big religious
bodies, Catholic and Protestant, are conducting an ecumenical dialogue, but a constantly growing number of human
beings—enough to represent a real force—are going their
own worldly way, with the result that Christianity is being
pushed out of everyday public life onto what can only be
regarded as a siding. The present situation of humanity
therefore requires that theological thought should do more
than institute an inter-Christian ecumenical dialogue; what
is also needed is a dialogue with the vast world of atheism; or
rather, to put it more accurately, with the exponents of that
form of religiousness, so widespread today, whose outlook is
purely of this world. Included in this is religion without God,
a posture which seems all the more attractive because it is
courageous and intensely sincere—"authentic." It may have
its source in an ineradicable loneliness; nevertheless it strives
to the best of its ability in human solidarity, justice and love
to give life meaning by a creative commitment to an absurd
world, thus at least radiating, on a purely human basis, a little
love in one's immediate vicinity.

However, it is not only the apostolic mission of theology
which invites us to include secular thought, the way of thinking deriving from man in this world, in its own gospel
thinking. The fully personal character of our faith itself in
confrontation with the most important phenomenon of our
time, namely religious apostasy and atheism, also demands
that religious thought should include secular thought in its
reflections on the mystery of our salvation. Because we wish

to live our Christian belief personally and freely, because we wish to think it personally, and desire in our religiousness to remain sincere towards the real problem of those who think differently—atheistically—this personal honesty and the free personal character of the religious act demand more than ever, and more urgently than ever, that we should resume the critical investigation of what is called *praeambula fidei;* that is to say, of the human person as a constitutive and at the same time important demand for religiousness. Unless there is some way or other in which the mundane problems of our existence as human beings in this world themselves raise the eschatological problem, God's kingdom in all its transcendency cannot satisfactorily adjust itself to the phenomenon of human freedom. Then saving history becomes an inherent contradiction, and the same is true of the idea of revelation itself. Further, the kingdom of God cannot then possibly be the breakthrough of divine salvation into our world. It is not that revelation and belief can offer us a solution on the plane of our secular life, and thus in the sphere of philosophy, but certainly that in the last resort earthly problems must, as a result of secular thought itself, imply a surrender to the mystery.

Man can only assimilate this mystery in his life, whenever it is revealed to him in grace, because of the inner demand to surrender of mundane reality itself. If the fundamental *eidos* of religiousness rests in the personal community of man with his God, in the dialogue between God and man, then this dialogue becomes senseless unless it presupposes that, expressly or not, on the natural level the value of the human personality can be recognized as a being in but nevertheless not of this world. If this spontaneous and prereflective acknowledgment common to all men cannot be maintained on the critical plane of philosophic reflection, our faith is hampered in advance, and free, personally accepted belief becomes impossible and untenable before the bar of human thought. The natural acceptance of the human attempt to grasp what is beyond ordinary earthly experience is the necessary presupposition both of revelation by grace and of our faithful acceptance of God's unconditional approach to us. In a pre-critical stage of belief and of the consciousness of mankind as a whole, the spontaneous prereflective acceptance of the constitutive attitude of a human being to the creative God is certainly sufficient, but in a more highly developed stage of human consciousness the personal and voluntary character of our religious life naturally demands critical recognition of the fact that the grace of God offered to us becomes inherently contradictory unless man has *not* already been compelled to surrender to the divine mystery as a result of his mundane outlook. Only if the natural affirmation of God in itself urges human beings to surrender to the divine mystery in a fashion which is either implicit and spontaneous or explicit and reflective can the phenomenon of religiousness be satisfactorily accepted as part of man's worldly life.

Indeed, when the Church puts forward its charismatic infallible doctrinal teaching in order to confirm[8] first of all the natural cognizability of God's existence, and, secondly, the natural cognizability of the personal value of the human being above and beyond this world—for which, in face of the reality of death, personal immortality is only another name[9] —then it does so not in a haughty attempt to conciliate a philosophy enmeshed in ignorance, but from a necessity which has its foundation in faith itself, and because in particular the natural cognition of these human values is of vital importance for the personal religious life itself. If faith itself did not demand it, such a pronouncement of its teaching authority would represent an illegitimate extension of its ecclesiastical authority to teach: a pronouncement concerning

[8] In the First Vatican Council. See *Acta et decreta sacrorum conciliorum recentiorum* (Collectio Lacensis, VII, 250). See DS 3004 and 3026.
[9] In the Fifth Lateran Council (Mansi, XXXII, 842; DS 1440).

the things of this world which are of no saving significance to the life of faith.[10]

Within the one act of religious orientation towards the living God there is thus a theistic aspect which is cognizable by human means: the fact that on the basis of his existence in this world man raises the question of God's existence, and, indeed, does it in such a way that in the absence of this constitutive need for God the Christian religion itself would be hard pressed to maintain itself. Thus if our Christian religious orientation towards the living God involves an autonomous aspect which is not yet faith, but the natural basis for faith, namely the relationship (whether expressly conscious or not) to the transcendental reality of God (which relationship God in his mercy accepts as the basis for religious intersubjectivity), then it is clear that thought on the basis of revelation is possible only if it includes secular thought: thought that proceeds from the immanence of this world to open up the approach towards the transcendental God, and thus naturally encourages the *surrender* of all human life to the divine mystery (irrespective of whether this mystery is then revealed, and if it is revealed how it is revealed). In this sense man is a being watching for a God who is on the way. In the absence of this personally established basis, which is only the breakthrough of God's creative act in our human experience, the *pointe* of the Christian act of faith is blunted to pure fideism and the door is opened to religious romanticism.

Although the clarification of the natural theistic dimension in our Christian faith is one of the tasks of theology, and particularly so in a time of atheism and unbelief like our own, nevertheless its specific task is to concentrate scientific

10 We should note that a solemn and infallible truth declared by the Church is not necessarily a revealed truth. Based on the fact that the Church is guardian of revelation, the Church can also expound the natural truths of life which have an organic connection with the truth infallibly defined. The infallibility of the Church's decree does not in these cases change such teachings into revealed truth.

theological attention fully on the content of the specifically
religious orientation towards God—namely, the "kerygma."
This brings us to the second of our two conclusions.

In and through the grace of faith, or, to put it in high
scholastic terms, in and through "the inner voice" of divine
revelation, our religious acceptance reaches the living God in
himself, but only to the extent that he is outlined in the
gospel story and, ultimately, in the life of the Church. From
this it follows that the explicit content of the inner evidence
about himself given by God to the faithful, and to the community of the faithful, can be drawn only from saving history.
If we then rightly maintain with St. Thomas the idea that
the living God—*Deus sub ratione Deitatis*—is the proper
subject of theology, because this is the way in which God is
our salvation, then it becomes clear that we can reach the
living God in theology only where he has revealed himself in
this way; namely, in the story of the Old Testament, in the
man Jesus, and in the whole mystery of the living Church—
all this, of course, against the background of general human
religious experience. Just as the philosopher cannot contem-
plate God except when proceeding from and remaining with
and in the created world in which the divine mystery is
cognizable, so theology can say nothing about the living God
except when proceeding from and remaining with saving
history in which God reveals himself as the God of our salvation. And yet the philosopher affirms God in his sovereign
transcendence of worldly affairs as a supernatural being who
is not a function of this world. In the same way the theologian affirms God in his transcendency—even in respect of
saving history itself.

In this sense theology is concerned with the history of
salvation on a christological basis, but in its profoundest
intention it remains formally theocentric, oriented towards
(or rather, "tuned in to") the inner majesty of the living
God. The more diligently theology investigates the temporal

economy of salvation the deeper it can penetrate into the nature of God himself. The ultimate concern of theology is the comprehensibility of God himself as the God of our salvation, but the gospel story is the only avenue along which such an understanding can be attempted. Just as the creation aspect enters into the manner of our natural knowledge of God, so the historical and christological aspect enters into the way in which every theological judgment is formed.[11] The fundamental theological question—for example, in seeking what has been revealed in reference to creation and the *eschata*—cannot be resolved unless theology first seeks an answer to the question, How did God make it possible for Israel, as God's people, to experience the reality of creation and of the *eschata*? In what way did God, the Father of our Lord Jesus Christ, allow his Son made man to experience these same realities? And finally, how does the Church, as the people of God redeemed in Jesus Christ, experience these saving realities? Or, to put it in a more general way, What does the old and the new Israel as the people of God think about itself and about God? This, it seems to me, is the fundamental question in any positive and speculative theological investigation. From this standpoint it is clear that theology is under a constant obligation to investigate how salvation was actually experienced by Israel, by Christ, and by his apostolic Church as it is expressed under divine guarantee in Holy Scripture. On this same basis it must investigate how this consciousness lives on, constantly clarifying itself, in the post-apostolic Church. The real life of man in its dialogue relationship with the God of our salvation is the treasure-mine and workshop of authentic and vital theology. In all this we must not forget that, although it was effected through the medium of the saving history of Israel and of the man Jesus, the divine call to salvation is addressed to all men,

11 Cf. St. Thomas: "utimur in (sacra) doctrina . . . effectu naturae vel *gratiae,* loco definitionis (Dei)." *ST* I, q. 1, a. 7, ad 1.

including those men who are now living. Contemporary
mankind hears the word of God here and now and must actu-
alize it in its life. Therefore this divine call must constantly
be brought into relationship with its particular spiritual
situation. Thanks to what Bultmann rightly calls a certain
Vorverständnis, or pre-understanding, each epoch of human
history is granted its own specifically coloured view of the
significance of divine revelation particularly adjusted to its
own time.

Perhaps the most sensitive point of this theological knowledge of God, which seeks to become a *theologia* by way of the
oikonomia, lies ultimately in its recognition that the living
God is totally different from the reality it knows in the
history of salvation. But even this conscious ignorance is
nonetheless a truthful, indeed, a life-giving, piece of religious
knowledge because it is embedded in a positive knowledge
of the history in which God is *personally* and effectively
present. Thus the incarnation of the Son in its Old Testament pre-history, in its historic fulfillment, and in its ecclesial
form as a mystery is the specific *locus theologicus* which
allows us to reach out hopefully towards the intertrinitarian
divine mystery that has given itself as the content of all our
lives.

3 Non-Religious Humanism and Belief in God

This contribution is intended to be not so much a positive expounding of Christian humanism as a confrontation of belief with non-theistic humanism.

What we discover in humanistic literature is a recognition, in many of its positive aspects, of the findings of modern anthropology which, as time goes on, are increasingly accepted both by believers and unbelievers. This amounts to a clearer recognition of that which is proper to man: man cannot be regarded as a *thing* which is naturally directed towards an end or purpose; man is a situated freedom which needs to live for a motive or a personal conviction. This may equally well be seen as a gain in the understanding of man by Catholics, Christians and other believers generally, as well as by non-religious people. This is not, however, in my view the *gravamen* of the problem. The specific nature of non-theistic humanism lies elsewhere.

THE NON-THEISTIC HUMANISM OF THE DUTCH HUMANIST ASSOCIATION

According to the declaration of principles of the Dutch Humanist Association, humanist ideology is "characterized by an endeavour to understand life and the world through human capacities and without proceeding from any special revelation" (adopted at the humanist Congress, which took place in Arnheim on April 23rd and 24th, 1955). From official comments made by Humanist sources it is quite clear that the phrase "without proceeding from any special revelation" is equivalent to saying: "without assuming the existence of a personal divinity" (earlier declaration of principles), and that, furthermore, it does not involve any positive rejection of the existence of God. The earlier declaration of principles had stated: "The inaugural meeting expressly rejected an amendment which proposed that the words 'without proceeding from' should be replaced by the words 'while rejecting.' "[1]

On the one hand this suggests that within the Humanist Association there are elements which clothe their humanism in a positively atheistic garb (as we can also see from the literature and the activities of organized humanists in France, Germany and Belgium), but, on the other hand, it also indicates that the association as such is not dominated by positive atheism. It is also interesting to note that at the Second International Congress of the International Humanist and Ethical Union in London in 1957 the term "non-theistic" was adopted—"non-theistic humanism." Thus there is a disinclination to be regarded as atheistic together with a desire to be a human being to the full "without God" and independent of all forms of religion and all recognition of a personal God. Thus when I refer to "Humanists" here I do so always in this narrower sense to mean the "non-theistic humanists."[2]

The justification put forward for the non-theistic character of this form of humanism is the contention that God cannot be encountered anywhere in human experience. Precisely on this account the Humanist neither denies nor affirms the existence of God. On principle he professes not just a temporary but permanent agnosticism—not a denial of the existence of God, but a denial of all knowledge of any such existence. On this account the adventure of living as a human

1 *Beginsel en doel van het Humanistisch Verbond,* Utrecht 1955, p. 4.
2 Where the words are capitalized "Humanism" and "Humanistic" refer specifically to the non-religious humanism of the Humanist Association.

being must be experienced apart from any form of theism, since if God exists he has neither theoretical nor practical significance for our human life.[3] Humanism is thus positively non-religious.

The motive of this exclusion on principle of all forms of religion is sought by the Association humanist in our human condition itself: human experience is the only starting point for any knowledge of reality, and the only form of access to reality. By reason of, and not in spite of, my faith I am in complete agreement with these two fundamental principles of the Association, apart from their interpretation of human experience. For the moment let us leave aside the difference in interpretation. From the specifically Humanist interpretation of experience it follows that by its nature this experience must be of *something human;* that is to say, related to man in the world, so that being human is not merely the starting point of any ideological outlook, but also its definitive horizon. In other words, man is the measure of all things. But in a very special sense: the contention that man sets the standard for every approach to reality does not mean either arbitrariness or nihilism. On the contrary, the Humanist accepts the mystery of the reality in which he finds himself. For him the quality of humanity is essentially determined by ethical values in life, and these are in and of themselves valid. This acceptance of inviolate ethical standards is described by the Humanist Association as "the cornerstone of Humanism."[4]

The fact that these standards are *essential* for man is of double significance: (a) the ethical conception of value belongs to the "existentalia" of human life; and (b) ethics are unthinkable without human beings. The meaning intended

[3] It is a different question whether there is in practice a distinction between the denial of God's existence and the denial of any knowledge of him. A God unconcerned with living people is by definition a non-God.

[4] In *Mens en Werweld* 8 (1953), n. 9, p. 1.

here is that by their nature ethical values are not religious, and that they are completely independent of the existence or nonexistence of a personal God. It is ethics which makes a man human. The reason why religion is rejected and ethics accepted must be ascribed to the fact that God is not experienced, whereas ethics is fundamentally a matter of experience requiring no proof and resting on intuitive clarity of perception.[5] "What is good is not good because the gods love it, but the gods love it because it is good."[6] Like modern Catholic theology, Humanism also acknowledges a certain variability within absolute standards, but the validity of the standard itself is absolute and inviolable. According to the earlier edition of the declaration of principles of the Humanist Association (explanatory note p. 7) the conception of value is normative, and independent of the free personal sphere of the individual human being. According to Doctor J. P. van Praag, the rejection of egoism and the practice of love represent "the only possible significance the human being can give to his life."[7] Although it is not scientifically demonstrable that this ethical conception of values is fundamentally the same in all human beings, Humanist inspiration assumes, and trusts, that this is nevertheless the case—at least, as Doctor van Praag adds: "as far as it is not refuted by rational knowledge."[8] Only facts can dispose of this Humanist belief in the universality of the ethical conception of values. However, since human intercourse becomes impossible if this fundamental conception of values is not similar in all men, this Humanist creed has a rational foundation. In the last resort it amounts to a *faith in man,* a faith in the possibility of lasting good in man despite the acknowledged existence

[5] *Het Humanistisch Verbond antwoordt,* Utrecht 1954, p. 13.

[6] H. J. Pos, "Socrates, Stoa en Kant," in *Mens en Werweld* 2 (1947), n. 9, p. 1.

[7] *Modern Humanisme,* Utrecht 1957, p. 74.

[8] "Humanistische verkenningen," in *Mens en Werweld* 5 (1950), n. 11, p. 2.

of malice and error. It is "a striving by man to determine his own personal fate, freely and responsibly." It is a purposeful striving to secure a better and more humane world in the future than the one we live in at present.

From all this it follows that personal responsibility for oneself is a central factor in the Humanist ideology. The Humanist accepts nothing that cannot pass the test of human knowledge based on experience; he insists on responsibility towards one's fellow man, and respect for the inviolable worth of the human personality. The Humanist supposes that this question of personal responsibility marks the great difference between Humanists and Christians, including Catholic Christians. He feels that personal responsibility, and therefore the specifically human in man, is "relativized" by belief in revelation.[9]

I feel that we are faced here with the perhaps unspoken but nevertheless dominating motive for non-theistic humanism as we have seen it develop in various countries. The real reason why the humanist denies the existence of God, or declares himself without knowledge of the existence of a personal God, lies in the fact that he regards the existence of God as a threat to his humanity. There are some non-theistic and atheistic philosophers who say so openly; for example, Sartre and Merleau-Ponty. But I also get the impression that the same underlying motive can be discovered in the publications of the Humanist Association and the writings of its members, although, in fact, the Dutch Humanist Association expressly separates itself from the atheism of Sartre and Merleau-Ponty. The Association frequently distinguishes between "religion" and "institutional religion," "religion" being regarded as a kind of secular mysticism. The existence of God, or at least the positive conviction that a personal absolute Being exists, is regarded as a threat to our humanity; in other words, as dehumanizing. This is taken to mean that

9 J. P. van Praag, *Ein poging tot plaatsbepaling*, Utrecht 1951, pp. 2–3.

one can speak of true humanism only in a non-theistic relationship. This is also clearly indicated by the fact that the
Association speaks of Humanists and Humanism only in a
non-theistic sense, and invariably considers Humanism alongside religion—for example, Protestantism or Catholicism.
That this is the chief reason, consciously or unconsciously, for
the rejection of religiousness can also be seen quite clearly
from the non-theistic Humanist's opinion of those who, for
example, call themselves Catholic humanists. For example,
J. P. van Praag says that "there is certainly a humanist Catholicism and a liberal Protestantism," but he immediately goes
on to question the authenticity of such an attitude since, as
he concludes: "The supporters of such tendencies should
closet themselves with their consciences to discover whether,
and to what extent, they may still properly call themselves
Christians."[10] This observation not only demonstrates how
from our point of view Catholic religiousness is disfigured in
the mind of the Humanist, but above all it reveals the real
reason for non-theistic humanism: one can make a choice
between either God or man. If God is chosen, then humanity
is compromised; if man is chosen, then the reality of God is
called into question. As a matter of our human experience
the unassailable reality of the human personality is evident.
The idea of God must therefore give way to this evidence,
particularly as we have no direct experience of the existence
of a personal God; uncertainty must then give way to intuitive clarity. This attitude can also be seen from discussion
among Catholics, Protestants and Humanists in the Nederlands Gesprek Centrum, in which Humanist speakers insist
that the Humanists "feel that faith in a personal God must
relativize the concept of value in an unacceptable fashion
because concern with the 'superhuman' must, with the best
will in the world, involve a temptation to close one's eyes to
practical human responsibilities or to turn away from them

10 *Op. cit.,* p. 4.

altogether."[11] Although I am prepared to admit at once that this Humanistic reproach really does apply to the actual way of life of some Catholics, I must nevertheless deny that this way of life can properly be called Catholic. But more of this later. In the meantime the thing that strikes me as really important in this and similar utterances from Humanistic sources is the fact that the dilemma—altogether false from a Catholic point of view—"God *or* Man" is at the bottom of the humanism of the Humanist Association. Therefore the openness of the Humanist Association to the world of men and things came to mean by definition the rejection of a personal God. Moreover, as far as Humanism is concerned, to be human is not only from its own point of view but also in itself the ultimate basis of any ideology. Everything beyond this human scope is a projection—or whatever other term they care to use.

The inexplicable fact of our existence in an equally inexplicable world is for the Humanist the mystery in which he lives, a matter for amazement, involving both happiness and suffering. And for him any attempt to resolve it by an appeal to a superhuman mystery is to devalue and tarnish this wondrous mystery.

From this brief summary of the fundamental nature of what the Humanist Association calls Humanism it is already quite clear that it would be very disobliging on our part merely to equate those who have turned away from the Church and ceased to practise their religion with this kind of elevated and inspired Humanism. A man can turn away from the Church for all sorts of reasons—and in doing so he need not necessarily become irreligious, or even cease practising religious duties. Humanism must also not be equated with nihilism; it is, in fact, an ethically based and courageous ideology which claims that its inspiration is exclusively

11 *Idealen von Opvoeding* (Nederlands Gesprek Centrum publication n. 3) Kampen 1956, pp. 5–6.

secular. In the same way, the members of the Humanist
Association cannot regard those who have thus turned away
from the Church as belonging to them merely because they
have so turned away.[12]

For the rest, if those who turn away from the Church and
become non-religious really adopt the humanism of the
Humanist Association, I can only thank God, since together
with Believers, the humanism of the Association represents
a real dam against modern nihilism and materialism. In
humanism we find the highest fundamental human values to
which any man can aspire on this earth without the express
affirmation of God and without an express faith in the living
God. As a believer, therefore, I can only welcome it with
thankfulness if those who are without faith nevertheless turn
towards such an ethically based, logical and courageous ideology and way of life. And this feeling of thankfulness is reinforced in particular since the principles of the association
remove all fear of anti-religious activities.

THE SIGNIFICANCE OF NON-THEISTIC HUMANISM FOR BELIEVERS

Personal Ideological Convictions and Tolerance

1. While remaining firmly convinced of the value and truth
of his own outlook the Catholic should always listen with

---

[12] Incidentally this difference is of quite fundamental importance in connection with the demand of the Humanists for official recognition (for sub-
sidies, broadcasting time, army "chaplains" and so on). As an organization
the Association is quite clearly entitled to claim equal rights in public life
with Catholics and Protestants—proportional equality anyway. However,
numerically speaking their claims, to be calculated, must be based on those
who are really members of the Association. They may not add automatically
to their lists those who have turned away from the Church. Otherwise the
appeal to the principle of tolerance would be a mere sophism.

respect to any honest voice that makes itself heard amongst us. Although none of us can determine for himself what is true and what is not, and reality discloses its own mystery to us, there can nevertheless be no truth without the perceptive spirit. Truth is disclosed reality; a disclosure at least up to a certain point, since we do not make reality but enter into its mystery. When we then say that truth must be the basis of our outlook we mean that the reality disclosed to us is the standard by which we live. Since truth alone must dominate our lives, no personally responsible and sensible man may attach himself to anything but truth or allow his life to be guided in any other way than by the evidence of his mind and conscience. It is precisely on this that the modern conception of tolerance, which is being more and more accepted by both believers and non-believers, is based.[13] The man who from his own experience knows what it means to hold fast to, and value, a conviction must respect the convictions of his fellow men because of the inviolable worth of the human personality, which experiences its full development above all in his outlook on life. Although, because of their imperfections, because of "perspectivism," and because of the growth of human consciousness unanimity amongst men is impossible, we can nevertheless not regard spiritual discord as good and acceptable in itself. Our tolerance goes therefore hand in hand with a zeal to convince our fellow men, and we extend a positive invitation to them based on our own outlook on life. At the same time our tolerance, and our respect for the human personality of others, requires that in our proselytizing efforts we should do nothing to offend the justifiable susceptibilities of our fellow men. Our proselytiz-

13 On tolerance see especially K. Rahner, *Würde und Freiheit des Menschen,* in *Schriften zur Theologie,* II, Einsiedeln 1958, pp. 247–277; Humanus, "Persoonlijke en burgerlijke verdraagzaamheid", in *Kultuurleven* 25 (1958), 245–257 and, an even more pointed work, J. H. Walgrave, *Verantwoording en uitbouw van een katholiek-personalistische gemeenschapsleer,* in *Welvaart, Welzijn en Geluk,* I, Hilversum 1960, pp. 119–127.

ing must be no more than an appeal to, and an invitation to
the conscience of, others. Every method that, for example,
exercises undue pressure on the conscience of others, either
from within or without, is unhumanistic and therefore at the
same time uncatholic. For the Catholic Church it is a matter
of dogma that faith can be accepted only in freedom and not
under pressure, especially not by means of any psychological
tricks. A prelate once declared in the French Chamber that
because of his Catholic convictions he demanded for his co-
religionists what on the basis of those same convictions he
must deny to others. Now this is an attitude I must condemn,
not only because it is unhumanistic but because it is uncatholic. What is more, it is pharisaical. That sort of thing is
a relic of the past. Such an attitude is not justified in Christian belief and dogma. It is a kind of dogmatism that the
believer should abhor every bit as much as the Humanist.
Only when the beliefs of others threaten the liberty of their
fellow men do we reach the limits of tolerance. At that
moment tolerance will be forced to oppose the threat in
defence of personal human values.

It is precisely this respect for every honest conviction that
has caused Thaumasia to put this lecture cycle on non-theistic humanism on the agenda—and certainly not in order that
as a final number of such an atheistic festival a Catholic
theologian should turn up to shatter non-theistic humanism
with a sledgehammer blow as if from God's own standpoint.
First of all, a Catholic (despite the ideas Humanists sometimes ascribe to him) can never place himself in the position
of God. Personal contact with the living God, present in
faith, can certainly be the deepest feature of our existence in
this world, shaping our behaviour and our views, but at the
same time this outlook, this behaviour and these views cannot
become tangible other than in the natural shape of our
humanity.

2. Our interest in non-theistic humanism is at the same

time tinged with anxiety, an anxiety caused not only by reasons of faith but also by humanistic considerations, since our own convictions tell us that outside the theistic outlook on life the value of human personality lacks its highest culmination. In our view the so highly praised humanity of man loses its ultimate personal significance if when he dies this human being disappears into anonymity. In this event the human personality is nothing but a temporary element in the cultural and ethical evolution of humanity. The personal value of the human being continues to exist merely as a relic in the culture which the dead man leaves behind as a heritage; as a personality, however, the human being disappears into anonymity. In the last resort we theists can only insist that non-theistic humanism amounts to a fatal attack on "human dignity." At the same time it is not a question of will or wish, since existentially there is no alternative. But we cannot possibly regard non-theistic humanism as, so to speak, thoroughgoing humanism. Despite our tolerance we cannot be glad that there are people in the world who do not share our profoundest convictions. As J. H. Walgrave says: "Thus I take upon myself a painful burden when I make the noble gesture of wholeheartedly letting my fellow-man be free to follow his own conviction."[14] Tolerance is not based on scepticism or indifferentism. And it is for this reason that our concern for humanism is tinged with anxiety.

3. Finally, our religious interest in the modern phenomenon of non-theistic humanism is inspired by the conviction that while in its totality we must regard it as an error there is nevertheless an element of truth concealed in it. A partial truth reveals its full content of truth only in the context of total truth. Each partial truth therefore includes a desire to be taken up and incorporated in its total context. Not merely in humanism itself, but even in its "atheism" there is a core of truth. Vestdijk and Szczesny see little future for religion,

[14] Walgrave, *op. cit.*, p. 120.

and it may well come about that as a believer I have to agree
with them. However, in that case, I may, like Dietrich Bonhoeffer,[15] find it necessary at a certain stage to draw a distinction between "the God of religion" and "the God of
Christian Revelation," taking the expression "the God of
religion" to mean: a projection arising from human weakness and human impotence, a mere experimental hypothesis
adopted because man is confronted with his own failure and
uses God as a stopgap for his own inadequacies and a way
out of his own embarrassments. We certainly do not need a
God like that nowadays. But then it might well come about
that real religion, as opposed to this projection, would appear in its true shape and as a new force in the modern
world. All that need be added to this is to say that "the God
of religion"—whose day is past and gone, and whose funeral
oration was delivered by Nietzsche himself—is not per se
merely the God of non-Christian religion, but also the God
of certain believers if we are to judge by their action and
their thought. For this particular reason if for no other, non-
theistic humanism is a salutary challenge for us believers
though we did not seek it. This now brings us to the following conclusions:

Non-Theistic Humanism as a "Catharsis" for Christian Thought and Christian Behaviour

After carefully reading the literature of the Dutch Humanistic Association and listening to radio broadcasts by speakers
representing its views, I think I may say that the reproach
Humanism levels at both Protestantism and the Catholic
Church does not in one fundamental respect (which I will
discuss later) properly apply to the Catholic Church. Where
Protestantism is concerned I propose to refrain from comment in view of the fact that another speaker is to represent

15 D. Bonhoeffer, *Widerstand und Ergebung*, Munich 1952.

it in the confrontation with Humanism. The Humanist reproach applies only to the distorted picture of theism and of revealed religion which is presented by some Catholics in their practical thought and action.

It is indisputably true that the idea of God held by some believers amounts to a projection of entirely human preoccupations to a superhuman level, and that their affirmation of the existence of God does, in fact, amount to an estrangement from or an alienation of what is human. It is regrettably true that, even if they do not actually say so in so many words, many Catholics do suggest by their practical way of life that the world and heaven represent an open book for those who believe, a book from which they can without difficulty extract eternal and absolute instructions for their behaviour, in the style of Cecil B. de Mille's film *The Ten Commandments*. The believer tends to be disquieted whenever man ventures to take his life into his own hands, and he is inclined to regard such independent behaviour as a kind of Godlessness, and to feel that man is merely setting himself up in competition with God. In his book *Le diable et le bon Dieu* Sartre shows very trenchantly that in the course of human history good and evil have been done, sometimes in the name of God, sometimes in that of the Devil. "In the name of God" believers have committed many atrocities and demonstrated both malice and lack of understanding. During the recent mutiny in the Algerian war I read that some of the "Ultras" on the French side in Algeria had placed their cause under the patronage of the Blessed Virgin even though it involved the frequent torture of fellow human beings. Believers have too often interpreted their faith in the existence of a Creator to mean that good citizens should always be the defenders of the established order and never the creative subjects of structural change. Under the cloak of "love" they have often supported an unjust system; and they have been inclined to believe too quickly that any

secular or political revolution meant the irruption of the
apocalyptic beast, never considering that almost certainly a
desire to establish a more just and humane world may have
played a large role in this revolution. This sort of new world
they have too often opposed, not on the basis of their religious faith, but because of their distorted conception of that
faith and on the basis of their false appeal to the God of
the creative order. They have often paid so much attention
to assuring themselves of heaven that they have quite overlooked their earthly responsibilities. They have often taken
their belief in the existence of God as a justification or excuse
for a selfish conservatism behind which they tend to overlook the urgent practical problems of mankind. They have
behaved as though their belief in an absolute God provided
them with a kind of instant, immutable, supranatural solution for problems which in reality believers—like Humanists
—can solve only tentatively and with difficulty while experi-
mentally grappling with constantly changing historical situations. They have forgotten, or failed to realize, that even for
those who believe in divine revelation such belief cannot
offer ready-made solutions—not even for such problems as
those of ethical behaviour. In particular they have exploited
the idea of God as though, released from their incarnation
in this world, they could judge from a divine standpoint. In
the last resort they felt they had God not merely behind them
but at their disposal. But this in fact amounts to the opposite
of true religiousness.

This criticism may be severe. But it would be unfair if we
failed to consider this particular distortion of Christian belief
in its proper historical context. First of all we should never
forget, as experience shows, that concealed behind the rather
primitive and, as a formula, positively aberrant idea of God
held by some simple people there is generally a profound
and altogether authentic desire for God. Furthermore, there
is an even more important factor which must restrain us

from being unjust in our judgment of this distortion of our belief in God: neither the members of the ecclesiastical hierarchy in their administrative work, nor ordinary lay believers can base their behaviour in this world exclusively on revelation. How they behave is influenced by all kinds of ordinary human beliefs, convictions, opinions, assumptions, and so on. Therefore when we speak of the "Catholic outlook" it is a term which is not altogether exact, since this outlook is not governed exclusively by revealed truths, but is also influenced by all kinds of ordinary human factors. Many of the ideas which are often regarded quite simply as part of the "Catholic outlook" are in fact ideas which are composed of an inner zone of absolute truth and an outer zone of views determined by the spirit of the age and shared by believers and unbelievers alike. Because of this we may say that a steady process of development and adjustment lies at the basis of what we term "the Catholic outlook." It would be much more accurate to talk of changes in the consciousness of peoples, changes which affect both believers and nonbelievers. The age of intolerance, for example, was not the natural result of revealed religion, but a temporary attitude of men generally, both believers and unbelievers, and confined to a particular period. In other words, intolerance was not behaviour exclusively confined to believers. Similarly our modern idea of tolerance is a new acquisition, and both believers and non-believers have contributed towards establishing it. The conclusion to be drawn from all this is that one should not ascribe things to the Catholic faith, or to belief in general, which are in fact due exclusively to a backward stage of general human consciousness. Thus the perspective would be utterly falsified if there were any attempt to compare the Humanistic outlook of our day with, for example, the Christian life of mediaeval man, and then to use the comparison as a stick to beat religion in general, since by such a comparison things would be ascribed to religion which were in fact due exclusively to a more primitive and backward stage of general human awareness.

However, it is certainly true that believers are often inclined to cling to outdated views although the general human awareness has already developed beyond them. It is also true that Catholics, for example in South America or Spain—and some Protestants in the United States and in South Africa— may lag well behind the more highly-developed views of their fellow believers in other countries in such respects. The believer certainly has a tendency to confuse time-honoured views with his religious faith as such, but this is not because of his faith but because of his distortion of it.

Apart from the distinction we must make between matters of revealed truth and the human views which are woven into the total outlook of the believer on life and the world, we must in addition not overlook the fact that even revealed truth, at least in its specific entry into human consciousness, is also subject to historical development, as all human affairs and things are, and this development, like any other in the sphere of the human spirit, proceeds tentatively and with difficulty. (It should not be overlooked, incidentally, that these other developments are important factors in the development of belief.) Many humanists erroneously suppose that a belief in the immutable nature of doctrine belongs to the essence of revealed religion.

From all this it is sufficiently clear that Humanistic criticism often embraces reproaches to Catholics with which Catholic belief is fundamentally in agreement, once they have been put forward. In this sense Humanism is, together with Catholic theology, a factor calculated to purge belief of those distortions for which believers themselves are responsible; not because they are believers but because of the imperfections of the *condition humaine,* and this is the real reason why we must show restraint in our evaluation. Anyone aware of human imperfections will not be surprised to learn that amongst both Catholics and non-theistic humanists there are those who do not always conduct their lives in full accordance with their convictions—for both it is always "an attempt" to do so. In the hurly-burly of everyday life an ideology always carries along self-contradictory elements. This is one of the reasons why the believer should constantly review and give himself an accounting of his personal convictions and his outlook. Like the attitude of the Humanist to his particular outlook, the believer should also admit frankly that there is no one among us whose life is fully permeated by the ultimate mystery at the source of our lives.

THE CATHOLIC SALVAGING OF THE TRUTH IN HUMANISM

The Starting Points of Humanism and Catholicism

Doctor van Praag has expressed the view that there can be no dialogue between Humanism and Christianity unless "it is realized first of all that it is a question of a confrontation of starting points,"[16] and I am quite in agreement with him. In this discussion, therefore, I shall deal primarily with these starting points.

1. As a believer I declare myself in agreement with the declaration of principles of the Humanist Association in the sense, namely, that those principles represent *the preliminary condition* for any true religiousness. Indeed I will even go so far as to say that whoever denies this humanistic preliminary condition cannot possibly give himself a true accounting for his own religiousness. In fact, it seems to me that such an accounting is just as essential for our human and Christian life as it is for the members of the Humanist Association.

[16] *Op. cit.*, p. 4.

However, when I say that the points of this humanistic program represent the preliminary condition of personal religiousness I am also saying that as a believer I cannot accept
them as the *ultimate* criteria which give sense and significance to human life.

I am at one with the Humanist in accepting independent
inviolability, the non-derivative significance of humanity, as
a worthwhile aim in itself. A human being can never be a
means for something or someone else. The human being, and
the human being alone—not the world and not God—is the
subject of the exercise of human existence. And here we must
grant that in the man Jesus, the Son of God himself was
also the subject of human existence. Precisely for this reason
Jesus Christ sets the standard for all true humanism for the
religious man. In fact man is the ultimate subject, and because of this he is personally and alone responsible for what
he does and leaves undone. Even if I am created by God—a
fact I fully accept—I remain the ultimate subject, and fully
responsible for my life; I alone am the subject of my actions,
of my good deeds and my evil ones. I alone, and not God,
am responsible to myself in these matters. This attitude is
clearly reflected in the Catholic attitude to sin: under no
circumstances can the believer shift his responsibility onto
God. Thus even though man as God's creature derives all
his freedom from the absolute freedom of God, he alone, with
the exclusion even of God, is himself the subject of his free
actions. Certainly, my ability to carry out free actions—and
also, and above all, the very origin of the free action I undertake at the sole initiative of my free if conditioned ego—
has, according to theistic convictions, at the deepest level its
origin in God. But it is precisely this origin which makes
me the unique, ultimate and responsible subject of all my
actions. In this respect, despite the radical difference in background, there is no discrepancy between the practical affirmation of the Humanist and that of the Catholic believer.

In this sense man is independent precisely because he has been created as a free person. Without this fundamental recognition of the personal and ultimate responsibility of man for his own life, religion would be compromised in its very essence, since revelation is essentially a divine invitation to free men to enter freely into a community of life with God. Freedom to accept this divine invitation is, by definition, part of revelation. Whether we are believers or not, the fate of man has been placed in the hands of man himself. It is on this account that we believe in the alternative of heaven and hell not so much as in an object, but as residing as an immanent possibility in all our free actions. It is in the ambiguity of the possibility of good and of evil that our humanity itself introduces this double perspective of heaven and hell. It is not revelation that teaches us that heaven or hell is an end possibility; it is implied in our humanity itself. Revelation tells us that only in and through Jesus Christ is there any possibility of bringing our lives to a definitively good end. I, and I alone, decide freely concerning the significance I shall give my life, not arbitrarily but with due respect for the auto-revelation of reality itself as it presents itself to me. Neither my fellow man nor God himself can replace me in this respect.

From this it follows that I am completely in agreement with this principle of the Humanist Association: Humanism (and I am prepared to add, Catholicism) "demands unfailing readiness to accept responsibility in thought and deed." Precisely because the believer is first of all a human being, the Humanist demand for reasonable responsibility and self-accounting represents a basic element for Catholicism too. In principle this demand is essentially humanistic for the believer too. Furthermore, it is a demand springing from this faith, which, according to Catholic dogma, must of its nature be a free and personally accepted belief.

The fact that I am not alone in the world either in my

experience of, or in my personal responsibility for, my life is something the Humanist will also concede. To be a human being is essentially to be a fellow human being. The social structure exercises its influence right into the most intimate core of an individual: it is only in the community that a man develops into a personality. From this it follows that my religious convictions are naturally influenced by my birth, my environment, and the contemporary civilization in which I live, and so on. The Humanist also agrees with this. It is something which belongs to the "existentialia" of human life. Thus the religious outlook of the individual is also based to some extent on, and is influenced by, the community of his fellow human beings. That I start off by being a Catholic, since I happen to have been born in a Catholic family, is reasonably accounted for by the *condition humaine*. For a child it is reasonable in a childlike way to accept as truth what its parents say. What would subsequently be wrong is if the adult were to remain rigidly in his original childhood stage. This is true of all human activities, and the Humanist is in complete agreement with us also on this point.

The fact that we are taught in the first place by others does not in the least relativize truth! It merely indicates the social structure of human consciousness, including the consciousness of faith.

2. Further, and here we are dealing with the central question, I am also in agreement with the basic contention of Humanism that no knowledge of reality is possible unless it is—no matter how—given in human experience. But the question is, Just what does human experience consist of?

First of all we may safely assume that this epistemological principle of Humanism, which I accept, contains a critical element directed against certain forms in which the proof of the existence of God has been couched—as seen by rationalist circles in the past. Very often it was seen as a rational transition from what was known by experience to the unknown of which there was no experience, and which therefore appeared to us as a wholly new conclusion. Such a purely logically constructed proof for the existence of God can only be a superstructure over human experience and therefore does not reach reality.

Any real proof for God's existence must be supported by experience. A proof of the existence of God is acceptable only if it is the *explicitation* of an experience, whereby what is implicitly experienced from the very beginning is clearly expressed through reflective consideration. Only in this way is the so-called proof, which is thus only an explicitation, not a superstructure divorced from experience, but the experience itself revealing its experiential content more clearly. Humanists will agree with us that there is more present in human experience than we are from moment to moment specifically aware of. If this were not the case, we should be at a loss to explain how the growth of human experience occurs in true continuity, and does not present itself merely as an atomized and incoherent awareness. The truth therefore lies not only in what Merleau-Ponty calls "prereflective experience," but every bit as much in the reflective expression of this same experience, even if to some extent this reflective knowledge is conceptualized. Rationalistic denial does not necessarily imply that we must regard a conceptual explicitation of experience as impossible. Rationalism should certainly be rejected by believers, but not the possibility of the conceptual expression of implicit experiential content. One gets the impression that Humanism restricts experiential knowledge to actual experience, and that as far as the Humanist is concerned the truth lies only in prereflective experience, so that all explicitation of this experience is properly transferred to the realms of subjective projection. Consequently the denial of all knowledge of the existence of God is perfectly logical. On the other hand, it is obvious also to us that God, who is absolutely transcendent, *by definition* cannot be *directly* experienced. If this were the case then he would, by definition, be non-God. At the same time the affirmation of the existence of God cannot be a logical conclusion from premises which are themselves "godless" in the first place. We can never draw a theistic conclusion from an atheistic premise (actually, a good many proofs of the existence of God are nevertheless so constructed). If God exists, then we can know it only through the medium of our own human world of experience, which is the *primum quoad nos* for us too; that is to say, our only access to reality. I am not prepared to quarrel with this Humanistic first principle; in fact it is postulated nowadays by all Catholic philosophers as the fundamental basis of all philosophizing. The question is only, Which elements and dimensions does human experience embrace, explicitly or implicitly? It is at this point that the ways of the Humanistic and Christian philosophers diverge. For if the phenomenological approach to human existence is thought to be all-inclusive, one methodologically confines oneself from the start to an atheistic conception of experience because thereby one evades the question, What is reality in itself? Although the Dutch Humanist Association does not expressly revert to Husserl's idea of *Wesensschau,* whereby reality in itself is put between brackets, the Humanistic idea of experiential knowledge reflects the same perspective. Reality is described to the extent that it appears directly to us. No attention is paid to the fact that just this has various implications which we do not notice straight away but which are nevertheless implicitly embraced in the experiential content.

When we consider the starting points of Humanism and Catholicism from this angle we see first of all that the Humanists lay down a starting point which we Catholics certainly cannot accept (for Protestants the situation is different). The Humanist declares that whereas human experience is his starting point, the Catholic starting point is faith in revelation. Against this assertion I must object—our starting point as Catholics is also human experience and not the doctrine of revelation; and this for the very simple reason that as a human being I cannot accept revelation unless I have previously come to the conclusion on the basis of my human experience that there is a personal God. The God of my belief is, of course, the God of Abraham, Isaac and Jacob, the Father of our Lord and Saviour Jesus Christ. It is the living God who in the Son became man with us all and thus realized in his person—to the benefit of all of us—the highest possible expression of humanism and religion. This is the basic conviction of the believer's life. Of course, it is also true that Christ is the ideal man as seen by God. But what in God's name can this statement mean to someone who cannot accept the existence of God? Here is the gravamen of the problem. "Grace presupposes nature"; that is to say, revelation can make no sense to me if I cannot already attach some meaning and significance to God. When the Humanist asserts that in order to evade the objection of religious projection the believer has to appeal to a particular faculty in man, namely the so-called *sensus religiosus,* or the sense of God, then as a Catholic I stoutly deny this. Man has no specific sense which would allow him to experience the existence of God in some special way independent of general human existential experience. All that is human—and therefore the natural recognition of the existence of God as the presupposition of belief in revelation is included—can be accounted for by the human mind.

As a Catholic I am therefore convinced that any appeal to a special revelation is impossible and even senseless unless a man "through his own human capacities and without proceeding from any special revelation"—to quote the words of the Humanist declaration of principles—can satisfy himself of the existence of a personal God from his own human experience. I am well aware that some, not necessarily consciously fideistic, Catholic circles think differently, but I also know that such views are rejected by ecclesiastical teaching as thoroughly uncatholic. The first Vatican Council most forcibly condemned the non-humanist aspect of fideism, which, furthermore, internally compromises belief in revelation itself. It laid down that Christian belief in revelation implies that in principle man possesses the natural and the spiritual capacity to arrive at the existence of God. Thus although belief in revelation exercises an all-important influence on our outlook, it cannot be regarded without more ado as the actual starting point of our ideology. If fideism were true, then I should have to admit that Humanism's attack on the Christian outlook accurately hits the mark. But fortunately such fideistic affirmations are not an authentic reflection of Catholic belief. With Humanism we acknowledge that humanity is not merely something we experience passively, but that it is essentially an existence reflecting on itself. Revelation is a revelation to mankind. It presupposes an existence which is already asking questions and which is seeking to give a sense and significance to life amidst the chaos in which we live. Professor Walgrave is right when he says: "Man's existence is a self-thinking existence; that is why no Christian view of man can be a pure datum of Revelation. A Christian view is possible only as a living synthesis born from the encounter between the man who tries to fathom his existence and God who expresses His judgment about man and reveals to him the meaning that He Himself gives to human life."[17] Man comes to himself in his encounter with the world and with his fellow man. Experience is experiential thinking. The living encounter of man with the world and his fellow men *is* itself an ideology. The exercise of our humanity is an outlook on life, a search for direction. Therefore from our standpoint too our humanity is the very first phenomenon, that from which all our considerations begin, and in which—in case there is a special divine reve-

17 Walgrave, *op. cit.*, p. 17.

lation—we must integrate this in a personal and justifiable fashion. Religion implies but does not grant to man that personal justification towards himself. I cannot free myself from this human, this humanistic starting point, not even as a believer. My life as an incarnated spirit in this world is the only means of access to the other, whatever the other is. Even revelation, in which God "vertically" enters our world, makes contact with our human experience.

When we thus contend that human experience, a human experience which must be in contact with God somewhere, lies at the basis of our belief in revelation, this means that the humanistic content of our human experience must embrace a *theistic absolute dimension*. But at the same time it also means that we cannot reach God himself through this human experience. What I implicitly experience, and only aim to explicitate by reflection, is the dynamics of the earthly reality we experience which objectively points to the mystery of God. This objective dynamics is implied in our experience: the so-called proof of the existence of God is only the reflective explicitation of this experiential content.

Here, in my view, lies the real difference between Humanism and Catholicism. According to the Humanist this dynamics, or this reference to God, is a projection of the human mind, and it is the human mind which is alone responsible for projecting earthly reality to a supernatural sphere.[18] The Christian philosopher, on the other hand, regards this dynamics as a projection of reality itself which, in and through what it is in itself, points towards a personal God. The problem which arises on the basis of our experience is not primarily a question of the human mind; it is a

18 Hence Maréchal's proof of the existence of God, which is based on the dynamism of the intellect, cannot meet with our acceptance. See, in this connection, D. De Petter, "Voor een integrale theodicee," in *TP* 1 (1939), 852–860, and E. Schillebeeckx, "The Non-Conceptual Intellectual Dimension in Our Knowledge of God according to Aquinas," in *Revelation and Theology* 2, New York 1968, pp. 157ff.

question of reality: the earthly reality which we experience is in itself a question. It is this question that enters the human mind. Reality reveals itself to man as pointing towards God. The human mind does nothing more, so to speak, than follow, by a projective act, in the wake of this dynamics which lies within reality itself. By acting in this way the human mind is carried along, not by a spiritual projection, but by the objective dynamics of reality itself, towards a recognition of the personal existence of God. Without this our experiential content would be intrinsically contradictory.

However, the explicitation of our experiential content leads us practically to the specific recognition of the existence of God. In any case the core of this spiritual movement lies in the experience of the contingency of all things, and above all of our own contingency.[19] On the one hand, we are conscious that by our own free will we can take the conduct of our life into our own hands, and be personally responsible for its course. On the other hand, we cannot take credit for our existence as free creatures; that is to say, of ourselves we (I and my world) cannot account in any way for our factual existence.

According to the Humanist this is precisely the great wonder, the mystery of our existence and that of the world around us, an existence that we can approach only in humility and diffidence. But I am afraid that the word "mystery" has been introduced too soon. I have a feeling that there is no mystery here, but an intrinsic contradiction instead—unless God exists. What is actually the content of our experience? Together with the Humanist we say: contingency, the fact that I exist and yet can adduce nothing of my own to justify or account for this existence. That is precisely what makes our existence so problematical. Our existence is prob-

[19] We do not wish to confine the proof of the existence of God to a proof of the contingency of man; all we are saying is that this contingency reveals itself more pregnantly in man.

lematic not because of the construction of the human mind but because of the mystery to which we ought to surrender ourselves. The contingency of my existence and that of the world is not primarily a notional question which needs explication, but a question of *being,* a question of reality. For if we cannot account for our existence yet factually exist, this experimental phenomenon is not—unless God exists—a mystery but an intrinsic contradiction. J. P. Van Praag's little joke about the simple soul who asks: "If God didn't create the world, who did create it?" really isn't so funny at all, but a straightforward question that touches the profoundest problem of our lives. And furthermore the question is raised by *reality* itself, not in the first place by men. It is just that men become keenly aware of the question after reality has raised it in the first place. For if things exist while having in themselves no reason for existence—as Humanists admit— then the more normal thing would be that they should not exist in the first place. We have no right to dodge the fundamental question, "to be or not to be?" put to us by reality itself, by talking vaguely about a "mystery." Here, the Humanist falls short of his fundamental principles of "giving an account of one's claim and of accepting a personal responsibility for life." The Humanist has depersonalized the idea of "mystery," turning it into a "non-mystery."[20]

20 From the moment one regards reality as exclusively secular there is no longer any room for a mystery *calling for one's surrender.* In itself nature is something foreign to man; it irritates him because it seems to lack any clear and definite sense. Nature is reality which knows no concern for man. Yet it is a reality which has no meaning without man. It is man who by hearing, seeing and feeling, by his culture and his technique, humanizes this world, gives it a sense and a significance, spiritualizes it, and turns it from something "uncanny" into something familiar. From a non-theistic angle the only mystery that remains in nature is the way it evades the human, technological and poetic grasp. In other words, its "non-humanness." It is a temporary mystery of sub-humanness which cries out for a human, contemplative, technical and poetic sense and significance. To humanize this indifferent, unresponsive nature and to put spirit and significance into it is the task of

We, on the other hand, hold that only if we have finally acknowledged the existence of God can our existence be a true and critically acceptable mystery which we can approach in humility and wonder. Thus, far from compromising my humanity by proof of the existence of God, I recognize my existence, which otherwise would be in itself contradictory, as a true mystery. How can reality be a mystery *in principle* for me and not merely a temporary obscurity, if this reality is an invention of man's mind, and unless I, consciously, enter into the realm of another, the realm of the Other who transcends me? Assuming that "mystery" does not mean a temporary ignorance concerning things we cannot explain, but involves recognizing that the reality in which we live is not an invention of man's mind and *therefore* transcends us, it becomes understandable that this inability to explain reality indicates its transcendence. Being present in this reality by interiority, the transcendent God testifies to his personal existence. The natural recognition of God and the experience of my contingent existence in this contingent world are one and the same experience. Therefore the natural recognition of God is really a spontaneous phenomenon in human history,[21] a phenomenon which is merely tested critically in the

---

secular man. If this were all, there would be no sense in being a believer. No one can sincerely surrender himself to something which in itself has no positive sense, apart from what man himself can give it. Mystery in the full sense of the word must therefore always have a personalist significance. Precisely because of the creative person of God, who transcends all reality by interiority, we and all the things around us represent an impenetrable mystery which will be revealed in its profoundest depths only in the vision of God.

[21] It seems that the spontaneity of this phenomenon can be disputed in our day. It is then a question of "interpreting" the phenomenon. The fact is that so-called "spontaneous atheism" *is only a present crisis.* Moreover, it is not an original and spontaneous attitude such as the spontaneous recognition of God used to be, but a reaction against the existing forms of concrete religiousness; in other words, it is a secondary "reflective" attitude which quite often conceals a spontaneous, implicit, but *authentic* belief in God.

so-called proof of the existence of God. Reflective thought, self-reflective human experience, gradually reveals the content of experience and is at the same time a critical check of this experience. The explicit argumentation shows the original phenomenon in the light of the implications discovered by experiential knowledge, which then appear to us as "conclusions" but which were, nevertheless, already present, though unnoticed, in our consciousness right from the start. In other words, the so-called proof of the existence of God can only be the explicitation of the implicit content of our experiential knowledge.

From all this it follows clearly that the natural recognition of the personality of God does not involve the destruction of our contingent existence but, on the contrary, the full realistic acceptance of the *mystery* of our factual existence as human beings. The first stage of the natural recognition of God is pre-eminently a humanistic affirmation which transforms our humanity into a mystery of hope and promise, where it would otherwise be intrinsically contradictory. Through and from within our human immanence, we obtain an objective perspective towards that absolute reality we call God. We cannot abandon the immanent humanistic standpoint for one moment, but within our humanistic experiential knowledge, God testifies to his existence. Our factual belief in revelation provides additional confirmation of this view, since we believe that the creative God is at the same time the God of our salvation. This means that in our created selves—that is to say, as creatures standing consciously in this world—there is a preliminary, if ever so vague, beginning of what God in his mercy seeks to complete in us. It is for this reason in particular that we can give a critical, independent justification for our supernatural act of faith, so that the sur-

---

The self-evident, matter-of-course attitude of a "life without God" seems, as far as modern man is concerned, to be structured quite differently from the self-evident, matter-of-course attitude of general human religiousness.

render of our life to the living God does not become a non-humanistic act. It is true of course that we do not believe because our faith can be rationally justified. The exclusive foundation of our faith is God's grace which inwardly impels us to accept it. This inner grace of faith, therefore, which we experience in an obscure fashion in and through the unexplainable inclination in us to believe, is the actual *intrinsic* reason for our security in faith. To believe is thus to give oneself to God relying exclusively on God's inward invitation. But this self-surrender is not an adventurous, irresponsible leap into a void, since on the basis of natural experience and natural evidence I already have a secure perception of the existence of a personal God.

Just because our humanity itself points to a personal God the special divine revelation opens up no new difficulties, a point some Humanists are prepared to admit. When we come critically to the acceptance of the existence of a personal God on the basis of our human experience, the acceptance of an eventual revelation from God can hardly offer any new difficulties; otherwise we would subsequently once again deny the personal character of God's existence and withdraw what we had in the first place already accepted. For this reason I do not altogether understand why in its declaration of principles the Humanist Association makes reference only to "a special revelation"—unless, as I suspect, they are thinking merely of the Protestant conception of revelation. The difference between theistic and atheistic humanism does not lie in any "special revelation," but in the question of whether with our natural capacities alone we are able to establish a perspective towards the existence of a personal God, since revelation, though it may well confirm this natural certainty, can never *replace* it. The security I have concerning God in and through faith itself, in and through prayer, and possibly even in and through the mystical life, is of its very nature a *certitude of faith* which stands or falls with faith itself. But without the natural, rationally justified, certainty concerning the existence of God which is at the basis of all this, an appeal to that certitude would merely involve us in a vicious circle. The mystics are always the first to adopt a critical attitude towards their own mystical experiences. Without the backing of our natural certainty concerning the existence of a personal God we could never critically establish the authenticity of a mystical experience. Proofs of the existence of God on the basis of mystical experiences in the way that Bergson, for example, seeks to establish them, necessarily lack the criterion of evidential clarity, the only thing to which the human mind can surrender itself.

· In accepting the natural certainty concerning the existence of a personal God we must naturally take the evolution of human consciousness into consideration. At a time when critical thought had not yet arrived at full consciousness and men believed in God as a matter of course, this spontaneous recognition of the existence of God was quite sufficient as a preliminary condition for belief in a special revelation. But in a more sophisticated era, in which the believer is also under an obligation to provide critical justification for his beliefs, the spontaneous conviction of the existence of God is not enough, since if that were all, the trend of the times could endanger faith itself.

Someone might well object: I can go along with everything you say, but I do feel that you interpret reality in a specifically theistic perspective, while the atheist interprets it in a different way, because you are a believer from the very start, whereas the atheist (at least explicitly) is from the very start not a believer.

This is fair comment, and I will not seek to deny it. On the other hand, it does not really affect the intrinsic value and truth of the natural and rational acceptance of the existence of God. The fact that I am a believer puts me in the best possible position to accept frankly and right away certain aspects of reality which might well otherwise have escaped me. Thus it is certainly true that for the believer his faith is the starting point for his rational justification of his existence, just as on the other hand it is not human existential experience as such which is the starting point for the Humanist's rational justification of his existence, but the fact that he is a non-believer. It is from this belief or lack of belief, then, that each—Christian and Humanist alike—proceeds to "question" his existential experience in order to provide, in each case, a critical basis for his own outlook. In both cases such a starting point can only exercise an irresponsible and irrational influence, whether it is for reasons of belief or unbelief that we fail to let our existential experience tell us objectively what it has to tell us; or if, on the other hand, owing to our belief or disbelief, we persuade ourselves that experience is telling us things which it is not in fact telling us at all. Very well, then; as believers who desire to justify our faith rationally and critically we are also convinced that the fact of our belief makes us more alert to those aspects of reality which speak to us of God; while at the same time we feel that the fact of the Humanist's disbelief so hampers his ability to understand these objective aspects of the content of existential experience that he does not even see them. And very often this is "not a question of not wanting to, but a question of being existentially unable to."

In the explicitation of the experience of contingency, therefore, I must remain wholly within the sphere of critical responsibility and accept only what appeals to my understanding because of its intrinsic clarity: belief or unbelief must play no role in the critical accounting itself. Any proof of the existence of God in which faith plays an intrinsic role and takes the place of mind would be of no significance at all for my faith, since then I should be secretly providing the missing links in support of my own beliefs. In the same way, the rational justification the Humanist looks for in his outlook would also be an illusion if he allowed his disbelief to play any part in the actual interpretation of existential experience. The influence of belief or disbelief means nothing more than that the whole human personality is involved in this question of justification. But this influence of the whole personality can be disciplined and accepted only if it is under the control of the mind and is not allowed to induce us to take any step which cannot be justified before the forum of human thought—whether our belief persuades us to accept things we could not factually perceive on the basis of our human experience alone, or whether our unbelief glosses over real aspects or problems of this experience which would otherwise not agree with our unbelief. Both for the believer and the unbeliever there can be a temptation to *mauvaise foi* here.[22]

When the Humanist says that he cannot accept belief in the reality of God, and then goes on to say that this attitude is a primordial datum of experience, we must object that this inability is not in fact a primitive datum, but already an answer. The Humanist says that his answer to reality is different from that of the theist because he, the Humanist, asks

[22] Professor De Petter has dealt very conclusively with this objection: "It is, after all, quite clear that the gradual embodiment of belief into human thought presupposes in the first place that it truly is human thought; that is to say, thought which must hold itself exclusively responsible before the forum of human reason. This is, incidentally, a quite general principle. . . . Faith is a gift to man, a gift which, consequently, presupposes humanity. There is no suggestion at all in the above-mentioned view that philosophy should be induced to borrow anything from belief, or that faith should function as a kind of a priori for philosophy." In a footnote he continues: "Naturally faith precedes philosophy (just as, in the same way, positive disbelief comes first with the non-believing philosopher), and as such it has an influence on philosophy (and the same thing applies to positive unbelief). However, this should be permitted only insofar as the consequences of this influence can be accounted for responsibly by philosophy on a philosophical basis. This is the only sense in which one can say that belief is the a priori of the philosophy of the believer." *Begrip en werkelijkheid*, Hilversum-Antwerp 1964, pp. 20–21, and footnote 14, p. 235.

a different question. However, one is entitled to wonder
whether reality does not first ask him exactly the same question as it asks the theist: the question of "to be, or not to
be?" of reality itself.

Related to these considerations is the view that the natural
critical acceptance of the existence of God need not necessarily precede belief (though the supernatural nature of the
act of faith implies, at least non-explicitly, a natural affirmation of the existence of God). With its pronouncement that
belief in revelation necessarily implies a natural certitude
concerning the existence of God, the Church means only that
Catholic belief requires these natural insights before it can
be regarded as personally and responsibly accounted for, and
be vitally integrated into man's spiritual life. The natural
recognition of the existence of God is not just an explanation
of our existence provided by an appeal to the absolute God.
With such a humanistic affirmation, proof of the existence of
God is only in its preliminary stage, and not yet actually in
the phase of its culmination. Should we go no further than
this preliminary stage, then our proof of the existence of
God would be itself atheistic, as it would mean accepting
God merely as a function of our human life; as a mental
crutch to make our own life comprehensible. The
"thaumasia" around the wonder of our existence would
then fade into a knowing, and become an "a-thaumasia,"
explaining the wonder by giving us an insight: "Oh, that's
how it fits together!" But that is not the case. God does not
exist thanks to the existence of man, but man's existence is
the direct result of God's love, although, of course, we naturally arrive at knowledge of the existence of God only via
our own existence. The objective orientation of our existence
towards a transcendental God reveals itself as a directive
towards a God absolute in himself, and absolute and freely
sovereign in his creation of the world.

The final point of the proof of the existence of God is

therefore an at least implicit worship of God, a recognition of the fact that our life can find its sense and significance only in God. The "proof of the existence of God" culminates in this religious summit, and without this culmination the so-called proof of the existence of God is the affirmation of a pseudo-God, a God expected to serve human ends and satisfy the human need for enlightenment. The natural affirmation of the existence of God is therefore only a critically based affirmation derived from this world and confirming that we are living safely in the personal mystery of God, even though we cannot *encounter* him from this world. Any arbitrary attempt to seize on God's presence merely pushes us still deeper into the isolation of our life in this world since it deprives us of the interiority which develops in us only when we come to ourselves in the security of the creative mystery of God. In this sense the existential experience of God's *absence* from the world, together with our attention to the intrinsic problematics of the existence of man and of the world, is the "experience" of our security in the all-embracing mystery of a transcendental but personal love. It is a love in which we personally desire to enter, but which, from the nature of things, we cannot enter on our own, although within ourselves we already experience his appeal to surrender on the basis of the creative act by which, through the ambiguity of our existence, God draws our attention to his presence as a loving person. Thus the natural evidence of our human existence compels us to surrender ourselves to the mystery of God, because by definition the mystery can be accepted only in surrender. By the explicitation of the experience in a "proof of the existence of God" the "thaumasia" becomes expressly personalistic, and therefore *religious,* admiration. This means that in its search for significance human experience fulfills itself in a religious surrender. This is— formally, at any rate—not yet the supernatural faith by virtue of God's grace, but a necessary preliminary condition for it.[23] Faith is therefore accepting the pronouncement of the "Totally Other" even before it has spoken. Supernatural faith, and supernatural hope and love, thus find in human experience a preliminary onset of natural faith, a natural hope, and a natural love in answer to God's creative testimony in himself.

I do not, of course, flatter myself that with all this I have succeeded in convincing the Humanist. In fact this was not even my intention. All I really wanted to do was to explain how I as a Catholic see the theistic factor in human experience. Further, I have spoken only from the necessity of providing a responsible and personal justification of my own faith, because free human actions, such as the Act of Faith pre-eminently is, can only be fully human in the light of a rationally justified certitude which is not subjective but based on reality itself. In doing so I have at least been able to prove that it is *because of* and not *despite,* my faith that in all seriousness I am able to accept the fundamental principle of humanism, namely, its insistence on a personal and rational responsibility for each "existential decision." In other words, as a Catholic I am also a humanist, and therefore I can only regret that so-called Humanists claim this patent of nobility which is open to all men exclusively for themselves, and pretend that it is the exclusive prototype of irreligious humanism, as though in this respect believers were inferior. At the same time it is interesting to note that once again this demonstrates that in the background of Humanist thought the dilemma "God or man" is very really and truly present.

I am well aware that a man cannot convey values and convictions by offering proof. Living truths can be conveyed

23 I say "formally" since in the existential experience of life such an attitude is more than simply "natural," for every human being is called to grace by the God of salvation. Through such an existential attitude he has, under the influence of grace, already implicitly said yes to this grace, just as the attitude of pride involves an implicit no to God's grace.

only by an appeal to the personal experiential thought of
others in the belief that the human mind as such is directed
towards objective reality; and that in consequence, in principle at least, the insight that one man has attained in a
rationally well-founded fashion is equally open to the other.
The whole exposition is therefore no more than an invitation
to the Humanist, an appeal to him to consider investigating
this path himself. The rest we can safely leave to God's grace.
The grace of God works slowly and unobtrusively but not
ineffectively, as I propose to show in my concluding observations which I would like to entitle "God's concern for non-
theistic humanism."

The Hopeful Aspect of Non-Theistic Humanism: God's Concern for Non-Theistic Humanism

There is really not much point in telling anyone, however
consolingly and understandingly, that although he insists on
calling himself non-religious he is in reality a theist, a kind
of anonymous Christian. In the last resort such an attitude
means that the Humanist is not being taken seriously. When
he tells us quite definitely that he doesn't want to be a theist
it is our duty to accept what he says at its face value. This, of
course, need not prevent us from asking him whether he is
being altogether logical with himself. The fact that non-
theistic humanism acknowledges the effective force and validity of ethical standards is something very promising indeed.
We are in agreement with Humanism that the ethical and
the religious are formally different in content. It would
certainly be wrong to insist that an ethical life is possible
only within the framework of an *express* belief in God. As a
personality man appears to us in our experience as an inalienable individual entity. This individual value as a personality
is the direct basis of the ethical awareness of value—for us as

well as for the Humanist. The question is, however, whether this spontaneous ethical awareness of value having an exclusively secular origin can in the last resort justify itself before the forum of reflective thought. The theist contends that this general, human spontaneous ethical awareness of value cannot ultimately maintain itself unless the ethical validity is regarded as the imprint in our human consciousness of the absolute significance and value of a concrete Being at the origin of all reality, namely, God.

Thus although the theist is prepared to admit that a secular personalistic morality is possible without any specific religiousness, he contends that there must nevertheless be an implicit acceptance and recognition of a personal God. Sartre insists that atheistic humanism (which he represents) implies the denial in principle of any absolutely valid standards (which, however, does not prevent his at the same time accepting an absolute standard; namely, human freedom as freedom). This is hardly altogether logical, and it becomes altogether incomprehensible without *positive* atheism. That, on the other hand, the members of the Humanist Association hold fast to ethical standards per se, and are moreover not anti-theistic but agnostic, allows us to maintain that in the sincerity of their ethical involvement their moral life implicitly contradicts what they expressly assert.

It is precisely this situation that strikes me as so hopeful. There is an important promise inherent in it; namely, that from this non-theistic humanism a cleansed and purged belief in God will develop. We are entitled all the more readily to cherish this hope not so much because Humanism in its historic shape as we see it today is factually unthinkable except against a background of centuries of Christianity in Europe, but in particular because we can discern all kinds of practical elements in the Humanistic outlook that we cannot but call implicitly Christian.

First of all, as the Humanist himself admits (although he

explains it in exclusively secular fashion), by dint of repetition man discovers that in his humanistic design he rises superior to what is merely human, and, secondly, that this bears more fruit than anyone would have thought possible: in the sphere of good, man often does more than could normally be expected of him. He penetrates to greater depths than he can consciously motivate, and because of this the Humanist describes such phenomena with an expression he has borrowed from Christianity, as "almost a miracle."[24]

Further, the Humanist himself describes his acceptance of moral standards not as the acceptance of scientifically non-proven truth, but as a "belief," a trustful surrender. J. P. van Praag, for example, writes: "Apart from religious considerations one can regard 'belief' as the complete acceptance of important convictions whose truth is not capable of exact proof. Humanism is also familiar with such beliefs."[25] Belief is interpreted here as a surrender to reality as it appears practically to us in our daily lives. It is a question of experiencing reality as a mystery, as a gift which is vouchsafed to us. Naturally, the Humanist does not admit that this gift comes from a personal God. Because of the factually ethical attitude of surrender to a moral standard accepted as inalienable we can only say that in this respect the difference between the Humanist and the believer is a matter of explicitness and maturity only. The theist declares that in experiencing the absolute validity of the ethical standard man *also* experiences God, and that he is in a position to assure himself responsibly and critically that just the experiencing of this ethical value involves, by its nature, personalistic implications; namely, that in the gift of his humanity man experiences the personal God. When, as a matter of our faith, we further know that God has created our humanity to enjoy a personal community with him, and that our lives

24 *Idealen van Opvoeding*, p. 6.
25 In *Mens en Werweld* 5 (1950), n. 11, p. 5.

—whether we desire it or not—are in fact sustained by God's personal and absolute love, which invites us to communion with him, then we know at the same time that God has directed this concrete human existence, from within and without, towards the God of salvation, so that whoever sincerely accepts this existence with its ethical directive, implicitly accepts the grace offered to him by God. The personal religious attitude develops precisely in and from the experience of a human being within his ethical life's design through which he approaches the mystery of reality with love and humility. It was Newman who said that God becomes an increasingly firm reality for us along the line of our fidelity to our :onscience. Religion is nothing but the true shape of a life design which approaches the mystery of that objective reality in which we move and have our being, in awe and diffidence, and allows itself to be guided by it.

At one point in *The Brothers Karamazov* Dostoevsky causes Zosima to say: "Whenever you actually love some reality you will also understand God's secret in things. One day this secret will be revealed to you, and then you will learn to understand it more and more every day." The manner in which many people are confronted personally with the reality of God is as yet provisional and obscure. The whole question is whether they experience reality as something they ambitiously embrace, or whether, on the contrary, they regard it as something that includes them, thus placing themselves in the service of others and experiencing their lives as lives lived for others in freedom, justice and love. There is an implicit theism in any trusting approach to the world of men and things, in the certainty that life can attain significance and dignity in it, even though I should deny it on the plane of explicitness. Whoever faithfully accepts reality, approaching the mystery of reality hopefully, will find that God speaks to him in it as though out of the cloud, and that the mystery gradually comes nearer to him and takes a firmer hold in his experience—at first perhaps in a still vague and anonymous religiousness, but then more expressly, and finally in complete acceptance of God's special revelation in Israel, in Christ, and in the Church of Christ. In any case, even if *he* does not find God, he will nevertheless be found *by* God. Therefore from the rich store of our convictions we say to the Humanist: "May you understand the gift of God, and may you also expressly grasp the riches from which you implicitly live."

The history of the Humanist Association is still too short to permit a final judgment. The fact that there are human beings in the world who are not religious is nothing historically new: the new factor is that these non-religious people should band together. Even so, this is not the specific characteristic of non-religious humanism, which, it seems to me, lies in the sometimes unconscious and sometimes even denied contention that God represents a competitor for man, and the dilemma is therefore "God or man." One of the two must give way if the survivor is to be fully himself. The difference between theism and Humanism does not lie in the acceptance or rejection of Humanism, therefore, but in the acceptance or rejection of *the loneliness of Humanism.* We feel that there is something extraordinarily chilling in Humanism. I mean that what the atheist does in this world together with his fellow men, and secure in their love, he does in the last resort in the innermost core of his personal freedom on his own. In this world the theist does the same thing as the non-theist, but he does it in the conviction that right down to the deepest roots of his existence he is secure in a love which embraces everything—namely, God.

It is quite true that for the theist life can be just as gloomy, just as uncertain, just as tentative and experimental, as it is for the Humanist. Nowhere does God appear in order to make up for man's impotence and ignorance. Even revelation does not provide him with the ethical standards he needs—

like the Humanist he has to seek them tentatively for himself
in constantly changing situations. What revelation does do is
to give these standards; we must ourselves find a divine direction, and this is experienced in the grace of faith, hope and
love. This means that what a man discovers from his own
human experience as absolutely ethical standards he must
then live up to as a child of God. In this way they attain a
deeper significance, but the ethical content itself does not
fall into his lap out of a clear blue sky. The fact that the
teachings of the Church are sometimes able to formulate
these norms is possible only as the outcome of long periods
of existential thought on the part of believers themselves.
The difference with atheism does not lie here. The believer
integrates his life in and with the world into his personal
dialogue with the mystery of the living God. Thus, far from
being a minus quantity compared with non-theistic humanism, Christian humanism is a plus. The believer also realizes
that he is responsible for the world and its future. His attitude towards human culture in its various forms is a positive
affirmation. He knows that he is one with all men, and that
there is nothing to prevent his working together with other
men, whoever they may be, provided such co-operation is
directed towards the maintenance and development of human
values and there is nothing in it to make him co-responsible
for any evil. In all this he stands firmly in his own faith. His
secular concern with the affairs of this world is a Christian
task.

Modern anthropology tells us that even as seen from a
secular standpoint the human personality becomes an auto-
possession in and through surrender to human community,
since the human personality comes to itself only in community with fellow human beings. We know in addition that it
is in this personal community in particular—not only with a
finite fellow human being, but with the personal God—that
the most profound being of man, far from being compro-

mised, is carried to its highest perfection. Human self-possession is the natural obverse of religious surrender to the living
God. Whoever loses his life for another, and in particular to
The Other, who is at the same time "intimior intimo meo,"
shall gain it.

I should like to close this chapter with one of the most
forthright humanistic utterances I know, and one which must
at the same time persuade us to pass a hopeful judgment on
non-theistic humanism. It happens to come from an unsus-
pected source; namely, St. Thomas Aquinas "Qui veritatem
tenet, non potest devinci, *ne a Deo quidem.*"[26] In order to
understand the full import of this text we must bear in mind
the Thomist view that "truth lies in the understanding." Let
us consider the following against the background of this text:
whoever holds fast to what appears to him in selfless orientation towards reality as truth cannot be overcome by anyone,
not even by God. No one may live in defiance of what his
mind tells him is the truth, and if a man lives in accordance
with what his conscience tells him is the truth, then God will
judge him as a good man with a good chance of reaching
heaven.

If someone should now ask: "Well, what do you really
think of the future of non-theistic humanism?" the first thing

[26] The literal text is as follows: "It would seem unfitting for a man to
dispute with God, so far is God exalted over him. Nonetheless we should
recall that truth does not differ according to who the speaker may be
(*veritatis ex diversitate personarum non variatur*); hence one who speaks the
truth cannot be overcome, with whomever he disputes (*cum quocumque
disputet*)."—*Expos. in Job*, c. 13, lect. 2. Placed in a modern context and
within the Thomistic insight *Veritas est in intellectu,* this text acquires a
great weight of meaning, both in connection with the objectivity of truth
(the point at issue here) and in connection with the personal conviction of
"being in the truth." I do not myself make the truth; the self-generating
insistence of the truth sets the standard for my witness of truth. Truth does
not draw its meaning from my assent to it, but I assent to it because it
declares itself to me as an absolute, although in my understanding of this
"declaration" I can be mistaken (either culpably or inculpably).

I would point out is that I am no prophet, but the second thing would be to tell him a story told by, I think, Karl Rahner. A boy was given a bicycle, and he found it so wonderful that for some weeks it occupied his whole attention. He even forgot to go to Mass on Sunday because he was out riding his bike. In the end, however, he went back to Mass—taking his bike along with him. And that's just how it goes in the rather larger story of mankind. Just at the moment people are fascinated with the great discovery of their new human existential experience, and in their eagerness and delight they are inclined to forget God. But after a while they will turn back to God again—taking their new experience along with them. It took the boy on the bike only a few weeks—it may take mankind with its existential experience a century. We need not be less hopeful on that account.[27]

27 The following literature on humanism should be mentioned: Kwee Swan Liat, *Bibliography of Humanism*, Utrecht 1957; J. Alleman, "De leidende grondgedachten van het moderne a-godsdienstige humanisme et hun onderlinge samenhang," in *TP* 21 (1959), 615–680, and 22 (1960), 13–76; M. Heidegger, *Ueber den Humanismus*, Frankfurt a. Main 1947; F. Jeanson, "Atheisme et Liberté," in *LV* 13 (1954). 85–96; and *Les caractères existentialistes de la conduite humaine selon J.-P. Sartre*, in *Morale chrétienne et requêtes contemporaines* (Cahiers de l'actualité religieuse), Tournai-Paris 1954, pp. 173–194; J. Lacroix, *Le sens de l'athéisme moderne*, Tournai 1958; E. Mauris, *L'athéisme contemporain* (Collection "Croire, penser, espérer"), Geneva 1956; M. Merleau-Ponty, *Sense and Non-Sense*, Evanston, Ill., 1964, and *In Praise of Philosophy*, Evanston, Ill., 1963; G. Rotureau, *Amour de Dieu, amour des hommes*, Tournai 1958; G. Siegmund, *Der Kampf um Gott*, Berlin 1957; P. Rostenne, *La foi des athées*, Paris 1953.

4 Life in God and Life in the World

SECTION I: CHRISTIAN SECULARITY ACCORDING TO DR. ROBINSON

Does being a Christian mean the same thing as being an authentic human being? Or is there perhaps some tension between the intimacy of a man with his God and that man's life amongst his fellow men in and of this world? It is a problem which has become vital for the men of our generation.

What was actually in the air as far as the religious life was concerned—often unspoken, but frequently suggested in practical behavior and put into words now and again—was explosively expressed in an "SCM Paperback" written by the Anglican Bishop of Woolwich, Dr. John A. T. Robinson and entitled *Honest to God*,[1] of which 250,000 copies were sold in five editions within the space of a month (from the middle of March to the middle of April 1963). Since then new edition has followed new edition and there have been translations into all the more important world languages and some of the not so important as well. The success of this paperback, which although it is popularly written is by no means easy to read, cannot be

---

[1] Philadelphia, The Westminster Press, 1963. All page references are to this edition.

accounted for even partly by the fact that Dr. Robinson himself introduced it to the British reading public in *The Observer*. This introduction appeared under the provocative title (which subsequently proved not to have been Dr. Robinson's idea) "Our Image of God Must Go."[2] It was followed by a discussion in which prominent figures in British intellectual life took part: these included C. S. Lewis, E. Mascall, A. Flew, A. Farrer, the Archbishop of Canterbury A. M. Ramsay, and last but not least, Julian Huxley himself.[3] But none of this is sufficient to explain the little book's outstanding success. The primary reason was that Dr. Robinson was saying what a great many people felt. And although, as we shall soon see, there is nothing original about what he had to say, his paperback (written as a popular synthesis) has done a great deal to bring these ideas to the surface of people's consciousness.

Before instituting a personal investigation into the Catholic significance of "Christian secularity" it would be as well if we seriously examined Dr. Robinson's views, as he has already wrestled with the problem. The sound intuitions and even the unsuccessful attempts of others can teach us a good deal. Our exposition will be divided into two parts: in the first we shall discuss *Honest to God* itself and Dr. Robinson's subsequent explanations of its meaning, in the second we propose to attempt to give a personal view of the problems of "Christian secularity" within the life of grace.

THE MAIN LINES OF *HONEST TO GOD*

Dr. Robinson is an Anglican bishop. He is aware that, as such, one of his obligations is to protect and defend the teachings of his Church, and this he points out right at the

---

[2] "Our Image of God Must Go," in *The Observer*, Sunday, March 17, 1963.
[3] Also in *The Observer*, especially Sunday, March 24, 1963, pp. 11–14; Sunday, March 31, 1963, pp. 11 and 12.

beginning of his book.[4] But he then goes on to say that nowadays it is going to become increasingly difficult to know what
the true defence of Christian truth requires. One can, for
example, just repeat what the Church and the theologians
have been teaching for years. But in doing this, are we really
defending the true faith? He rightly comes to the conclusion
that the best defence of true faith may well lie in a re-stating
of traditional orthodoxy in modern terms and a radical renewal of our ideas and practices.

Dr. Robinson, like many others who agree with him, does
not doubt the fundamental value of Christianity, but he
wants to see what he calls "a Copernican revolution" in our
outlook and our practice and its concrete working-out. He
doesn't in the least want to be an iconoclast, and in fact he is
constantly defending those believers who can't go along with
him in his ideas and who still live their Christian faith in
"old concepts." He is therefore well aware that a man can
live religiously with outworn and misleading images. His
personal Christian misgivings derive from his firm conviction
that nowadays our belief, particularly where intellectuals are
concerned, cannot be maintained within the framework of
the old vision and experience. It is for this reason that he
feels that his "Copernican revolution" is necessary, though he
frankly admits that he is not going to enjoy it and as far as
he is concerned it is "a reluctant revolution" (p. 27), though
an urgently necessary one, if Christians are not to be driven
into out-and-out humanism, and even atheism. He is aware,
too, that much of what he is trying to say will be seriously
misunderstood, and that to some extent this may be his fault.
Nevertheless he feels confident that if he is subsequently seen
to have erred, it is in not being nearly radical enough. His
attitude—and it goes to the root of the matter as far as
modern man is concerned—is: "All I can do is to try to be
honest—honest to God and about God—and to follow the

4 *Honest to God*, p. 7.

argument wherever it leads" (p. 28). Well, where has his
argument led him?

*God as the Transcendent Third in Interpersonal Human
Relationships.* Dr. Robinson contends not only that Christianity's traditional formulation of a Supreme Being en-
throned in heaven as "the highest being" is a myth but also
that the statement that God is a transcendent *personal being,*
with knowledge and a will, an entity whose existence can be
demonstrated by so-called proofs of the existence of God, is
a myth. The traditional idea of theism strikes him as at least
problematical. As he indicates in Chapter 3 of his book, "The
Ground of Our Being": "To say that 'God is personal' is to
say that 'reality at its very deepest level is personal' " (p. 48);
in our own interpersonal relationships we touch upon the
greatest spiritual profundity of our lives. God is the depth of
our secular relationships, and in the first place in and through
our interpersonal relationships. God is present in our love
for our fellow human beings as a transcendent third. "The
eternal *Thou* is met only *in, with* and *under* the finite *Thou,*
whether in the encounter with other persons or in the response to the natural order" (p. 53). To believe that God is
love is to believe that in our interpersonal human relationships we not only *should* encounter the most fundamental
truth of reality (which is not yet a belief) but that, in the face
of all the evidence, we do in fact encounter it. This can be
achieved, according to Dr. Robinson, only by an act of faith.[5]

Theology must therefore be the analysis of the depth of our

---

[5] "To believe in God as love means to believe that in pure personal
relationship we encounter, not merely what ought to be, but what is, the
deepest veriest truth about the structure of reality. This, in face of all the
evidence, is a tremendous act of faith. But it is not the feat of persuading
oneself of the existence of a super-Being beyond this world endowed with
personal qualities. Belief in God is the trust, the well-nigh incredible trust,
that to give ourselves to the uttermost in love is not to be confounded but
to be 'accepted,' that love is the ground of our being, to which ultimately
we 'come home' " (page 49).

human intersubjectivity. A contention is theological not because it purports to tell us something about an individual entity we call God, but because it tells us something about the ultimate sense of our existence. And this deepest ground of our being is love from which no one can separate us. Precisely what is *implicit* in all our historically conditioned human relationships is God. God is the "ecstatic" character of our existence, our self-transcendence. We can never encounter God in a "religious" turning away from the world, but it is in unconditional concern for "the other" *seen through to its ultimate depths* that God is found (p. 61). There is no way of encountering God by himself because God is the profoundest depth of all our human experiences and encounters: "God is the depth of common non-religious experience" (p. 62).

Jesus "the Man for Others." All this is seen in its most significant form in Christ. Nowhere in the gospels is it said that the man Jesus is personally God: "Jesus never claims to be God, personally; yet he always claims to bring God, completely" (p. 73). The profoundest sense of our being is revealed in the man Jesus: he loves until the end. Here too the point is that Jesus has experienced his humanity to the end as a humanity for others, for his fellow men. God is revealed in Christ's *self-transcendence.* This transcendence is not a transcendent personal Supreme Being, but—and here Dr. Robinson uses an expression borrowed from Bonhoeffer— "the nearest Thou at hand" (p. 76), just the first fellow human being we happen to meet on our way through life. To be authentically a human being—that is, a human being living for his fellow human beings—means a life based on transcendence, self-transcendence directed towards fellow human beings: that is Christ crucified.

But here too Dr. Robinson seeks to "de-mythologize" the absolute transcendent person. He refers only to the human ecstatic self-transcendence of Jesus. God has revealed himself

in his Son as the profoundest significance of all reality. Jesus
is "the man for others" (p. 76), the man who lives and experiences his humanity for others, but "as united with the
ground of his being, God." (These terms are also borrowed
from Bonhoeffer.) Therefore our "being Christians" is no
more than "being human beings," living for others from the
depths of our being, from which no one can separate us. It is
a question of "worldly holiness," wordly holiness and Christian secularity. To pray does not mean to go to church and
turn your back on the world in order to find God. God can
be found only in the world, and above all in our fellow human beings. Dr. Robinson certainly realizes that now and
again peace and quiet are necessary in our lives, but then
only as a function of our secular activity. Liturgy is holiness
in secular matters (bread, wine, water, oil . . . above all,
solidarity with one's fellow human beings). If we are to be
honest with ourselves, we shall ask, Who really succeeds in
meditating? He understands that cloistered human beings
can practise meditation with greater success, and he admits
that there must be times of engagement and disengagement,
a "need for times of withdrawal," but for ordinary human
beings real life is lived in meeting their fellow human beings; and it is "in this incarnational relationship that deep
speaks to deep" (p. 99), and that is prayer. The "high moun-
tain" that he needs in order to pray is his relationship with
his fellow men. It is there and thus that he receives his revelations. After that he may need to retrace his steps and
analyze the revelations received in prayer; that is to say, the
revelations obtained in contact with his fellow men. To
pray for anyone means "to let *God* into the relationship.
Intercession is to *be with* another at that depth, whether in
silence or compassion or action" (p. 99). The best way to
petition God on behalf of a fellow human being is to be with
that man at the depth of both your beings—a togetherness
which can come about in stillness, in compassionate sympathy

—or by doing something for him personally. Anything else is mystification. Thus in order to pray and meet God we must go out into the world and not withdraw and sit at the side of the road. Unless we go out into the world we shall never experience the miracle of those who went to Emmaus. St. John tells us that God is always love, and that he who does not love his fellow men does not know God. Dr. Robinson quotes George Macleod as saying that whoever does not realize this seeks to "fill a vacuum with 'spiritual thoughts.' " Thus, Christian life is a life for others, and it is therefore also a "worldly life," as Bonhoeffer insisted. There is nothing particularly religious or Christian in giving oneself to a fellow human being—people often do—but to open oneself to another *unconditionally* in love, that is a Christian act.

Dr. Robinson now contends that, on the basis of this new Christian insight, Christianity has been freed by Bultmann from the "mythological," by Tillich from the "supernatural," and by Bonhoeffer from the "religious." The result is, Dr. Robinson finds, that he can be "an agnostic with the agnostic, even an atheist with the atheists" (p. 127); and he also finds that when he listens to discussions broadcast by the BBC between Christians and Humanists, most of his sympathies are with the latter. However, he is against any form of naturalism in the sense of Julian Huxley's *Religion without Revelation.* Religion for him is not just "faith in the possibilities of man," as it is for Huxley. The difference between them is that according to Huxley love *ought to be* the last word as far as human life is concerned—but that belief doesn't require a revelation—whereas according to Dr. Robinson love —against all the evidence—*is* the last word where everything is concerned, and that is something we can know only from revelation. For this reason Dr. Robinson regards the kind of secular Christianity he upholds as something different from either atheism or humanism. His form of Christianity sets out to hold the golden mean between humanism and the "orthodox" belief in supranaturalism, according to which God is a personal being who created the temporal world out of nothing and then entered into a personal relationship with man. Certainly, God grounds everything wholly in love, but to see God endowed with a centre of consciousness and will like ourselves and yet "wholly other" is mythological.

All this is fraught with consequences for ethics. Only love is an ethical injunction; everything else must be judged by reference to love. The result is, as Dr. Robinson points out in Chapter 6 of his book, "The New Morality," that judged from the standpoint of love, divorce, for example, can sometimes be good, sometimes bad. And, finally, this new outlook involves a variety of consequences for the Church which must become the servant of the world, as Dr. Robinson points out in Chapter 7, "Recasting the Mould." But for the moment we propose to leave this aspect of the matter to one side.

The "God of Religion." Dr. Robinson's book may well be regarded as a reaction to the contention that man is naturally religious. Bonhoeffer has already sharply opposed this idea and contended that Christianity must be freed from this dependence on the *anima naturaliter religiosa*. Both Bonhoeffer and Dr. Robinson say that the so-called *need* for God, which is then ontologically reinforced by proof of the existence of God, is a myth. The "God of religion" is a *deus ex machina*— a God who, when we are unable to provide the answers and the explanations, provides them for us, a "stop-gap or long-stop" (Bonhoeffer used the term *Lückenbusser,* a stop-gap or make-weight). In the meantime "such a God" is constantly being pushed farther and farther out of this world. The "last secret place" that he still occupies today is the private world of the individual's need for God. This is what both Bonhoeffer and Dr. Robinson call "religion" (as distinct from "divine worship and faith"), and it is here, according to Dr. Robinson, that the Churches still operate, attending to the needs of those who feel, or can be induced to feel, in this way. Very well, it is clear that this "religious premise" of Christianity must now be discarded, just as St. Paul had the courage to discard circumcision as a precondition for Christianity. If we are honest with ourselves, we must recognize the necessity of living in the world even if God is not there: this fundamental premise of Bonhoeffer's is adopted by Dr. Robinson. Further, the protest of atheism against such a Supreme Being, against a "personal, transcendent God" is valid: "This was the God they must *kill* if man was not to continue dispossessed and kept in strings" (p. 41). We must bring Christianity to the "secular world," which has no need of religion. This secularity is God's greatest gift to our age. In the future "secular man" can believe in God, who is love, without experiencing any need of religion. The future of "religion" is "secular holiness." Dr. Robinson now takes leave of the "God of religion" by quoting the grisly words of Julian Huxley: "Operationally, God is beginning to resemble not a ruler but the last fading smile of a cosmic Cheshire Cat."[6] Whoever attacks this god preserves the transcendence of the real God. But at the same time, Dr. Robinson tells us, he has completely reinterpreted Christianity; its idea of God, its dogma, its public worship and its evangelism. We may conclude that what he aims at is the "secularization" of religion and Christianity in an attempt to explore the full consequences of Christianity in face of a *total absence of religion* (p. 104).

The Wider Context of Dr. Robinson's Experiment. The foregoing represents essentially, though only in broad outline, the content of *Honest to God.* Is Dr. Robinson really in favour of a radical secularization of Christianity? Merely to ask this question is a serious matter, but it is justified because we see definite symptoms suggesting that this is not simply a question of seeking a Christian attitude towards the

[6] *Religion without Revelation,* New York, New American Library, 1959, p. 58.

phenomenon of secularity. Certain signs indicate that on all sides there are Christians who hold views about religion which tend to coincide more or less with those which the non-religious Dutch Humanist Association (or at least some of its representatives) bring to their approach to the world and their fellow men. One is reminded of the crisis in the Middle Ages when a peripatetic heathen philosopher was appealed to against the traditional teaching, and Christians brought up in the Augustinian tradition believed that the Anti-Christ had appeared. Galileo's demythologizing of the Bible was another such crisis, and so was the Modernist reinterpretation of the articles of faith at the beginning of this century. But the present crisis seems to call Christianity into question more radically than any of these. At the same time there is no cause for "alarmism." Not that this means that everything is now going to come all right on its own. The feeble cry "Oh, it'll all come out all right" will not do, as far as I am concerned. There was not only a Thomas in the Middle Ages who rose above the crisis, there was also a Siger of Brabant who, in the same crisis, went under. And besides the Modernists who succeeded in "reinterpreting" dogma in an authentic way (though only in a preliminary fashion, since the same problem is still with us, still unsolved and still of real importance) there were also Modernists who hollowed out the faith with the knife of their human reason, not guided by God's word but reshaping it to fit human standards. The present reaction towards secularization (which has been facilitated by our own outmoded theology, and above all by our factual experience of Christianity) is salutary—on condition that we keep our ears attuned to the word of God and remain humble towards his revelation of truth as an existential and saving revelation. It is salutary because the fact that a tendency is so obstinate, and so intensified by contact with ordinary men and women of our day and their problems, appears to suggest that this tendency is justified and undoubtedly touches somewhere on a real but partial truth which was formerly hidden. But just because this truth lay outside the view of our "outmoded" practice and theology and has nowadays become existentially self-evident, its one-sidedness brings the faith itself into question. The fact is that what is new, and profoundly experienced, can obscure earlier truths which remain believable only insofar as they are thoroughly rethought right down to the core of their original formulation and become, as it were, newly discovered. It may appear paradoxical, but the recognition of old truths sometimes demands a more profound conversion than the recognition of attractive, freshly discovered truths which have the advantage of a new and surprising brilliance, although they shock us because they upset our familiar ideas.

Although theological reflection can help us in the renewed discovery of old truths, it is nevertheless only a subordinate servant. Only the breakthrough of a new appreciation of God, of God as a value in and of himself worthy of love—and the heart and centre of all other values, a source that appears constantly vaster and richer than all that we can draw from it in human luxury and secular enchantment—can show us the one-sidedness of the radical secularizing tendency. At the same time, though in the second place, the authenticity and frankness with which this new Christian part-truth is posited is itself promising. But the honest recognition of this candor, which is really a tacit plea for clemency (if not acceptance), does not excuse theology from the task of showing that this candid affirmation is only partial, and that if it is posited as the total affirmation of Christianity it will undermine Christianity in its very foundations. This task must be carried out in a clear-minded way while at the same time we listen carefully to what this secularization has to say to us. God is most assuredly above all concepts and formulations, and we can

keep him in clear and precise perspective only to the extent
that we recall all our ideas of God one by one and constantly
try to see beyond our expression of them. Precisely because
God transcends our concepts there is the inherent danger that
Christian belief will pursue the quest for understanding into
a void, a process which has been exemplified again and again
by the pseudo-mystics. But on the other hand there is the
constant danger of making our religious beliefs dependent on
outworn ideas. Hence many of the reactions against the "horizontal" course of contemporary Christianity may be arising
from an inaccurate idea of the "vertical dimension" in religion—in other words, the reaction is not always one deriving from the Lord. Finally—and here is the crux of the question—by reacting against certain traditional religious ideas
and formulations one may distort the values these aim at or
their authentic *meaning* or *trend*. To horizontalize Christianity in this way would be to produce the most radical evacua-
tion of the meaning of the Christian faith (and indeed of any
kind of theism) ever experienced in the history of the
Church. We can see in Holland, too, evidence here and there
of such a radical secularization.

Before we test the radical secularization of religion against
what we believe to be Catholic conviction let us first be perfectly fair to Dr. Robinson's own vision, and ask ourselves
whether he must be termed a complete "horizontalist."

I am quite convinced (and the following analysis will make
it clear) that a dissection of *Honest to God* on its own will
take you just anywhere. In the book itself there is nothing at
all to show the reader clearly the one valid direction which
the author himself intends to take. It is just because of this
that *Honest to God* has given rise to so much misunderstanding; some readers have even declared that Dr. Robinson
would have been more honest if he had frankly written himself off as a Christian. There has been a quite embarrassing
lack of what Dr. Robinson himself calls "charity of interpre-

tation,"[7] an amiable good will which, according to him, he has more often experienced at the hands of non-churchgoers and "non-believers" (who, incidentally, also reject his book), than from churchgoers. This embarrassing fact provides practical proof, at least in part, of Dr. Robinson's own thesis: practical Christianity is often estranged from the world around it and bothers its head very little about real human problems.

On the other hand, one never reads a book which deals with definitely modern problems quite apart from what is already on the market in that milieu. The conjunction of a religious terminology with an agnostic, even atheistic, way of life, which yet insists that love *is* the ultimate meaning of life (and not merely that it ought to be), is no longer a matter for surprise in our society. That a bishop should write as Dr. Robinson does is of course not an everyday affair, but our insecure and uncertain age is hardly shocked by anything at all. He does touch, however, a real problem which demands a daring solution; it is a bold venture precisely because the "solution" cannot be made crystal clear. When in *Honest to God* Robinson remains vague, even in really fundamental matters, there are certain to be divergent interpretations for which the responsibility really cannot be placed on the readers.

Some guidance to a deeper understanding of what Dr. Robinson himself actually means can be found in his own contributions to *The Honest to God Debate*.[8] Though, as we shall soon see, these explanatory articles themselves re-

[7] John A. T. Robinson and David L. Edwards, *The Honest to God Debate* (S.C.M. paperback), Philadelphia, The Westminster Press, 1963 (hereafter cited as *Debate*), p. 240. C. J. Hoekendijk also has said a few amiable words on the subject in "Open Kaart. Nederlandse reacties op *Honest to God*," in *Wending* 18 (1963), 682. Hereafter this particular issue of *Wending* will be cited as "Open Kaart."

[8] See also the contributions to "Open Kaart" and O. Fielding Clarke, *For Christ's Sake: A Reply to "Honest to God,"* Wallington-Surrey 1963[2].

quire a laborious analysis if we wish to reveal the core of
Dr. Robinson's contentions clearly and without prejudice,
they do show clearly how wrong those people are who contend that *Honest to God* speaks for itself. The Bishop of
Woolwich begins by posing a pastoral problem and wants in
this way to deal with the gravamen of the problem. But his
pastoral approach to our present age has essential theological
implications, and these must be judged theologically within
the perspective of the word of God to which we are bound.
But in this respect care must be taken not to fall into a
"magic" of the *word,* which is not so very different from what
was formerly experienced as the "magic" of the sacrament.

DR. ROBINSON'S APOSTOLIC CONCERN: A REINTERPRETATION OF THE FAITH IN THE LIGHT OF SECULARITY

A Confrontation of Christian Belief with Present-Day Secularity

One thing is beyond all doubt: Dr. Robinson's fundamental
concern relates to the living reality of God. Yet he approves
wholeheartedly of the secularity of modern man. The present
generation of mankind is the first which is wholly the product
of our modern society in which technology embraces the
whole of life, and which turns its face away from classic
humanism, the Graeco-Latin *humaniora,* and dismisses all
"metaphysics."[9] A third of the world's population regards
atheism as "the one true faith" ensuring political and social
progress.[10] Dr. Robinson's pastoral work lies south of the
Thames, and his latest articles show very clearly that he likes
the kind of modern people among whom he has to work.

[9] See G. Hourdin, *La nouvelle vague croit-elle en Dieu?,* Paris 1959.
[10] See F. Perroux, *La Coëxistence pacifique,* Paris.

Christian charity impels him to bring the living God to these twentieth-century men—"I want God to be as real for our modern secular, scientific world as He ever was for *the ages of faith*."[11] God must also be a living reality for such people as these. It is from this solicitude that we must interpret *Honest to God,* for that is what is at stake. The men of the twentieth century in Britain believe in God: this has been shown with striking clarity by various public opinion polls. "I would submit that the creed of the English is that there *is* a God (the polls bear this out, whatever it may mean, with striking unanimity), that it *is* wise to pray to Him from time to time, but that, in terms of *that* God, they are practical atheists."[12] A man interested in the cure of souls cannot just accept this.

There is something about our theology and our preaching that makes it impossible for the modern man to believe, to believe in practice, in God. For this reason Dr. Robinson proposes to launch a dialogue—not so much between Christians and those who stand outside the Churches,[13] as between Christians and secular man whether he is inside or outside the Churches.[14] Actually, even this is not very accurately expressed; it is really a question of a dialogue between "the religious man" and "the secular man," who, if he is "religious," is so in the specifically unfavourable sense Dr. Robinson attaches to his "religiousness." Secularization, complete worldliness, implies the breach, not with Christianity, but with what he calls "religiousness": the factor which is seen as against the social-economic and technical progress of our society. In other words what Dr. Robinson calls "religion"

11 Robinson, *Debate,* p. 279.

12 Robinson, *Debate,* p. 229.

13 In this respect H. Jonker, in an otherwise remarkable article, mistakes Robinson's meaning ("Open Kaart," pp. 747–749).

14 "It is a dialogue between religious man and secular man. And secular man is just as much inside the Church as out of it, and just as much inside myself" (Robinson, *Debate,* p. 275).

means a God who has no reason to manifest himself except when man lacks something, an "intervening God" about whom there is no need to bother one's head when everything is going smoothly in life, and who is blamed when things go wrong—in sickness, war, disaster, and so on. According to sound Catholic theology we should call "religious" in this sense "pseudo-religious." I think Dr. Robinson would be able to accept this distinction: he too is well aware that the whole Christian tradition has always reacted against such false piety. However—and he is quite right—he refuses to be fobbed off with it. It is all well and good that in the seclusion of theologians' studies true religion has been defined and this is clear in their books (which are inaccessible to the average man), but the fact remains that ordinary church people (and they are the ones we are dealing with) are fed up with "religion,"[15] that the ordinary man looks on God as a "stop-gap," a God necessary to him to fill up the lacunae in his science. Bonhoeffer's statement that as human beings we can get along without God is explained by Dr. Robinson as always meaning "without having to bring him in,"[16] without having to see him as one of the many links in our understanding of the world. God is not an element with which the exact sciences can concern themselves: he manifests himself in a totally different sphere. "Secular man" is thus a man who does not need God for his secular understanding, as an element *to be added* to the secular factors, something without which this vision of man and the world would not be complete. I am well aware that secularism can be given another sense, but we must use the word in the sense that Dr. Robinson gives it (and for this the "scientific" attitude of the twentieth century is decisive). As Christians we too can fully accept this secularity. On the other side, there is what he

15 *Debate,* pp. 269–270.
16 *Debate,* p. 271.

calls "the religious man," the man who believes in God, although he regards the living God in a naive, prescientific-age fashion as "a stop-gap," an attitude which often leads to anti-progressive reactions in our society—for instance, such a man might well oppose inoculation against poliomyelitis on the ground that it cast doubt on divine providence.

The fact that *Honest to God* is intended to be an enthusiastic affirmation of God precisely for the secular and anti-"religious" man is confirmed by Dr. Robinson's own admission that his book is rejected by both atheists and "religious" men.[17] It is perplexing to hear Mr. MacIntyre charge Dr. Robinson with using "religious language to mask an atheistic vacuum"[18]—in order, in fact, to be able to proclaim atheism in a way acceptable to Christians. The dialogue that Dr. Robinson proposes is one between the secular man and the religious man in the sense described, and Dr. Robinson conducts his side of the dialogue as a Christian; that is to say, as anti-"religious" and completely open to secularity, of which he fully approves. If one fails to grasp this, it is impossible to understand *Honest to God* in its own sense, and one becomes unfair to Dr. Robinson. He tells us that his book was born of the fact that he knew himself to be committed without reservation to Christ, and also a man committed, without possibility of return, to modern twentieth-century secular society.[19] He tells us further that his book was written out of the belief that both these convictions must be taken with equal seriousness and that they *cannot* be incompatible. His aim is to bring the living God to a secularized world which is threatening to slip into atheism, and he wants to do it in such a way that the modern man need not feel religion

17 *Debate*, p. 231.

18 *Debate*, p. 229; MacIntyre, for his part, calls Robinson "a very conservative atheist" (p. 216); the atheism is, he finds, most evident in *Honest to God* (p. 215).

19 *Debate*, p. 275.

as a naive, prescientific, and for him unacceptable, encroachment on his unshakable secular ideas and practical outlook.

It therefore strikes me as inaccurate to regard as Dr. Robinson's chief anxiety the problem of the way to present the
faith and the language in which to do it. That is after all a
question with which the theologians have wrestled again and
again, and it has always given rise to tension between "con-
servatives" and "reformers." Of course one is entitled to ask
whether the weak spot of his undertaking is not perhaps to
be found in this, though it is a subordinate part of his pastoral program. However, the thing he is above all interested
in is the extent to which our Christian religion is foreign to
this practical world in both doctrine and practice. He regards
this divorce from the practical world in an age of secularization as highly dangerous for Christianity. The numbers of
those who have turned their back on the Church and the
misgivings of those who still cling to the Church are proof
that his anxiety is well founded, and it is because of this that
he is anxious to crystallize the attitude of Christianity to the
world clearly and sharply. The *consequence* is that he under-
standably attacks the patterns in which our faith is expressed
and the pattern of life of churchgoers. The problem of religious language is therefore only a subordinate part of a
more radical and more fully formulated problem: What is
the place and the significance of religion in the life of man
who, precisely as man, is attached hand and foot, anxiously,
lovingly and in suffering, to this secular world? In his attempts to resolve this problem, Dr. Robinson believes he can
see helpful suggestions in the writings of Tillich, Bonhoeffer
and Bultmann, so he eagerly seizes on them and quotes their
observations to us gratefully, irrespective of whether the con-
texts of these three authors are reproduced or the meaning
of each seen within his own particular perspective.

Undoubtedly there is a close connection between problems
of this kind and the question raised in a special number of

the *Tijdschrift voor Theologie*,[20] and it may be that the line Dr. Robinson has taken in providing a solution will strengthen the connection, or perhaps even fuse the two problems—the problem of religious language and that of the place of religion in the life of man—into one. Nevertheless the primary concern in each case is quite different. Dr. Robinson, for his part, is not concerned with marshalling arguments to bring back into the Church those who have turned their backs on it;[21] his undertaking is simply "a venture in evangelism," and it is intended to interest not only those inside but those who have always been outside the Church as well. The fact is that Dr. Robinson has received thousands of letters about this and, as he tells us, his little book has brought many people "back to God" or to a profound spiritual freedom.

"Aggiornamento" for Our Religious Conceptions

The methods Dr. Robinson adopts in his efforts to grapple with the problem of "Christianity and the present spiritual situation" become immediately clear from the previous sketch of the general position. It is in view of the fact that there is such a direct clash between the "religious" interpretation of Christianity and the "secular" attitude of modern man that Dr. Robinson is anxious to "revitalize" the Glad Tidings that God sent to us through Christ.[22] It is natural that he should try to reshape the imagery and practice of the faith because for him secularity is a matter of course. In Dr. Robinson's view, when there is a conflict between faith and science it is "faith" which must give way, for the very good

---

20 "De verwereldlijking van de godsdienst: een genade of een verzoeking," in *TT* 3 (1963), n. 3.

21 Robinson says of his book: "It is not addressed from inside the Church to those outside" (*Debate*, p. 275).

22 The word is Robinson's own (*Debate*, p. 251), although he refers to it only indirectly in connection with the *theologia naturalis*.

reason that in that case it can't really be faith at all, but mere imagery. And formally speaking, if this "science" is true science—and that may well be an inescapable fact—then he is right. Dr. Robinson thus aims at making true faith preachable and acceptable once again, insofar as it is not in itself[23] an obstacle to true acceptance by modern man, merely an out-of-date "religious" image. What he is aiming at is what Pope John XXIII called the "aggiornamento" of Christianity. The Pope pointed out that it is not so much a matter of formulating the faith in an orthodox fashion as of formulating it so that men can understand it. Dr. Robinson is also anxious to point out that his "aggiornamento"[24] "will, I am convinced, leave the fundamental truth of the Gospel unaffected."[25] We must take this assertion very seriously. There can of course be a great difference between what one intends to do and what one in fact does, but all the same we must not doubt that Dr. Robinson intends to be orthodox. He does not want to preach any new faith, and he stands with heart and soul behind the gospel Good Tidings. All he wants to do is to translate the Good Tidings into a form which will mean something to the men of the twentieth century. His orthodox confession of faith rings out clearly: we men of the twentieth century must use other means of communicating the rich

23 It is of course true—and this aspect Robinson leaves out of consideration—that even if faith is declared "acceptable," the solution is not very self-evident. In any event this seems to me to be the original contribution in the otherwise harsh, and to me unjustified, criticism in "Open Kaart," especially that from the orthodox Protestant side: "In my view Robinson is asking for too total a concentration on the survival chances of the Christian faith as it is now formulated, and too little for the legitimacy of its reinterpretation" (H. Kuitert, p. 743). C. Dippel, it seems to me, puts this more perceptively: "the fear that the gospel does not fit into this world, and the effort to make it fit" (ibid., p. 813).

24 "A radically new mould, or meta-morphosis of Christian belief and practice" (Honest to God, p. 124), a remoulding of the entire life and practice of the faith.

25 Honest to God, p. 124.

heritage of Christian tradition which up to now has been expressed in prescientific and pre-"secular" categories.[26] Even if it appears that he has not succeeded in doing what he set out to do, this must not make us forget the validity, and above all the urgency, of the task he undertook. I feel that the real reason for the wide sale of his book lies precisely in what he tried to do, and for this we should be deeply grateful even if the actual result is not successful.

Orthodoxy is not primarily a question of adherence to the precise conceptual formulation of the articles of faith but of assent to the intent expressed in the formulation. As St. Thomas Aquinas says: "The act of faith has its term not in the proposition as it is enunciated—that is, in the conceptual image—but in the *reality itself*."[27] It is primarily the assent in faith to the saving reality of the gospel which makes anyone's faith "orthodox." On the other hand, this assent in faith cannot be given in the absence of a conceptual image or expression through which this saving reality can be aimed at. This formulation of the faith must not be replaced simply by something arbitrary, for then we should be affirming something without really knowing what we mean, and in that case we could say practically anything and believe that it was the Christian faith! The intent of the faith has its repercussion on the expressed affirmation of faith itself. Thus orthodoxy also lies—but secondarily—in the formulation of the faith, but only insofar as and because it is an inner (not merely intrinsic, pragmatic or symbolic) *reference* to saving reality. Hence the *mot juste* is important for faith. But there is more to it than that. Not only is the *mot juste* involved in what one ordinarily means by "orthodoxy"; there can like-

---

26 *Debate,* p. 230.

27 *ST* II-II, q. 1, a. 2, ad 2. By "intention" we mean in-tending (not "intention" in the modern sense of the good intention); that is to say, an awareness of direction which views the truth without absorbing it with understanding.

wise be a *mot juste* for the conceptual image, the word which seizes my understanding, unveils concrete reality to me, allows my understanding to make contact with reality. In this sense it is the crucial word. Now for Dr. Robinson the *mot juste* in the first sense is a presupposition, but he speaks of it expressly only in the second sense. It is as though someone were to say, "You are the loveliest girl in the world—there is no one like you." As an expression of admiration the remark is perfectly orthodox, but judged by the standards of the exact sciences the orthodoxy of the statement looks a trifle doubtful, if it is not altogether untrue. Dr. Robinson means something of the sort. For the man who is living in a pre-scientific and naive stage of human culture the old imagery of belief is not only orthodox, but, in addition, the *mot juste;* that is to say, as far as the prescientific believer is concerned it is calculated to render the truths of the gospel real and tangible. For a man of the twentieth century, on the other hand, a "secular" man, such imagery will have lost all significance. To quote the Provost of Derby Cathedral, "most traditional, conservative theological writing of today is lucid, correct and dead."[28] The old imagery has in fact become a hindrance to belief; it is, as Dr. Robinson says, "irrelevant and incredible."[29] Traditional views, he says, are neither true nor false, an attitude which Sperna Weiland has formulated clearly: it is not a question of the *truth* of an image or a conception, but "of the suitability or not of that image or that conception to make the truth of the Gospel in the given situation visible, audible, tangible—in short, real."[30] It is a question of how the imagery and the conceptions *work,* and not of giving a different content to the declarations of faith.[31]

The reproach that some people have made to Dr. Robinson

---

28 *Debate,* p. 41.
29 *Debate,* p. 230.
30 "Open Kaart," p. 803–804; see *Debate,* p. 230.
31 *Debate,* p. 41.

that he, a well-known biblical expert, did not turn to the profoundly human language of the Old Testament, shows very clearly that they have failed to grasp his main intention. He is thinking above all of "the scientist," the man accustomed to work in the exact sciences, and of the ordinary twentieth-century man whose life has been thoroughly shaped by these same sciences. For such twentieth-century people there is no place for "metaphysics" or theology side by side with "science": any scientific validity is denied them because in this modern world of ours "science" means exclusively "the exact sciences," and the social sciences in the broader sense. In these kinds of science there is—and quite rightly— no place for God. Again and again Dr. Robinson speaks of "the modern, secular, *scientific* world." Incidentally, for him secularization is a neutral fact which applies to Christians too since we all—Christians and non-Christians alike—take the assumptions of modern science seriously, and this naturally has its effects on our idea of God and on our experience of God.[32] Apart from this scientific contact between man and the world there is only "the quite different" sphere of human relationships and love. Dr. Robinson wants to provide the scientifically-minded whose outlook is so slanted—a slant he unquestionably accepts—with a new religious language. But seeing that this has to be looked for outside the sciences, all that remains is the language of love. As an expert student of the Bible, Dr. Robinson knows better than anyone that this kind of language is spoken par excellence in Scripture. But he also knows that this biblical language is interwoven with a prescientific and naive form of expression. Therefore, though he certainly reverts to the biblical way of speaking about God, he tries to free its expression from the prescientific mode of thought.

He does this with the subtitle to a contribution to the debate, "A Currency Crisis," and in a very practical inventive

[32] *Debate*, p. 228.

English fashion.[33] A crisis has arisen, he tells us; a breakdown
of communications between the proclamation and those who
listen to it. One thing that Dr. Robinson fails to ask himself
is whether this breakdown might be due to some defect in the
receiving apparatus: he is quite convinced of the justification
of secularity. The result is that he looks for the cause of the
breakdown exclusively on the other side; in the imagery of
the proclamation—behaviour which, to say the least of it,
strikes me as one-sided. "Currency" regarded as a means of
communication is made up for Dr. Robinson of the doctrinal
dogmas of the faith, the moral standards which are set up, the
ritual forms of the liturgy, and so on. This currency derives
its whole value from the "gold standard" on which it is based;
that is to say, the existential involvement with God's covenant
in Christ with us. As Dr. Robinson points out, "in times of
economic stability we do not give a thought to what lies
behind our paper money; we take it at its face value and use
it as a ready and acceptable means of communication and exchange" (p. 245). But as a result of various circumstances men
may be forced to give some thought to the factual value and
validity of their country's currency system. When men begin
to ask questions in this way the result is a crisis. What is
nowadays called an "in-group" continues to regard the currency as valid, while a steadily growing group of "outsiders"
can see no validity in it at all. In Dr. Robinson's words: "the
uneasy suspicion is growing that churchmen may find themselves holding wads of paper money whose exchange value is
virtually nil" (p. 245). Because of its out-of-date imagery
dogma is beginning to look as though it had no content at
all: it is therefore time for revaluation. There are two ways
of reacting to such a situation, Dr. Robinson tells us; one is
to stress the value of the old money at all costs, to strengthen
its purchasing power by internal reforms, and to try to extend its area of exchange. But before long it becomes clear

[33] "A Currency Crisis" (*Debate*, pp. 243–248).

that this can be no more than a short-term policy, and in fact there is only one solution: to replace the currency with as little real loss as possible, while there is still time. The Church must therefore ask itself how much of the baggage it is carrying around with it is really essential if it is to remain loyal to the gospel of Jesus. A currency crisis that forces us back on our *real assets,* says Dr. Robinson, can be a salutary shock. Only then can the Christian message hope for a hearing amongst modern, secular men.

Proceeding from the related phenomena of the drift away from the Churches and the misgivings and anxiety of those who are still in them, Rahner has said very much the same thing as we have just heard from Dr. Robinson: "The only permissible tutiorism in the practical life of the Church today is the tutiorism of boldness. . . . We must ask ourselves how far we may go, using all the theological and pastoral possibilities open to us, since the position of the Kingdom of God is certainly such that we must dare the utmost if we are to stand firm as God demands of us. . . . It seems to me, in this as in many other questions, that if *this* tutiorism were adopted—that is to say, adopted as an imperative for our time (not as a principle valid for all ages)—and if we proceeded from the conviction that the safest thing to do is the boldest and that this stands the best chance of success— not wariness, but the utmost allowable boldness—then many an idea in the Church would take on a different form."[34] This quotation seems to me to illustrate precisely what Dr. Robinson has in mind. But then I would like to extend this view (which Rahner propounds quite independently of Dr. Robinson) with a quotation to the effect that this new form of tutiorism does not by any means suggest that "we must let everything and anything be perpetrated in the Church, that no one at all must summon up courage to oppose some other

[34] *Blust de Heer niet uit,* Hilversum, pp. 16–17

tendency in the Church, to utter a warning against it, and to challenge it to a real and serious battle. Otherwise what we have said has not been adequately understood."[35] In this spirit we are prepared to go with Dr. Robinson's "tutiorism of boldness" just as far as we think we can reasonably go, and we shall call an unmistakable halt as soon as we have in all honesty to say that in our opinion he is going further than loyalty to the evangelical message permits. The fact is that there is an obvious misunderstanding between God and our generation, and this misunderstanding urgently demands dissipation if we wish to prevent more and more people from drifting into atheism and agnosticism, a state of affairs where "religious" language cannot really conceal practical atheism.

THE CORE OF THE CHRISTIAN KERYGMA ACCORDING TO DR. ROBINSON

The message of salvation that the Bible proclaims tells us—translated into Dr. Robinson's "new language," which is to be understandable and credible for everyone—that a Christian is a man who lives in the world with and for others, thanks to his belief in the depth dimension of life which cannot be expressed in any other way but as *personal love*. This love which buttresses and sustains everything is God, and has revealed itself as love precisely in the man Jesus. Dr. Robinson regards the world, the reality in which men live, as a "mercy," a gift. There are elements in our being which betray a depth of reality in which all human love and everything else find their ground and source. We find the shadow of God everywhere in our existence. As Dr. Robinson says: "God is known through his effects."[36] The Bible calls this absolute ground "the love of God *and* the grace of our Lord Jesus Christ *and* fellowship *in* the Holy Spirit" (2 Cor.

35 *Ibid.*, p. 19–20.
36 *Debate*, p. 254.

13:14); and "these three" are one absolute reality because in each of them the Christian experiences the absolutely unconditional. The Trinity is therefore the only legitimate Christian name for the reality we call God. With this Dr. Robinson does not mean "a God conceived in some vaguely impersonal pantheistic terms," but "the God of Abraham, Isaac and Jacob, the God and Father of our Lord Jesus Christ."[37]

And *Honest to God* has been written, we are told, to bring us word of this Trinity, revealed in the man Jesus in a manner credible to the men of our day.[38] It is not a matter of a confession of faith in a word or a formula. God must be found right there where men live and work, and not "far off," outside ordinary life, and not only when a man comes to the end of his life and lies on his deathbed. Those things in life which people find most interesting seem to have nothing to do with God; hence Dr. Robinson's desire to bring God back into the centre of human life. "He is not far away," *Dominus prope est.* Therefore, says Dr. Robinson, let us start from what people find most interesting in their daily lives: it is there we must find God. And what really interests them most is not in the last resort money, nor sex as such, but love. We need to love and be loved: we need to be fully accepted as individuals "for our own sake." This is precisely what love does; it accepts a man for what he is; it gives him dignity, it "makes his life." And now when we open the Bible we see a man who made and remade men through his love. We can see love at work in a way never seen before that time or since. In Jesus the gospel sees God at work, because God is love. "There's love for you," says Calvary—that is, unto the death of Jesus. The Good Tidings: love is there for me too. And his resurrection teaches us that even death cannot break the power of this love to transform and save: "Love is still

37 *Debate,* p. 262.
38 *Debate,* pp. 276–279.

supreme!" A Christian is therefore nothing but a man who believes in love as the ultimate meaning of his being. Love for him is the ultimate, conclusive reality: God. Only in this way can "modern, secular man" understand that life and the universe represent something more than scientific formulas. The real key to reality and to humanity is love. It is truly love that makes the world go round.

It is a simple message, a true biblical message, a message such as we hear regularly from the pulpit. Of course, one must ask just what Dr. Robinson means by it, but for God's sake let us allow his words to get through to us first, before entering into a theological analysis, necessary as that is, and let us not forget the message of love when we start to wrestle with precise meanings. Dr. Robinson teaches us that even in a theological journal it is necessary first to listen to this simple, matter-of-fact message before we start worrying about orthodoxy. You can theologically reason yourself away from the message altogether by demanding, for example: What exactly does Dr. Robinson mean by this? Personally I think that his meaning is crystal clear without any need of theologizing, namely that love is love and means surrendering yourself to the other. That is what a Christian does because he knows that God is love, and that he has given proof of this love, pressed down and running over, in his Son Jesus Christ. Despite all difficulties, a Christian believes that his life is sustained by this absolute love in every hour of the day and in all that he does. Isn't this the authentic gospel message? Theology can illuminate all its implications, but it cannot add one jot or tittle to it. Dr. Robinson's express profession of faith, not merely the intention of his faith, would appear to be perfectly Christian and orthodox. It still remains to be seen whether his theological explanations are the same. With this I do not mean whether he takes over the traditional imagery of the Christian confession of faith, but whether his conception does not destroy this message itself by contradicting fundamental, or even less central aspects of it. This is important too. But even if in this respect he should be found wanting, that is no reason to cast doubt on his primary, and for him decisive, orthodoxy. Incidentally, isn't there in practice a trace of unorthodoxy in all theology just because we are still on the way to a full and clear revelation of the *Eschaton?*

DR. ROBINSON'S THEORY OF KNOWLEDGE

It is hardly necessary to demonstrate that the interpretation of the act of knowledge is also a matter of extreme importance for the faith. Even though religiousness is not in the first place a question of knowing but one of surrender in faith and confession, this surrender implies in the nature of things a consciousness of value. The interpretation of this consciousness is all the more important because the believer professes to live in a relationship to the absolute. The critical theoretical question of how in his life and his self-understanding man comes into contact with the absolute is therefore a vital question which must precede any thematic exercises of his religious convictions. Dr. Robinson is also inclined to this opinion, and he is therefore willing to make a place in his faith for the once despised *theologia naturalis,* as he calls it, meaning the naturally given possibility of talking sensibly about God.

Very little of his theory of knowledge appears in *Honest to God;* and this is one of the reasons why the exegesis of it could arrive at almost any conclusion, even that it is almost atheistic, or at least, exhibits a vague kind of "religious agnosticism." Incidentally, even if this theory of knowledge should turn out to be the weak spot in his theological vision, we should nevertheless guard ourselves against putting a question mark against his faith. A relativistic theory of knowledge should certainly objectively and logically call into question the orthodoxy of his beliefs, but no human beings are logical in all things. The lack of logic should therefore be seen as not so much in his faith as in his theological interpretation of it and in the theory of knowledge it implies. A positivist who explains all human phenomena, including love, in terms of chemical stimuli may nevertheless truly love his wife. If she were to tell him what he could do with love "like that" and send him packing, she would indeed have recognized his lack of logic, but be ascribing it to the wrong sector. And this is what we often do with "heretics."

But none of this means that the lack of logic does not urgently need adjustment, because the longer it is left to establish itself, the greater the danger that even the original orthodox intention will in the long run be worn away, and then the bad logic will set everything awry. Our human existence does not halt at prereflective experience; it is an auto-thinking and expressing existence that comes more completely to itself precisely in reflection. In the same way the existence of faith is a self-interpreting existence, a reflective existence in faith. Reflection is not an ideological superstructure. It is in the explicitation of, for example, the experience of love that love first comes completely to itself. In the same way faith will attain its validity in reflecting on its own experience. Faith therefore demands a thinking that respects the intention of faith. Otherwise this very human assimilation itself could guide the life of faith in a wrong direction and in consequence bring life based on faith into the wrong path. Without orthodoxy in the expression of faith (however malleable it may be within the framework of the attachment to God's word) we shall in the long run falsify the experience and the confession of faith as well. And what is more, in the last resort we shall also thereby make any tradition of faith, the handing on of the fund of faith, impossible. What we have called secondary orthodoxy—that is to say, the orthodoxy of our expressions of faith and our conceptual affirmations—is therefore of vital importance for the faith if it is to be true to its fundamental intention.

What foundation does Dr. Robinson provide for an understanding and discussion of God? He has never explained this systematically. But in reference to the debate about *Honest to God* he does venture a theory of knowledge. We can work this out from his explanation of our knowledge of God and the Trinity.

The Question of Meaningful Language About God

The basic question is: Can our words about the Absolute have meaning? Dr. Robinson answers: The atheist says no, I say definitely yes. And he goes on to conclude that it is precisely here that the difference between an atheistic and a religious interpretation of life is to be found. In order to grasp the full import of this we must first go back to John Macquarrie's contribution to *The Honest to God Debate* entitled "How Is Theology Possible?" on which Dr. Robinson's ideas are clearly based. This title can be paraphrased, "How is it possible to talk about God?"[39]

The author, who is a professor of systematic theology in New York, says that the problem of God is not a matter for *proof,* but a problem of life which can be resolved only in an analysis of our existential experience. The finitude of human freedom, Macquarrie tells us, can be grasped only as the constitutive *gift* of an absolute being. We must therefore be careful with the expression that Dr. Robinson adopts— "the existence of God cannot be proved"—because his argument is factually the same as what we ourselves have elsewhere referred to precisely as "proof of the existence of

[39] "How Is Theology Possible?" in *Debate,* pp. 187–193. See also J. Macquarrie, *Twentieth-Century Religious Thought,* New York 1963.

God."[40] With both Macquarrie and Robinson such words as "proof" and "objectivity" have been given an unambiguous significance; they are used just as they are in the positive, exact sciences. They mean therefore only (a) that we cannot reach God with the methods of exact science and (b) that God can therefore not be discovered by the approach of natural science to reality. But that goes practically without saying: Philosophers and theologians would therefore be well advised to take the one-sided and positive, scientific use of words such as "proof" and "objectivity," and "reality as such" into account, if they want to be at least understood by their contemporaries. Both Macquarrie and Dr. Robinson contend that as far as the believer is concerned, to affirm either the existence or nonexistence of God is irrelevant, for both these authors (and many others with them) regard "existence" and "nonexistence" as a neutral reality which can be observed or proved by the positive sciences. To give a positive answer to the question "Does God exist?" is much the same as giving a positive answer to the question of whether in addition to the planets we know of there are also planets, so far undiscovered, of which we know nothing. One might say that in 1966 one would be forcing open already open doors with that sort of affirmation; yet the traditional "proofs" for the existence of God, as they appear in the older textbooks, have given every encouragement to it.

In order to present discussion about the Absolute as having meaning, Macquarrie therefore starts in an altogether different direction. His actual question is: "Can we regard Being as gracious?"; in other words, can we show that reality is a gift, freely given, so that we may be convinced that we really can "live from grace"? "God," says Macquarrie, "is the religious word for Being, understood as gracious" (p. 189),

[40] Compare the previous chapter, especially pp. 52-56. Also the articles published earlier in the collection: *Begrip en werkelijkheid*, Hilversum-Antwerp 1964, pp. 150-167.

reality as love. God is the ultimate value of life. "Being," existence in and of itself, is understood by this author as an "entity"; that is to say, a separate reality side by side with other realities. Understood in this way God quite obviously is not "an independent being," not an independently existing reality. As though in addition to Mars and Venus there were another reality which we called God! Seen from this angle there is no reason at all to accuse this author (or Dr. Robinson, who joins forces with him) of concealed atheism or fideism.

We must thus encounter God on an altogether different plane as the wholly Other, who is at the same time the wholly Intimate. This is what Tillich means (and with him Macquarrie and Dr. Robinson) when he calls God the ground of all being. Reality will reveal its deepest secrets to and in us. We do not have reality in our power, reality has us in its power.[41] Dr. Robinson adopts Macquarrie's analysis with the following words, which quite clearly reveal the background from which he is thinking: "is reality ultimately gracious, or is it in the last analysis impersonal or neutral?"[42] The personal plane is clearly opposed to the "impersonal or neutral" nature of "objective existence." His answer to the problem raised is: personal love is the reply to the question concerning the ultimate significance and ground of reality.

No honest believer will deny this; the only question is: just what does he mean? And is the previously mentioned question adequate? Is there not an active openness in man for reality in itself, and does not this become significant to us precisely on that account? The fact that the word "creation" is never once mentioned doesn't mean anything in itself. There can after all be no real objection to an attempt

41 "We are grasped by it and brought into subjection to it; but in such a way that something of its character is disclosed to us" (Macquarrie, *Debate,* p. 192).

42 Robinson, *Debate,* p. 230.

to describe in other words what is usually described with the word "creation." On the other hand, that Dr. Robinson positively rejects the idea of creation might seem greater cause for misgiving. But any hasty judgment is to be avoided here too. A background of non-conformism (of which he gives every evidence) would explain it. Fundamentally he might well mean the same thing as traditional Christian belief means by the expression (incidentally, not always clearly understood) "created out of nothing."

Is Metaphysics Possible? Dr. Robinson: "I do not know"

When we begin to probe a little deeper into what Dr. Robinson (and Macquarrie) mean by their profession of faith in God we immediately come across one of his central ideas: he radically rejects "a shadowy Something behind the phenomena."[43] The suggestion that the reality we call God lies *behind* what is apparent to us, thus "in another world,"[44] Dr. Robinson regards as meaningless: such expressions can lead us anywhere. In any case, since the days of Kant so-called "naive realism" has been finished off once and for all. We must thus reckon with the possibility that Dr. Robinson is really—and quite rightly—merely attacking naive realism. But this ought to become clear from his more detailed explanations, and in my opinion this is where we come up against the real "Robinson" problem. And it is not going to be easy to find out exactly, even with the help of Dr. Robinson's subsequent explanations, just what he understands by his belief in the existence of God.

The problem which confronts us here is connected with what has been taking place in our own country with, for

43 Macquarrie, *Debate*, p. 191.
44 Robinson, *Debate*, p. 252.

example, Luypen on the one side and De Petter, Geurtsen and others on the other side.[45] What, in the last resort, is *being* or *reality?* Is being exhausted in having significance for man? Or is it an independent entity which, thanks to the "light" of man's intellect, comes to itself in man, but then in the nature of things by way of history, whereby the independent entity becomes the matrix for our human meaning-giving existence? The conception of the Absolute is at stake here. And we have already heard Dr. Robinson say that Christian belief stands or falls with the Absolute.

He introduces the problem by raising the question of "the whole possibility of *metaphysics* as a meaningful enterprise."[46] For himself he tells us he just does not know. We must take this statement exactly as it is intended: Dr. Robinson doesn't know, so he neither denies nor affirms. Nevertheless it is a real problem for him, and he doesn't know any sensible answer. However unprejudiced and understanding we may wish to be where Dr. Robinson is concerned, the utmost caution seems advisable here because there may well be hidden implications that would in effect undermine all real faith. From this standpoint certain expressions such as "God" and "secularity" can really take on a significance which would jeopardize the authenticity of Christianity. And we can't disengage ourselves cheaply by a guileless indication of Dr. Robinson's non-conformity. There is an obligation to the Absolute and to the word of God that must transcend any non-conformism!

45 W. Luypen, *Existential Phenomenology*, Pittsburgh, Duquesne University Press, 1960, and *Phenomenology and Atheism*, Pittsburgh, Duquesne University Press, 1965; D. De Petter, "Een geamendeerde Fenomenologie?" in *TP* 22 (1960), 286–306; and H. Geurtsen, "Fenomenologie en Atheisme," in *Bijd.* 24 (1963), 302–312; J. Plat, *Traditionele Metafysiek en Fenomenologie*, Nijmegen 1962; also A. Kockelmans, "Het standpunt van de phaenomenologie met betrekking tot de vraag over de verhouding tussen zijn en verschijnen," in *TP* 22 (1960), 544–587.
46 *Debate*, p. 249.

Dr. Robinson himself says that the answer to the question of whether it is possible to think metaphysically must depend on what you mean by metaphysics. If it implies a very naive conception of reality, then he would attack only this kind of metaphysics; for example, a simple representational or essentialist metaphysics. In our country to say "that is a metaphysical view" is in popular parlance to say more or less that it is "up in the air," or much the same as is popularly understood in England. And according to Dr. Robinson, to say "that is theology" is to say much the same—"theoretical statements about things that make no practical difference."[47] The fact is that the exact sciences have narrowed down the broader significance which *scientia* once had and monopolized what is left of it for themselves, so that nowadays nothing apart from them is recognized as scientific at all. We may well deplore this, but we must not fail to take it into account. If we do not, no dialogue at all will be possible. This changed usage has at least the advantage that it is now possible to keep philosophy and theology more clearly separate from the exact sciences. The true essence of the "moral sciences" of philosophers and reflective religious conviction can gain by this.

At first the way in which Dr. Robinson understands "metaphysical" thought in the affirmation of God appears negative: through his reaction to a book by P. Van Buren, *The Secular Meaning of the Gospel* (a book which had not previously come my way, and which Dr. Robinson summarizes).[48] He tells us that he found Van Buren's book "one of the most exciting and disturbing" he had ever read. It first appeared at about the same time as his own book, and he regards it as "a major contribution" which tends to bear out his conviction

[47] *Ibid.*, p. 276.
[48] *The Secular Meaning of the Gospel*, New York, Macmillan, 1963. See *Debate*, pp. 249–254 (and also p. 242).

that in retrospect *Honest to God* "will be seen to have erred in not being nearly radical enough."[49]

The problem posed by Van Buren is: "How may a Christian who is himself a secular man understand the Gospel in a secular way?" (p. xiv). Hence also the problem of "horizontalizing" religion itself. According to Dr. Robinson the gravamen of the problem posed by Van Buren lies in the interpretation of John 14:9: "He that hath seen me hath seen the Father." Whatever "God" may mean we see him in Jesus, the Christ, and we need look no further. Dr. Robinson does not approve of this interpretation by Van Buren, and he tells us he regards it as "unscriptural." According to him, Van Buren turns the whole of theology—that is to say, the way we speak about God—into a Christology, a speaking about the man Jesus. Dr. Robinson is unable to accept this, since one of his main aims is to defend the proper rights of "natural theology" within the faith. According to Van Buren, theological assertions do not tell us how things *are* but "how things are for, and what has happened to, a man who sees a certain piece of history in a certain way" (pp. 198f.). Affirmations about God therefore characterize only a "particular perspective on life," "a way of life."[50] Talk about God involves the giving of meaning by the human mind, and nothing is said about whether there is any absolute datum present in it through which the particular meaning which is given could be judged. Statements about God therefore tell us nothing about God; all they do is tell us about the personal convictions of those who utter them. Van Buren tells us that "God" is in and of itself a strictly meaningless term.

As I have not read Van Buren's book, it would be premature to pass judgment, but from what Dr. Robinson tells us about it, it can scarcely be understood as anything but an

---

49 *Debate,* p. 250.
50 "The particular perspective on life" (*Debate,* p. 251).

attempt at the complete secularization of religion. In his own
book *Honest to God* Dr. Robinson has made observations
which can be understood in a similar sense. According to him
a statement is theological not because it tells us anything
about an individual entity we call God, but because it tells
us something about "the ultimate ground and depth" of our
existence.[51] In the light of this the affirmation of God's transcendency can best be understood agnostically. Dr. Robinson
gives us no more detailed explanation. The fact that Van
Buren's book so moved him may suggest that in a flash he
saw a new possibility, and this induced him to ask himself
whether Van Buren had not in fact drawn his conclusions
from the premises he, Dr. Robinson, accepted—a vague
cosmic-religious agnosticism centred around the man Jesus.
However, in the last resort—and this is very important—he
vigorously resists Van Buren's way of looking at things,
though he admits that it by no means involves relativism.

The human life perspectives of which Van Buren speaks
are, according to Dr. Robinson, neither arbitrary nor completely subjective: the Christian affirms the Christian perspective on life because he is urgently persuaded to do so by
the love which Christ has revealed. This—and no other—
vision or perspective on life is possible for him. This, he
says, is classic objectivity.

Despite this kindly meant interpretation of Van Buren's
book, Dr. Robinson would like to solve the problem in a different way himself. He is not altogether convinced that in
order to be honest both as a Christian and as a secular man
one must so radically dismiss all talk about God himself that
one can't say anything about how things actually *are*. To
judge from this reaction Dr. Robinson clearly tends to confirm the independent being of reality, although he does not
put it quite like this. As against Van Buren he insists that

[51] *Honest to God*, p. 52.

whoever sees Christ certainly sees the Father, but this, he goes on to point out, does not make the question about the Father superfluous. All it means is that we have no need to look *further* for the Father—to look, so to speak, beyond Jesus. Dr. Robinson agrees with Van Buren that the question of the nature of reality has meaning only when it is posed in relation to man. Man must be involved in the matter. He obviously does not deny reality as it is in itself; he says only that our affirmations about God imply an experienced relation to this reality: they are existential affirmations, "not objective propositions" about "things in themselves."[52] Note that "existential" is used in opposition to "objective" and to "things in themselves." Now I must first of all deplore this one-sidedness, yet it is clear that Dr. Robinson's conceptions of "objective propositions" and "reality in itself" derive from a positive-scientific standpoint; he does not mean to deny every metaphysical implication in existential relationships. The question thus remains open.

From Dr. Robinson's denial that our statements about reality are "objective propositions about 'things in themselves,'" it does not at all follow that they indicate purely subjective, human perspectives. A statement about God touches on a reality in which my life finds its ground and source when I approach it from a totally human standpoint and not only from the particular standpoint of the sciences.[53] Both statements, the totally human (Dr. Robinson calls it "the level of ultimate concern") and the specifically scientific are true on their own plane. The former relates to ultimate reality, and the latter relates to a phenomenon as it can be approached by the methods of the natural or special sciences. Thus Dr. Robinson is dealing here with what people on the Continent call the multidimensionality of truth. Let me say:

52 *Debate,* p. 252.
53 *Ibid.,* p. 253.

Up to now he has been talking in the accents of true classi-
cism. Or better, perhaps: Metaphysically speaking, we can
arrive at any and every conclusion on the basis of what he
has to say. It is up to him to tell us in what direction he wants
to go. So far his original confession, "I do not know," still
holds good.

Dr. Robinson and the Trinity

When Dr. Robinson deals with the Trinity the main lines of
what he believes can be seen a little more clearly.[54] He tells
us that "The doctrine of the Trinity is not . . . a model of
the divine life as it is in itself. It is a formula or definition
describing the distinctively Christian encounter with God.
Hence all the features in the Trinitarian formula are in the
last analysis representations of elements in the existential
relationship" (p. 254). Detached from this relationship they
are senseless as far as we are concerned. We cannot, for example, map out the Trinity, or represent it by sketching a
triangle. It is clear that here Dr. Robinson is condemning an
"objectivity" of the kind usual in the exact sciences for fear
of some sort of tritheism in the popular conception of God.
We can only approve of this and note that Dr. Robinson does
not say that the reality of God becomes senseless outside our
existentialist relationship to God, but only that it has no
meaning *for us*.

After this denial of "the Trinity in itself," Dr. Robinson
turns just as sharply against "the doctrine of a purely 'economic' Trinity"; that is to say, against the theory of theologians who contend that God himself is not trinitarian, but
that he "appears" to us in saving history "as one in three."
Thus Dr. Robinson also rejects this purely functional idea
of the Trinity, and at the same time—and quite definitely—

[54] *Ibid.*, pp. 254-256.

Sabellianism, or the idea that the Trinity consists of "three successive modes."[55]

To sum up: the dogma of the Trinity does not (a) tell us anything about God as he is in himself; there are not three *persons* in God; (b) or anything relating simply to our attitude to God ("our way of looking at it"); (c) or tell us anything even about God's appearance in saving history. The question that immediately arises of course is: Well, what does it teach us then? There must be some indication somewhere of how Dr. Robinson sees any *human* knowledge of the *absolute*. Let us go back to what he says about the one God; that is to say, apart from the dogma of the Trinity.

Just as he denies that there are "three persons" in the Trinity, so he refuses to call God a *person*,[56] although when referring to ultimate reality, the ground of all our being, God himself, he repeatedly says that this is "a personal love."[57] From our point of view we are entitled to see a lack of logic there, but the important thing is to find out how it comes about that Dr. Robinson himself sees no lack of logic in it, since we can hardly suppose that an intelligent author would vigorously deny in one context what he upholds with equal vigor in another. The contention "God is personal" must mean that the profoundest sense of reality, and thus the ground of all Christian life, cannot be approached through the necessarily impersonal (Dr. Robinson also uses the term "neutral") and mathematical scientific structures of the world. It always comes back to the same thing: we must seek God on another plane, thus in the nature of things, not through scientific but through totally human ways of ap-

55 *Ibid.,* p. 255.

56 *Honest to God,* pp. 29–44; *Debate,* pp. 253 (God) and 254 (Trinity).

57 *Debate,* p. 253; and see p. 262; "a gracious *personal* reality," "God as dynamic *personal* love," "the *personal* character of God as gracious." (Italics mine.)

proaching reality: "at the level of ultimate concern." Dr.
Robinson denies only (quoting Kierkegaard) that truth "beyond the level of mere information," can be "apprehended in
a purely objective, 'spectator' relationship, but only as a man
is prepared to stand, as subject, in an I-Thou relationship
of engagement, trust and commitment."[58] No one will want
to deny that! The only thing that arouses some irritation is
that he not only insists on forcing a long-open door and
making a great to-do of it, but after that he just twists and
turns in front of it; he doesn't go through. God is not a conclusion which can be rationally arrived at from given premises in the way the physicist concludes from his study of the
known structure of the physical universe that certain as yet
unknown elements must exist. We are all well aware of this.
But as a pastor in his contacts with the average believer in
our technological society Dr. Robinson seems to be constantly running up against such misunderstandings. Incidentally, it is not so very long ago that theologians were inclined
to regard the new scientific discoveries concerning the infra-
structure of the universe as indicating some new sort of
proof for the existence of God! For Dr. Robinson, God is
quite rightly a reality which can be experienced only in love
and worship as truth and reality. That is as much as he has
said at this stage of our analysis. However, even this is not
without significance in view of the dictatorship and the
monopoly that "the sciences" claim and arrogate as their
right where reality is concerned.

Only now is it possible for us to pass through the open
door with Dr. Robinson. Does he accept that *within* this
existentialist relationship there is room for a metaphysical
dimension; or, rather, does he recognize that this existentialist relationship is possible only if inherent in it there is a
"pre"-factor in the shape of a *consciousness* (to be further
determined) of the reality of God itself? Does he explicitate

[58] *Debate*, p. 244.

this existential phenomenon right through to the end, or does he stop halfway?

"God in Himself"

The problem is this: What can we say about God from an existential—that is to say, non-scientific—relationship with him? In this connection Dr. Robinson's admission that "what lies outside or beyond this relationship we can never say"[59] strikes me as important. His old contention reappears. It is capable of bearing various meanings up to and including the banal: "We can know nothing—without knowing it"! One would suppose that "un au-delà de la pensée est impensable" in this sense belonged to the philosophic thought since the days of Immanuel Kant.

It is a matter of course that we can only say anything about God within and on the basis of our creative and saving relationship with him; yet we must admit that within this existential relationship God himself can reveal himself to us precisely in his own independent being. Thus we cannot really grasp God conceptually, but nevertheless we can obtain a *knowledgeable perspective* of his independent being, of him as he is in himself. For Dr. Robinson the expression "to know God (no matter how) as he is in himself" means to know him precisely insofar as he does not appear in our cognitive experience; in other words, insofar as he *is* precisely when we do not know him. He then identifies this with the formula: to know God according to the reality he possesses independent of his recognition by man (since this is of course "absoluteness"). The meaning attached to this is very often: to know God insofar as he is unknowable to us. This is of course nonsensical. The misunderstanding lies in the fact that what is experienced and known of God is set without more ado against what God is in himself. God as

59 *Debate*, p. 253.

reality is completely independent of our knowledge of him, but in the nature of things we can only say anything about this reality of God from our own cognitive consciousness. And there is the whole problem that Robinson poses with his denial of "a knowledge of God in himself."

We are helped on our way by something he says himself: "We must be modest and moderate our metaphysical claims. . . . God is known through his effects. . . ."[60] This strikes us as a matter of course. On the other hand, what he says here strengthens the suspicion that he has a rather extraordinary idea of the knowledge of a reality "as it is in itself." From a certain standpoint one can approve of such a statement: to know God "as he is in himself" is, after all, the beatitude of the heavenly vision of God. But the problem is whether in our human statements about God we do actually touch the *reality* of God, what he himself is, irrespective of what we are and what we think. He does not need us in order to be what he is, although there are of course scholars who make this reality of God the object of their inquiries. But we must not forget that Dr. Robinson has said that he really doesn't know whether metaphysics is possible at all. In telling us that "we must be modest and moderate our metaphysical claims" he is also telling us that in any case—and rightly so— he is against what is called "naive realism." But so much can be concealed under that expression that we must leave all possibilities open.

Referring to our knowledge of God in faith and in dogmatic definitions, Dr. Robinson says that on the one hand they are not mere subjective projections, but on the other hand, they do not tell us what God is in himself. Summing up, he then tells us that they are descriptions of a reality by which the personal experience of the believer is constituted and sustained.[61] Or, put differently (and this is more in ac-

60 *Ibid.*, pp. 253–254.
61 *Ibid.*, p. 244.

cordance with his usual views): they are descriptions of our
existential relationship to God precisely insofar as this is
constituted by the reality of God and not otherwise. Whoever
wishes to determine more closely the real meaning of this, in
my opinion, fundamental statement will find that Dr. Robinson himself adds to the difficulties by his own interpretation.
Let us quote him word for word: (Theological statements)
"are not objective propositions about 'things in themselves';
but neither are they simply affirmations of my outlook or
perspective on life. They are statements about the reality in
which my life is grounded *as I respond to* that reality at the
level of 'ultimate concern' (as opposed to proximate concern
—the level at which scientific statements, etc., are true)."[62]
When we referred previously to this particular passage we
deliberately avoided dealing with the highly significant condition "as I respond to." Perhaps, after all, it isn't so very
significant except that in view of Dr. Robinson's skeptical
attitude towards metaphysics and metaphysical thinking there
is a priori a possibility that his words conceal an interpretation which stops short at mere existential phenomenology
rather than carrying the analysis right through to its metaphysical core. As it stands, this passage can be interpreted:
My life is founded in God only and exclusively when I consciously and deliberately engage myself in this reality. Episte-
mologically it would mean that existentially man can know
nothing unless he knowingly co-determines the meaning of
what is known. This is the standpoint adopted by the atheistic phenomenology of Merleau-Ponty, who concludes—quite
rationally—that any knowledge of the Absolute is radically
impossible. In my opinion we have now arrived at the real
problem—and in fact the only problem—which *Honest to
God* poses. If we can master it without further trouble, then
we may regard it as merely one of those many theological
studies with which Christian tradition has acquainted us—

---

62 *Ibid.*, pp. 252–253. My italics, E.S.

with this difference, that a laborious study of Dr. Robinson's other works is required before one can recognize, clearly and without prejudice, the authentic Christian character of a book as hazy as *Honest to God.*

In order to come to a better understanding of the contention that a man's own view co-determines reality and to discover whether Dr. Robinson himself adopts this proposition, we must analyze it a little more closely. The proposition is first of all clearly different from what we have said above: God's interiority in us is the reason why we affirm his reality. God is not a reality because we are, even though our sentient presence in this world is our only access to his reality. Hence it is a matter of course that my human consciousness of reality is *for me* what it "becomes" or "is made to be" through my conscious activity. I can speak of reality only insofar as I see it, as it is in fact *for me,* by the act of my consciousness. In relation to the knowledge of God one must observe in addition that this consciousness is not the experimental scientific consciousness but the total human, existential consciousness. All this seems to go without saying. However, this proposition is altogether different from a second proposition, which is that man can know *nothing* without himself having contributed towards establishing the meaning of what is known (I say "nothing" because of course there is human knowledge which contributes to the significance of what is known). Very often this second proposition is regarded as the logical implication of the first, and sometimes the two propositions are even held to be identical. In that case sight has been lost of the fact that the qualification of reality which is derived from its being "for me" need not necessarily be an immanent qualification *of that which is known;* it does not belong to the conscious *content* but is simply a condition of consciousness for me. In the latter case it is of course possible that what is known or conscious "for me" corresponds precisely to *the being of the object in itself,* or its independent reality (although in the nature of things the mental image will be imperfect because the human perspective, "our way of looking at it," plays a certain role in the *representation* of what is known). But in the former case *any* knowledge of the Absolute is by definition impossible.

Now in the quotation from Dr. Robinson the condition "as I respond to" appears to point in this direction: my existence in God will be confirmed precisely when, and only when, I personally acknowledge God. The quotation would have sounded very different if it had meant that my pre-established grounding in God is able to penetrate through to me only in my active consciousness and in this way becomes an existential relationship in which I know that I am sustained by the ground of my being. However, the expression: "My life is grounded in God, *as I respond to . . .*" would seem to go off in quite a different and a less fortunate direction.

Perhaps Dr. Robinson has merely expressed himself clumsily, and I believe, in fact, that this is the case (though once again we are struck by the extent to which he leaves us in the dark even in his explanatory articles). In a brief footnote he reacts to something MacIntyre has said about this: "What is at issue is the reality (to use Professor John Macquarrie's term) of 'being as gracious,' though *we,* of course, can only speak of that Being as we are grounded in it."[63] This sense can to some extent remove the ambiguity of "as I respond to": the ground of all being is a personal love, although—as a matter of course—*we* can speak of it only within our existential context of "grounding everything in God." For this reason and despite his ambiguity of expression, I feel that I must interpret Dr. Robinson as follows: in saying that "objective propositions about God in himself are impossible," he still means by "objective" and by "in himself" the data which the scientists can reach. On that plane one can reach truth without an existentialist involvement. We are obviously still

63 *Ibid.,* p. 230, n. 1.

standing in front of the open door: God is a reality which cannot be approached by scientific means, but only and exclusively by existential ones. A matter-of-fact contention is repeated in a constantly changing key.

Negative Theology

It has not yet become altogether clear in Dr. Robinson's view whether in God's self-communication, and thus in our religious life, the Absolute is granted to us to experience *directly*, even as a mystery which is only *indirectly expressible*. Nevertheless these two aspects appear to me essential for any authentically Christian understanding of revelation. Incidentally, we have already pointed out that Dr. Robinson refuses to call God a person, or to regard the Trinity as "three persons." The Absolute, which he along with all other believers acknowledges, can of course be approached only on a personal plane, but according to him it is illegitimate to call this "not-personal" entity ("the impersonal" belongs to the sphere of the sciences) a *person*.

This might seem to be a purely academic question, but how can we make the language of the Bible, which speaks of God's covenant and his "personal relationship" with men, real for us if we deny that the God who co-operates with us is a person? Certainly, if we overhumanize the "person" there is a danger of "trivializing" God's saving action. Holy Writ has overcome this difficulty by not providing any definite picture of God. He is referred to by all kinds of names, both personal and impersonal. He is a "rock," and he is a "staff" on which we can lean. This stream of "names for God tumbling over each other" preserves the unutterability of God. God exceeds all human, physical, anthropological and purely spiritual categories. On the other hand, it is clear that the core of God's revelation—his covenant activity—can best be expressed in existential categories. According to Dr.

Robinson, God is "personal," not "sub-personal," and yet not
a person. The distinction he draws here speaks volumes. The
fact that he is prepared, without feeling the least difficulty,
to use the adjective "personal" while rejecting the noun
"person" tells us that for him "personal" is an *existentialist*
category (indicating intersubjectivity), whereas "person" is
metaphysical, and, as he has told us himself, where metaphysics are concerned he pleads ignorance.

In any case, in saying "God is not a person," Dr. Robinson
is certainly saying that God is more than a person, and not
simply a person as a man is a person. However, if we reject
the humanly understandable word "person," we not only
cause him to disappear "in the pillar of cloud" where, according to 1 Cor. 10:1 (cf. 1 Kings 8:12) the Lord always
dwells, but we also reduce him to a vague principle making
any intercourse with him psychologically impossible. After
that it isn't even a step—only half a step—to saying that we
can experience God only as a transcendent Third *in* our interhuman relationships; and that in consequence if we serve
men, whom we can see, then we are doing our full duty
concerning God, whom we cannot see. This is really rather
more than "a purely academic question"!

Dr. Robinson's denial of God's personality means that,
where the so-called God analogy is concerned, his eye is fixed
exclusively on the negative aspect. The whole of Christian
tradition has always emphasized the fundamental importance
of recognizing that God is not a person in the way that man
is a person. Referring to the Trinity, Dr. Robinson says:
"Nor can the experience be depicted adequately by three
relationships to separate 'persons' in the modern sense."[64] For
him, to say anything more about God than this negative
statement means "to look behind phenomena," to say what
God is while we do not know him! However, we can know
God only as he is in reality (and he is, in the nature of

64 *Ibid.,* p. 254.

things, *independent* of our knowledge), even though it may
be imperfectly—"in a glass, darkly," as St. Paul says—because
he is revealing himself as God. Where Dr. Robinson is concerned this is not fully accounted for. It looks very much as
though he regards every metaphysical affirmation as "prescientific" in the sense of "primitive" and "out-of-date." In
direct connection with his denial of God's personality he
writes: "But the process of secularization, with its distrust of
any proposition going beyond the empirical evidence, is forcing the Church to strip down its statements and be rigorously
honest about what it can claim."[65] The difference between
our way of looking at things[66] and his lies in the difference
between "talking *about*" and "talking *from* or within" existential relationships. According to Dr. Robinson our affirmations about God do not refer to God himself, but to what
comes through to us about him *in* our relationship to him
(he sets the two kinds of knowledge against each other, however). We, on the other hand, say (and believe that we are
doing no more than thematizing the best of Christian tradition) that we can talk about God *from* and *within* our existential and religious experience, and that in so doing we
truly have an objective and real view of what God *is* in himself, and not merely an idea of how we are in fact in and
through God. In other words, revelation as absolute self-
communication of God implies in the nature of things a self-
giving on the part of God; that is to say, his being itself as
a gift to men, though under the cloak of faith.

The difference may seem subtle and minimal, but it is
vital.[67] Dr. Robinson talks about man, not arbitrarily, but

65 *Ibid.,* p. 253.

66 Further on we shall call *this* negative knowledge of God (which is more
differentiated than the pure negative knowledge of God according to Robinson) the "to be or not to be" of a true encounter with God.

67 Compare our exposition with the "functional names" ("nomina de Deo
dicta ex tempore") which we give God: "De zin van het mens-zijn van Jesus,
de Christus," in *TT* 2 (1962), 149–152.

insofar as he is in the hands of God. We can say that in an age-old problem: "When we call God good are we saying anything about God's goodness, or merely something about the goodness constituted in man by God?"[68] Dr. Robinson is siding both with Rabbi Moses Maimonides (God is neither good nor a person; that is to say, "He is not good or a person in the way that a human being is good or a person"),[69] and Alanus ab Insulis (God is a person means: thanks to God's constitution of him as such man is a person).[70] Thus the independent reality of God is not denied, though nothing is said about it: we know only what God makes of man. And this is really one aspect of our knowledge of God. St. Thomas, taking over the core of the patristic utterances about God, consistently answers the question as to what we really know about God: *quid non est,* "what God is not," and *qualiter alia se habent ad ipsum,* "what other beings are thanks to their constitutive relationship to God."[71] But for Christian tradition this "ignorance" is merely an aspect of our knowledge of God (and faith) since this negative and relative aspect is sustained by the implicit, unexpressed positive knowledge of what God is, without which this negative and relative would collapse.

It is precisely this aspect of our knowledge, which suggests its metaphysical depth, that we do not find in Dr. Robinson. The example he provides us with in order to clarify his theory of knowledge strikes me as significant. He asks us to

---

[68] See Thomas, *ST* I, q. 13, a. 2 ("utrum aliquod nomen dicatur Deo substantialiter"); see E. Schillebeeckx, "The Non-Conceptual Intellectual Dimension in Our Knowledge of God according to Aquinas," in *Revelation and Theology* 2, New York, Sheed and Ward, 1968, p. 157f.; see also F. Ruello, *Les "noms divins" et leur "raisons" selon Albert le Grand* (Bibl. thom., n. 35), Paris 1963.

[69] *Doctor perplexorum* I, 58: *The Guide for the Perplexed,* ed. Friedlanger, London 1928², p. 82.

[70] *Theologiae Regulae,* reg. 21: *PL* 210, 631; and reg. 26: *ibid.,* 633.

[71] See "The Non-Conceptual Intellectual Dimension in Our Knowledge of God according to Aquinas," in *Revelation and Theology,* 2, pp. 174ff.

suppose that we know a child but not its mother; how much could we then say about her love for the child? All we know is what the mother in her love has made of the child. The love of the mother is a co-constitutive element to what the child is concretely. We can certainly analyze the phenomenon —the child—and we shall really find elements constituted by the mother's love. But it is senseless to try to look beyond this in order to get to know the mother's love itself.[72] Dr. Robinson is quite right to say that we know nothing about the mother *outside* our experience of what the child is. And so it is with our knowledge of God. However, this does not mean that we therefore know nothing of God's love itself; all it means is that our concepts and images must point to our own human experiences, which are precisely what they are because of their constitutive relationship to God. Dr. Robinson condemns—rightly—naive realism, but he himself is so much impressed by what "a phenomenon" is for the exact sciences that he quite overlooks the metaphysical significance of "the phenomenal."

Implicitly, however (though in contradiction to what he says positively), Dr. Robinson evidently agrees that our knowledge is determined by God's reality itself: "God is known through his effects. And what theology analyses and describes is the existential relationship in which those effects are known."[73] St. Thomas also says: "In theology we use his effects as a definition of God, whether they are the natural (creative) or the saving effects."[74] This implicit acceptance of absolute reality as the norm for our human interpretations is to be found most clearly in Dr. Robinson when he speaks of "the opening of oneself to that utterly gracious personal

72 *Debate,* p. 254.

73 *Ibid.,* p. 254.

74 "Licet de Deo non possumus scire *quid est,* utimur tamen Eius effectu, in hac Doctrina, vél *naturae* vél *gratiae,* loco definitionis, ad ea quae *de Deo* in hac Doctrina considerantur" (*ST* I, q. 1, a. 7, ad 1).

reality which Jesus could only address as 'Abba, Father!' "[75]
It becomes quite clear here that according to him—and rightly
so—the absolute reality of God is precisely realized through
the symbolic action of calling God our Father (as Jesus does).
However, he is certainly not adept at the systematic working
out of these questions, as can be seen from such remarks as
that the statements belonging to the dogma of the Trinity
"are not statements about metaphysical entities beyond our
ken."[76] Seeing that Dr. Robinson seems to be acquainted
with realism only as "naive" or "scientific"—rejecting the
former category and accepting the latter in a private sphere—
and for the rest accepts existentialist relationships without
their *metaphysical* dimension, it would appear to be a matter
for misgiving that he equates the expression "God is a person" (even if this is so in a divine fashion which escapes us)
with a "pre-scientific, supra-naturalistic world vision." If he
were confronted with non-essentialistic metaphysics (which
he doesn't seem to know anything about) he would presum-
ably approve and perhaps recognize it as seeking to express
his own most intimate meaning. Now his own *theologia
naturalis* does not merely—and rightly—defend a "negative
theology," it is itself *to some extent* agnostic with regard to
God as he is in himself.

This insecure and uncertain attitude is seen with particular
clarity in Dr. Robinson's discussion with Donald Evans. Tillich says, and Dr. Robinson in *Honest to God* agrees with
him, that one who calls God the ground of his being cannot
call himself an atheist: "If you know that God means depth.
. . . You cannot then call yourself an atheist or unbeliever,"
since no one can say that "life has no depth." But if you
could say that, then you would be an atheist and unbeliever.
Dr. Evans puts this observation of Tillich's back in the context in which it was originally made and which Dr. Robinson

75 *Debate,* pp. 261–262.
76 *Ibid.,* p. 256.

had overlooked. "As it stands, the utterance is false," says Dr.
Evans, since "a depth experience by itself brings, at best, only
an unconscious knowledge of God."[77] With this the meaning
of a human depth experience is qualified in an important
respect, and Dr. Robinson accepts the correction. He admits
that Dr. Evans is right when he contests his statement in
Honest to God that "the question of God is the question
whether this depth of being is a reality or an illusion."[78] Dr.
Robinson then tells us that he would like to rephrase his
statement (clearly under the inspiration of Macquarrie): "The
question of God is whether these experiences of depth (and
everything else in life) are to be interpreted in terms of 'Being as gracious' " (p. 261)—in other words, to the extent that
man experiences, or does not experience, the core of his being as a gratuitous gift. It becomes obvious at once what an
enormous difference there is, not perhaps in Dr. Robinson's
meaning, but certainly in the formulation he used on which
the readers of his *Honest to God* had to rely. The version
provided in his book may well be properly called atheistic,
and one that leads directly to the vague cosmic-religious outlook you encounter among members of the Ethical Union
in Britain and the Humanist Association in Holland, many
of whom likewise accept a depth experience in their lives as
a reality and not an illusion. Many of them even speak of
reality as a gratuitous gift, though they do not ask the important question "a gift from whom?" but dismiss it as irrelevant.

It is precisely on account of Dr. Robinson's doubt as to the
value of metaphysics that such vague affirmations leave his
readers in a fog. Perhaps the wide sale of *Honest to God* is
partly due to the fact that it is so vague as to allow anyone

[77] *Ibid.*, p. 261. Cf. P. Tillich, *The Shaking of the Foundations*, New York,
Scribner, 1962, p. 62.
[78] *Honest to God*, p. 55.

to read anything he likes into it. Our own laborious analysis, not even yet at an end, already shows quite clearly that the reader can draw practically any conclusions he likes from it. Therefore its success with the public and the violent emotions it has aroused for and against leave an aftertaste which is difficult to describe in words. Anyone can find in *Honest to God* just what he has a mind to, or loathe everything in it that appears to contradict his own firmly held views on the faith. Either case clearly reveals how much insecurity and uncertainty have been produced by the secularizing tendency, both in the belief of those who are still in the Church and the "unbelief" of those who are churchless. It also unmasks the false security and overconfidence which in former times expressed itself in the fierce persecution of heretics by the orthodox. When we analyze and "demythologize" *Honest to God* the book seems of slight importance: as we said before, it forces doors that are not locked, and nowhere does it conduct us through them. And yet it acted catalytically in the prevailing insecurity and uncertainty concerning the profoundest problems in our secularized world; and, of course, the catalysis worked all the more effectively because the meaning of the book was so misty. Promises of future performance were thought to be in it which in fact it had not made and would not have wished to. All the same one is impressed by Dr. Robinson's acceptance of secularity, though this is interpreted rather one-sidedly as "scientific," and by his enthusiastic acceptance at the same time of living Christianity.

But we have not yet finished with his epistemological views. Up to now we have advanced no further than a consideration of what he calls his plea for a *theologia naturalis*. It is a matter of some urgency to discover how Dr. Robinson interprets the relationship of his views to the biblical proclamation of the gospel.

THE RELIGIOUS ATTACHMENT TO THE
WORD OF GOD

Posing the Problem

Dr. Robinson has been reproached because in his attempt to
reinterpret our religious conceptions he did not turn again
to the still fresh and living biblical images, but introduces
instead such ideas as "the ground of our being" and quite
clearly prefers this sort of thing to the biblical idea of "God
the Father." The reason for his action is, of course, that he
regards these biblical concepts as deriving from a prescientific
stage of human consciousness in which all secular reality was
charged with a sacred and mythical character. In a secularized
world such religious concepts have ceased to communicate
their meaning to believers; hence they must be replaced by
modern thought forms.

Here we come to the delicate question of the extent to
which we are bound to these fundamental biblical concepts,
a question which places in the balance the whole sense of
revelation. I do not conceive revelation as an objective, impersonal reality coming down, so to speak, vertically from
heaven; nor, on the other hand, do I take it purely as a reflection upon the general human experience of life, a sort of
self-interpretation outside the influence of grace. "Flesh and
blood have not revealed this," Christ said. In Scripture faith
is inevitably expressed in words, images and ideas. Are these
arbitrary human constructs, or do they draw their meaning
from reality's revelation of itself; or, again, are they given
their meaning by human beings, to be sure, but *on the basis
of* and *according to the norm of* the saving truth which,
though it is given directly, can be expressed only indirectly?
The answer we give to this question will determine our

adherence to the biblical concepts of the Christian faith. It is important to realize, in this connection, that we find the *definitively* spoken word of God only in the man Jesus and in the preparation for his coming in Israel; hence in the prophetic and in the apostolic witness in Scripture. This means that in the final analysis the authentic history of salvation, with its revelation of the word, has come to us in Hebrew dress. Doubtless all mankind, wherever it might be in the world, is reached and addressed by the living God of salvation; thus the experience of human life, wherever it occurs, is most assuredly a *locus theologicus,* a source for the tenets of faith. Nevertheless we must say that these truths represent only the crumbs which fall from the table where the man Jesus is sitting. That human life constituted by Jesus the Christ, nurtured by the people of Israel and the biblical piety of the Old Testament, is the only authorized source of revelation. As a "source of revelation" the ordinary human experience of life has no authority; its witness is valid and legitimate only insofar as it conforms to the *norma non normanda,* the independent norm which, according to the testimony of apostolic Scripture, is constituted by the human life of Jesus.

From this it is immediately clear that the modernization of the concepts of our faith must not be the direct translation of the contemporary experience of life into concepts modified with reference to itself: it must take place via the intermediary of the authorized representations and concepts of the Bible. This means that if there is to be a reinterpretation of our formulations of the faith, this modernization will have to be guided and determined by the sense of the biblical language of faith.

On the other hand—and here we are analyzing the meaning of what we have just called "the sense of the biblical language of faith"—biblical representations and concepts function as a norm for us only inasmuch as they are bearers of a revelatory meaning. *Truth* lies formally not in a concept or representation, but in a judgment; in this case a biblical judgment of faith. Now, as we know, the Bible itself uses quite pliable concepts. For example, when, in speaking of heaven, the biblical writers address themselves to people who have experienced the dry, scorching wastes, they represent heaven as a place of refreshment and comfort "where the burning heat of the sun is no more"; or they present it as a joyful family party: a marriage-feast. When they concentrate on the Oriental taste for processions and liturgical celebrations, they represent heaven as a religious ceremony with solemn processions and an adoration of the majesty of "the Lamb." From this it is evident that variations in the language of faith are possible and the Bible itself does not, always and of necessity, try to pin us down to one single scheme of representation. Therefore absolute status need not be conceded to the biblical language of faith. Here we perhaps differ from the opinion of at least some Protestant Christians, who do sometimes consider themselves bound to biblical phraseology in its precise representational aspect. We consider ourselves bound *only* to what is intended and thus expressed by these images and ideas. And yet one must still wonder whether or not the Bible does in fact bind us to certain conceptual contents. As St. Thomas Aquinas pointed out: "When it is a question of talking about God, one may not too lightly speak in a fashion different from that of Holy Scripture."[79] Some people seem to treat the subject as if we could divest biblical statements of the whole of their Hebrew conceptual context, peeling from them, so to speak, all that is the product of that particular cultural history until we retain only the *nuda vox Dei*, a "divine language," which we shall then be able to translate afresh into modern concepts. But if we did that nothing would in fact be

[79] *Contra Errores Graecorum,* c 1., *Opusc. Theolo.* 1, ed. Marietti, 1954, n. 1032.

left. We can turn our attention, in knowledge and faith, to divine reality only in and through a particular conceptual representation: without that there remains nothing to consider.

This problem becomes urgent when we find Dr. Robinson stating that he does not consider himself bound by biblical notions such as "God, the *Father* of the *Son*, Jesus Christ," by the biblical concept of creation, and so on. At this point we must ascertain whether he believes and accepts the fact that in our affirmation in faith that "God is Father," "God is Son" we are governed by the objective norm of divine reality itself. Or is his position that whereas in the patriarchal society of those former times this affirmation was indeed a meaningful religious formulation of the experience of faith, now, in another age and under changed circumstances, it should be replaced by more modern ideas which have a real function in our society? We are dealing here with an extremely subtle question which involves the very meaning of the Church's proclamation of the faith and leads us back again to the fundamental question discussed above: Does the believer co-determine the meaning contained by the reality believed in, or does this co-determination involve only the conceptualization of faith? And, if the latter is the case, is the believer in his theological conceptualizations bound also by the interpretation of theological concepts in the Bible?

Dr. Robinson poses none of these questions. He is only concerned with stating that contemporary secularized man can no longer accept the faith in the prescientific language of the Bible, and as a pastor of souls he goes in search of theological concepts which are in fact viable in our society. And in this search what serves as his guide and norm? After all, an enterprise of this nature is by no means free of complications and cannot be undertaken without any frame of reference. Let us investigate the concrete way in which he

envisages this modernization. We shall start with those "re-
interpretations" which actually raise no difficulties in principle; those schemes of representation of our faith which
clearly do not derive from God's proclamation but are determined purely by cultural history.

The Rejection of Three Outdated Plans of Representation as Legitimate "Reinterpretation" of the Teaching of Faith

The fact of secularization has brought this whole problem
to life: How can a Christian still live and think in a Christian way in a world which, thank God, is secularized, a
world in which man has become mature and adult? *This* is
the spiritual sphere and the general atmosphere ("Thank
God," because secularization is a "God-given fact"[80]) within
which Dr. Robinson finds himself faced, as pastor and
preacher, with a real problem. It is just this secularization,
which for him is to be simply accepted, that is in opposition
to three ("perhaps four," he adds) outdated world-views.
The fourth, to which he hesitatingly adds a question mark,
is the metaphysical view (which we have already considered);
the other three are: the supranaturalistic, the mythological
and the "religious" views of the world. Dr. Robinson rightly
holds the opinion that the revitalization of Christian faith
in a secularized world requires that we be freed from the
last three frameworks of representation. But it is the dubiety
with which he regards metaphysics (for him most probably
to be relegated to the category of outmoded world-views)
that will *in fact exercise a determining influence* on his
attitude towards the three world-views which he does de-
nounce as outmoded, depositing there the poison which has
its source in his ambiguous epistemology.

[80] *Debate*, p. 249.

(1) In Dr. Robinson's terminology a "supranaturalistic" world-view[81] is not the same as what is often meant in Catholic circles by "supernaturalism"; he calls the latter "religious," since for him it involves insisting on an immediate, supernatural intervention by God where intramundane, created causes would suffice to explain an event. It is worth noting this because the traditional distinction (within an existential unity) between "nature" and "supernature" is not directly attacked by him, although many have sought to find precisely this in his work.[82] For Dr. Robinson, however, "supranaturalism" involves a conception that represents God as a being existing of and in itself in a world other than ours, a sphere of being which is supposed to lie somewhere above and beyond our world. Here his rejection of metaphysics, however hesitant, can be seen to be plainly exerting its influence; for this kind of supranaturalism has never belonged to the authentic tradition of Christian theology, even in the more naive epochs of the past, though it may well have belonged—and may still belong—to the spontaneous, ordinary expression of the faith. We ourselves may say that the sun rises and goes down while we know full well that the scientific explanation is quite different. In any event, in our natural scientific world *this* way of speaking about God has encountered an obstacle in the fact that "supernatural" has come to refer not only to God and the angels but to occult phenomena such as telepathy and all that is involved with the so-called "sixth sense." Once, in the course of studying Henri de Lubac's *Le Surnaturel*, I bought another book with the same title, and it turned out to deal only with occult phenomena, diabolic possession, and so on. Let us therefore eschew such words, which are productive of misunderstanding on sight; language is rich

81 *Ibid.*, pp. 256–263.

82 This question is nowhere treated by Dr. Robinson, although it is important for the situation of Christianity with regard to secular reality.

enough for us to say what we really mean in a different way.

Dr. Robinson states explicitly[83] that he does not deny God's transcendence and immanence, but that he certainly does reject "supranaturalistic" schemes of representation. This is a candid admission that by his "anti-supranaturalism" and his statement that "God is neither above nor beyond, but the absolute ground of our being" he has not meant to say anything new, but only to bring out the best in Christian tradition.[84] This will disappoint yet another group of admirers of *Honest to God*. Nevertheless, his appeal to the "Deus superior summo meo et interior intimo meo" of Augustine is somewhat ambiguous, for he uses this idiom, he says, because he is speaking to post-Freudian people. This makes me wonder whether he is not too much influenced here by his pragmatic attitude. For although it is possible that there are some advantages in this method, the ambiguity involved can, as we see it (and we have evidence at least of this), ultimately produce only confusion. Metaphysical depth is, after all, rather different from the phenomena of depth psychology. Still, one can see what he is aiming at. He argues roughly as follows. Our clumsy efforts to express orthodox faith result in representations which fall ludicrously short of the reality. In earlier times, for example, God was envisioned as a benign father with a long beard, who lived in heaven, from whence he kept a watchful eye on everything with a view to rewarding the good and punishing the wicked in due course. If no other method is open to us, let us by all means indulge our folly in borrowing our means of representation from areas which will engage the serious interest of contemporary man—that is, those of modern physical and psychological science—instead of groping our way back into the prescientific, primitive world which is outmoded in everyone's eyes. As a pragmatic argument, this

83 *Debate,* p. 259; see also pp. 256–257.
84 *Ibid.,* p. 257.

is not so bad. But I rather suspect that Dr. Robinson takes only "the sciences" seriously (owing, perhaps to his pastoral experience) and gives too little consideration to the fact that even the "modern, secular scientific man" has prereflective experiences which are expressed and projected in a non-reflective way. Has he not observed that our technological world is beginning to long for a return to the resources of nature, is eager to "get away" in order to dream, to be idle, to indulge in fantasy and create new "myths" wherein this whole scientific approach can, for the moment, be forgotten? If we view everything from the standpoint of a technological secular world, then instead of making faith credible and open to experience we shall within ten years render it intolerable for human beings who have become satiated with this—irreversible—process of technologization. When Dr. Robinson—rightly—asks metaphysics to moderate its "claims"[85] is it not fair enough to reciprocate with the modest request that he should moderate his *pragmatic* adaptations of the faith? Furthermore, I believe that from a sociological standpoint nothing is so dangerous as a hasty adaptation of structures which have been the product of centuries of rigid conservatism.

(2) The "mythological form of thought"[86] is a pictorial representation, a way of representing the relation between God and ourselves vividly, so that it says something to us. It is especially primitive man who feels at home in this thought pattern, and for this reason such schemes of representation are necessary to him. The problem then naturally arises as to what in the Bible is historical and what is mythical—which is not the same, as Dr. Robinson rightly affirms, as the difference between "true" and "false": a myth attempts to disclose the meaning of a fundamental historical fact. Dr. Robinson shows great care in sorting out these

[85] *Ibid.*, p. 253.
[86] *Ibid.*, pp. 263–268.

various elements; he does not go nearly as far as Rudolf Bultmann but remains within the bounds of what contemporary exegetical science considers proved. The only objection one can maintain is to Dr. Robinson's hesitation in recognizing the validity of a metaphysics within the interpretation of the gospel. Nor is it possible to conclude from these articles the way (precisely in connection with the mythological element) in which he conceives of the "secular man Jesus," as he calls Christ. True, even if one left aside the Graeco-Latin concepts of Chalcedon (one person, two natures), one could still speak in an orthodox fashion about the mystery of Christ as long as one actually intended to say the same thing as is meant by the dogma, and in terms which seek to give *objective* expression to the revealed mystery of Jesus, the Christ. But Dr. Robinson says of Jesus only that in him God's own love has been revealed. From here one can go wherever one wishes, and it is difficult to make out from his writings just which direction one should choose.

However, my personal opinion is that one cannot refuse to regard him as orthodox in his acceptance of the christological dogma, particularly since in connection with the Trinity he explicitly contends that the Christian encounters one and the same absolute reality in the Father, in the Holy Spirit and in the *man* Jesus Christ, our Lord. What more can one ask? If more is indeed wanted, then there is a real danger of confusing the mythical with the actual theological affirmation. I have the impression that he is really recanting his agnosticism concerning God's independence of being (in the sense analyzed) and admits to a *positive knowledge* of God, namely of the God who reveals himself *in* the man Jesus: "He who has seen me has seen the Father." And, seeing that the man Jesus is situated in the context of our world, it is in this man that we see and experience *how* and *what* God really is, without needing to search behind this phenomenon to another world. I should say that Dr. Robinson's christology reverses his agnosticism to some extent. This comes out clearly in his theology of the Trinity; even though he also says here that we do not know the Trinity in itself, he nevertheless affirms that in the Father, the Spirit and the *man* Jesus, Christian experience encounters one and the same absolute reality, so that "these three" are equal and yet one.[87] As regards the "secular man Jesus," this phrase in fact means, to express it in the Western terminology of the dogma: Jesus, the Christ, is (for Dr. Robinson too) "one person in two natures." Does this last phrase say more to us than Dr. Robinson's expression? More than is said by the synoptics, and Paul and John? Perhaps—at least for those who have studied the Western philosophy of "nature" and "person"—the statement contained in the dogma is the clearer. But what do these concepts say to the average man or woman of our time? That seems to me to be Dr. Robinson's problem. I do not believe that one needs to seek further for something extra, although I know that one could perchance take the same verbal expression to mean something completely different. But for the moment it seems to me that this cannot be charged to his account. And hereby, in fact, he has once more disappointed a group of admirers who wanted to find something in his work which he is neither able nor willing to give.

(3) About the "religious" conception[88] of God not much more need be said. All Dr. Robinson wishes to deny is that there is somewhere in this world a separate "quartier religieux," as he calls it,[89] evidently in the sense in which there is a "quartier latin" in Paris. It is precisely in this.

---

[87] *Ibid.*, p. 255.
[88] *Ibid.*, pp. 268–275.
[89] *Ibid.*, p. 269.

domain that secularization is the result of the grip which
the sciences have on our modern world, whereby the pseudo-
religious and all sorts of "forms of religious sublimation"
are unmasked. Dr. Robinson wants to "exclude" God from
separate worldly sectors, because God is to be found *everywhere* in life, not amongst or beside the things of this
world, but as the deepest ground of their being. In this way
he is able to bring Christianity into the midst of the secular
life of man and to bridge the gap between Christianity and
the world.

Here again Dr. Robinson's indecisive attitude towards
metaphysics produces a certain vagueness in his conception
of secular reality. He also seems (still with hesitation) to
conceive of secularization as a rejection of metaphysics.[90] On
this ground one would expect him to be consistent and
classify the metaphysical human need for God under the
category "religious" (pseudo-religious). But once again he
does not seem to wish to accept this "objective consequence."
He acknowledges that in man there is a "quest for God"; he
likewise recognizes all the various traditional religious categories from Christian and general human tradition: dependence on God, reverence, adoration, repentance, etc.[91] "Christianity" in an entire absence of "religion," as he said in
Honest to God and repeats in *The Debate*,[92] could thus be
safely translated as: Christianity without pseudo-religious
factors.[93] Faced with his hesitation concerning metaphysics,
we must say only that he reckons human statements regarding
that which God-in-himself is (n.b., to be understood as seen

[90] *Ibid.*, p. 268.

[91] *Ibid.*, p. 270.

[92] *Ibid.*, p. 270; *Honest to God*, p. 104.

[93] I do not think, however, that Dr. Robinson has been successful in
interpreting the authentic Christian meaning of the prayer of petition for
temporal things. Is this form of prayer "pseudo-religious"? See the sixth
chapter of this book, "Dialogue with God and Christian Secularity."

from within our relation to God) as among the pseudo-religious and supranaturalistic elements. In this we cannot follow him, a fact that will have unavoidable repercussions on the last point which we wish to consider.

Testing New Theological Concepts Against the Norm of Meaningful Biblical Expressions of Faith

If the Good News as offered to us in Scripture were stripped of all that Dr. Robinson calls outdated forms of representation, what remained should be more or less what we described above as "the Christian kerygma according to Dr. Robinson," namely: God is love, and he has shown us this in Christ; this love is stronger than death. And, as we have also said, this is in fact the heart and soul of the Good News. But all the categorized concepts used by Scripture and the ecclesial articles of faith used to describe in detail the meaning of this event of love—incarnation, resurrection, redemption, Father, Son, Spirit, to name but a few—seem, as far as their role as dogmatic concepts is concerned, to be reducible to one of the three "outdated schemes of representation" mentioned. And whatever escapes this reduction in any case ends up in the fourth category, the metaphysical, which he does not condemn so completely but to which he can attribute no real meaning. But does not the whole meaning of the incarnation lie precisely in the fact that the transcendent God who is beyond all our categories has become a secular reality in the man Jesus and thus provided us with access by means of human concepts to his intimate mystery?

With his whole heart Dr. Robinson believes in the reality referred to by the Christian creed as Father, Son and Holy Spirit, but he finds himself unable to address this God as

"Father" or to call Jesus Christ "the Son." In his own religious situation Christ certainly did find it possible to do this. Must we, then, seek another interpretation in order to express what we experience in our relation to what the Bible calls "the Father" and "the Son"? Now here one is playing with fire—nor is it certain that the tragedy has not already occurred. The absolute reality of God, of the Trinity, is completely accepted, but it is human beings, not revelation, that must give it more precise expression. Dr. Robinson does not wish to proclaim any God other than the biblical God,[94] and indeed he does not have an arbitrary or merely subjective conception of human projections. He speaks of the reality of God as "the loving, personal reality which Jesus could not address except as Abba, Father."[95] He does not say that the first divine person is "Father," but that he is such that in the relation of the man Jesus to God he can only appear as Father. With a little effort we can make good sense of this: God is truly Father, but in a way which we find impossible to represent, and yet he is Father in such a way that he falls within the objective perspective indicated by our human experimental concept of "father," although we do not know precisely how that experiential content applies to God.

But, in his explicit formulation at least, Dr. Robinson does not wish to go as far as this; Jesus' experience of the Father is the repercussion in his human consciousness of what God really is. This is completely correct. But (another consequence of his hesitant attitude towards metaphysics) Dr. Robinson does not see this paternal characteristic as reality in God as he is "in himself"; the human meaning which Jesus attributed to him helps constitute this divine content. This is not an absolute name for God; it does not define him as he is in himself; it only defines him as that which in

94 *Debate,* p. 263.
95 *Ibid.,* pp. 261–262; also p. 230.

our religious relationship we human beings can call "Father."
He is Father not as "God in himself" but as "God for us":
which means, strictly speaking, that in the actual life of the
Trinity there is no question of "Father" or "Son." Taken to
its logical conclusion this leads us to a Trinity belonging
merely to "salvation history." Dr. Robinson is unwilling to
accept this conclusion, and the fact that, however inconsistent
this position may be, he himself is unaware of incoherence
at this point goes to show that he prefers any awkwardness
which may be involved in his attempt to resolve his difficulties to outright skepticism. His trouble is an insufficient
advertence to the fact that in the revelation through salvation history the absolute meaning of God communicates
itself to our faith even though we can then express the
reality of this datum of faith only indirectly. His hesitation
in recognizing the metaphysical element in "the phenomenal" influences his conception of the element of revelation
in our experience of faith.

In point of fact Dr. Robinson does not accept that, in the
actual notions of Christian faith (e.g., "God is Father"), there
is present, independent of our interpretation, an objective
meaning which God himself has invested in Christ through
certain of our human relational concepts (such as father
and son). By reason of their objective import we are thus
bound in faith to these concepts. Consequently he has a
more pragmatic conception of the fundamental ideas in our
language of faith. For him biblical concepts have no intrinsic
epistemological value. And yet, on the other hand, we find
him again and again making statements in which, though
perhaps in other words, he speaks in a way that necessarily
betrays an implicit acceptance of the objectivity of faith,
while continuing to expressly contradict it.[96] He says that

---

[96] One example: "They (the dogmas and concepts of faith) say, in greater
detail or in less: This, when you spell it out, is what is involved in *loving*
God with all your *mind*" (*Debate*, p. 244).

our theological concepts are expressions of our trust in the
Reality (of God) that merits that trust.[97] They are thus
"inspired" by trustworthy Reality itself, and not by an
arbitrary human interpretation of meaning. However, the
manner in which he verbally expresses this attachment to
the objectivity of that saving reality seems to me unsatis-
factory and gives him a greater independence with regard
to the biblical notions of faith than one can like from a Christian viewpoint.[98] I have now realized that the tendency of
many of his passages nevertheless places him not so much
among the *ideengeschichtlichen* problems of modernism, but
rather among the *realgeschichtlichen* problems of a down-to-
earth Englishman who, with an orthodox viewpoint, is concerned with making the faith comprehensible to human beings of the twentieth century. His pastoral-theological interest
leaves him little solicitude for the matter of the truth of the
fundamental concepts of the Christian faith.

We may conclude that the problematic element in Dr.
Robinson's theology lies in his doubt concerning the human
mind's active openness to reality-in-itself. Even in view of the
fact that what we make our own in this reality and express
in ideas does definitely include a human perspective, his
epistemological background betrays a too limited conception
of human consciousness. This unavoidably has a curtailing
influence on the way in which he interprets revelation.

97 *Ibid.*, p. 244.
98 *Ibid.*, p. 236. While maintaining the dogma of the Fatherhood of the
first divine Person and thus of the Sonship of Christ (conceived, both of them,
not as based on what Dr. Robinson calls a "supranaturalistic" world-view,
but as the only correct language of faith concerning God) I would undoubtedly be able to accept a certain pastoral pragmatism. For instance, in a
culture in which the idea "father" evoked only repugnance or contained all
sorts of additional meanings, the missionary would need, guided and inspired by his theological conception of God's Fatherhood, to look for other
concepts which for that people might serve to suggest what biblical revelation means.

IN RETROSPECT

Theological Orthodoxy, Philosophical Ambiguity

(1) This much is clear: Dr. Robinson accepts the fullness of Catholic tradition as it lives in the Anglican Church. Only one shadow lies across his book: the hesitation regarding metaphysical thought. And even then, for the sake of honesty, we must add that he actually reacts only against a conceptualistic or essentialistic metaphysics. Unfortunately, he seems to know of no other. He suspects that there is another, for his hesitation is understandable only on the basis of such a suspicion (hesitation with regard to a purely conceptualistic metaphysics seems impossible to me). Here we notice how theological interpretation is clearly qualified in part by a philosophical anthropology and metaphysics! We see how at its heart the modern difficulty concerning the Christian faith is, fundamentally, also a philosophical problem: that of man's thought about himself. And how, precisely for that reason, this reflection of man upon himself can only achieve clarity within God's self-communication to mankind, in which he at the same time reveals mankind to itself. If Dr. Robinson has made mistakes in his evaluation, then these derive from his theory of knowledge, not from a lack of faith or of a sincere desire to remain orthodox.

The clamour about *Honest to God* can therefore be explained only by reference to contemporary unrest and uncertainty on the level of the philosophy of life, which is due to progressive secularization, within which it seems to be getting more and more difficult to find room for Christianity.

Eventually Dr. Robinson's problem affects the relation

between evangelical purity and human authenticity, Christianity and secularity, and finally the "relationship" between what we may—in pictorial terms that are forever insufficient —call "horizontalism" (the intramundane, secular) and "verticalism" (depth, introspection, silence-with-God). It is precisely because he wanted to react against the estrangement from the world characterizing so many concrete forms of Christianity, past and present, that Dr. Robinson sought to lay emphasis above all upon what our being Christian (our faith in God's love revealed in Christ) means in this world. And a look at the past shows us that this is just where stress was needed. But the contrast effect of this factually justified accentuation has been to push the real meaning of prayerful, personal intercourse with God into the background; in addition, this intercourse has, through the pragmatism of Dr. Robinson's character and apostolic aim, been misrepresented more than what was perhaps his deepest intention. As far as his orthodox intentions are concerned, the following statement speaks volumes: "I would say at once that I do not pray to the ground of my being. I pray to God as Father. Prayer, for the Christian, is the opening of oneself to that utterly gracious personal reality which Jesus could only address as 'Abba, Father!' "[99] Such an affirmation is decisive! An "honest to *Robinson*" would certainly not be out of place after the intense denunciations experienced by this "radical Christian" in an English Christian society which, while retaining a theologically liberalizing tendency, preserves a lofty detachment and is not engaged in what is actually going on in the world. But on the other hand, we must also remain loyal to those who have read and commented upon *Honest to God* (especially before the appearance of *The Debate*). For a book is always read in a particular spiritual situation: in the case of *Honest to God* this was our concrete situation, in which the problems touched on

[99] *Debate*, pp. 261–262.

by Dr. Robinson have long been present and have been receiving all sorts of solutions, including atheistic, various kinds of pseudo-atheistic, and vague cosmic-religious types. If one does not take Dr. Robinson's commentary and his epistemology into account, one can interpret *Honest to God* in almost any way. I do not wish to deny that people who knew him were perhaps able to recognize the full Christian tradition in *Honest to God* almost from the very beginning; but as the objective expression of Dr. Robinson's own thought—and for the reader it is the only access to that thought—there is no question that the book is enveloped in an obscurity which inevitably evokes misunderstanding. Furthermore, the unfortunate headline in *The Observer,* "Our Image of God Must Go," which Dr. Robinson himself now deplores (though it was not his), put the book in an undesirable light from the very beginning, although the success of a *bishop's* paperback must be partially attributed, as Dr. Robinson himself admits, to this sales technique.[100]

(2) To this I would add a few further considerations. There is also much that Dr. Robinson left untouched; in particular, the problem which is in fact causing so much of the trouble: that of the place of the Church in Christian life. Naturally, he did not need to describe the whole of the Christian kerygma; indeed, like any straightforward Englishman, he seems to deal only with what he has set himself to do—nothing further is considered. And yet it is just this hiatus that worries me. Dr. Robinson's problem was that of presenting the faith in a way which would be credible to people who are in all sorts of difficulties with regard to it because of modern secularization. Now all sociological investigations into religion (and also our concrete experience) tell us that the chief difficulty is not the problem of God, nor even of Christ, but that of the Church: why this mediation by the Church in our relation to God and Christ? A rather extensive

[100] *Ibid.,* pp. 233–240.

investigation among the French "nouvelle vague" (young
people from eighteen to thirty years old) revealed that only
9% term themselves confirmed atheists, 5% "don't know"
(agnostic), 13% are non-practising Catholics with atheistic
tendencies, while 73% acknowledged that they vaguely believe in God as the ground of being of all there is, although
they are not attached to any church. The objections made
against religion in a "secularized France" in fact concerned
not God or Christ, but the Church and its demands. A few
hastily consulted English investigations point in the same
direction. Thus the actual area of uncertainty of faith receives no mention from Dr. Robinson. This, in its turn,
unavoidably gives opportunity for misunderstanding. A book
which is intended as an answer to the concrete difficulties of
faith of our generation and which leaves this problem aside
seems to me to miss a fundamental element in the matter.
Unintentionally, Dr. Robinson raises expectations that he
neither can nor even intended to satisfy.[101] Moreover, the
failure to mention this problem seems to me to be one of the
factors in the success of the book, since some, judging by
what they themselves say, interpret it as taking the side of
a "Christianity without a Church" which at the present
moment has such a strong attraction. But they cannot find
support for this view in Dr. Robinson's book.

Finally, there is in *Honest to God* an even more remarkable omission; I mean Christian life as an eschatological
gift.[102] It is true that as an exegete Dr. Robinson has written
an earlier book on the *Eschaton*. In *Honest to God* he could
not say everything; yet in it he formally deals with the problem of secularity in connection with "being a Christian." We

101 See, among others, the pointed utterance of Monica Furlong, who
speaks of "the splendid farce of established religion" (*Debate*, p. 246), to
which Dr. Robinson has no decisive answer, but only a distant smile.

102 See, for example: "De ascese van het zoeken naar God," in *TGL* 20
(1964), especially pp. 153–158.

are therefore justified in asking whether a vision which—
and rightly so—aims at bringing together Christianity and
the world satisfies the demands of the gospel if the eschatological aspect is completely left out; in other words, if the
Christian "existence in the world" is not shown to be at the
same time an existence which is "not of this world." This
omission must necessarily bring about misunderstanding.
The secularization of religion itself is without doubt a
tendency also found among Christians: Dr. Robinson has
unintentionally strengthened this.

Dr. Robinson's work seems orthodox but incomplete, and
the danger threatens that it may be read as though it were
complete.[103] As far as the various diverging appraisals and,
above all, the general reaction to it are concerned, I would
quote with approval Professor A. de Froe's remark, which is
unfortunately all too true: "We do not use the written word
in order to stimulate thought, but misuse thought in order
to judge the written word."[104]

It only remains for us, stimulated by Dr. Robinson's vision
of things, to personally reflect upon the place that a Catholic
Christian must give to Christianity in a secularized world.
This we shall do partly in confrontation with some of Dr.
Robinson's views and partly without reference to the prob-

---

[103] Another suppressed theme, which we cannot deal with here (and which
I shall thus also leave out of my critical appraisal) is the secularity of moral
life. Of what is the "secularized man" capable in the field of morality? Dr.
Robinson does not analyze this, and surprisingly lets slip the statement that
the whole of secularization and intramundane emancipation is not yet moral
progress (*Debate*, p. 270). An analysis of precisely this fact would seem important in order, for instance, to be able to take up a position, for or against
Augustine's statement that "A man cannot live an authentically human life
as a man, unless he has become a child of God." Further, we shall also leave
Dr. Robinson's moral theology outside the consideration of this article because, in connection with the elements of "situation ethics" therein, this
would require a separate exposition; a hurried discussion of it would either
be hopelessly superficial or could easily lead to misconception.

[104] "Open Kaart," p. 721.

lems posed by his book. In other words, here Dr. Robinson
will be a stimulus rather than a signpost.

SECTION II: EVANGELICAL PURITY AND HUMAN AUTHENTICITY

In order to avoid misunderstanding I should like to make it
clear that I am not directly concerned here with a reflection
upon the pastoral approach towards believers who have detached themselves from the Church, who contend that they
have abandoned their belief in God and find salvation only
in an authentic devotion to man and the world. To such
people[1] we can say, with Han Fortmann[2] and Karl Rahner[3]:
"Carry on, wherever you may be, follow the light in which
you stand, however small it is: tend the fire, even though it
is only smoldering." This is not to say that anyone sincerely
seeking will expressly find God in his life. This kind of
optimism is inspired by human sources and often contradicts
actual experience (so far as we are competent to judge). But
what is certain is that such a person is *found by God*, by the
One he is seeking. This is the optimism of grace, and it is
real. But however important it may be, we are not concerned
with it here. Here we wish to consider the experience of

---

[1] Here I am making a generalization, for where priests and religious are
concerned all sorts of implications, including social ones, enter in and com-
plicate the situation, but we cannot go into these. We shall also consciously
pass over the psychological backgrounds and implications of earlier up-
bringing which may be at work in some people, even though such aspects
would have to be included in a full consideration.

[2] "De onmacht des geloofs," in *TT* 2 (1962), 3–10.

[3] *Ueber die Möglichkeit des Glaubens heute,* in *Schriften zur Theologie* 5,
Einsiedeln 1962, pp. 11–32.

faith of the believer who expressly accepts Christ and his Church. And with others I would then pose the question: Can we and may we experience this Christianity in its envangelical purity and human authenticity in the spirit of a radical "horizontalism"?

The following analysis will deal with two aspects. For in his concrete structure man is a secular being that surpasses this world, and he transcends it not only horizontally, but also vertically in trans-ascendence or openness towards God; he is a being, moreover, who is personally addressed by the God of salvation precisely in his transcendence. Within the one concrete, integral act of a person's religious orientation towards the living God we therefore can and must distinguish two moments: the *natural* moment of human orientation to God and the *theologal* aspect[4]; both of these orienta-

4 The author explains, in a footnote: "The meaning of the terms *natuurlijk* ('natural') and *theologaal* ('theologal') will become evident from the analysis which follows. In anticipation of this we may make the following brief statement. The qualifications *natuurlijk* ('natural') and *bovennatuurlijk* ('supernatural') concern man in his relation to God. Insofar as man is able to discover his immediate relation to God only through an autonomous (spontaneous or reflective) self-interpretation, he is from a theological point of view termed *natuur* ('nature')—which therefore has nothing to do with the Aristotelian concept of nature. In contrast to this, the term *bovennatuurlijk* ('supernatural') concerns that immediate relation as personal intersubjectivity with God, which is possible only through grace because it is beyond human power. Since the term *bovennatuurlijk* only directly refers to the surpassing of human powers and says nothing explicitly about the reciprocity in the intersubjectivity with God (with which we are formally concerned), we give preference to the term *theologaal* ('theologal'). Despite the fact that this word is not included in such Dutch dictionaries as, for example, 'van Dale,' it is on the way to acceptance in Dutch. *Theologaal* is the adjective for 'intersubjectivity with God.' Formerly three *theologische deugden* ('theological virtues') were spoken of, but the semantic development of the word *theologisch* ('theological') has been such that one cannot retain this usage, and we should quite definitely speak of three *theologale deugden* for the further reason that the expression *goddelijke deugden* ('divine virtues') is ambiguous." There is a similar need for a new term in English, and I therefore render *theologaal* by the neologism "theologal" in the remainder of this translation.—Translator.

tions, although real, are but moments of the one religious outlook of a human being; that is to say, of a personal being who comes together with his fellow human beings in and towards the world to personal—including religious—activity. Only an analysis of this integral datum can provide elements for a reply to the challenge of the basic tendency towards secularization, a reply which at the same time honours the worthwhile elements in this vision, without thereby failing to appreciate man or God in their deepest sense. On account of its extent I wish to bring out only a few of the aspects of this far-reaching question, and then only in a highly compressed way, even though each point of detail would require a more ample analysis.

THE "VERTICAL" DIMENSION OR "DEPTH" OF HUMAN TRANSCENDENCE

Human Freedom in Its "Vertical" Origin and Its "Horizontal" Situation

Even within an "atheistic" or at least agnostic perspective, modern philosophy speaks about man's transcendence of the world. This we may call secular transcendence, "horizontal-ecstatic ex-istence" (Heidegger). Through this transcendence man surpasses himself within the horizon of this world, and human freedom is (according to Heidegger and Merleau-Ponty) the native soil of the meaning of this world. Man finds no rest in what he has already achieved. Emerging from the past, he is continually finding himself in a particular situation, from which he projects a new future. Thus, as freedom, man is an openness and self-transcendence situated in this world: he is a being that possesses the capability of determining himself in this world and of continually transcending that determination.

At the same time, as the source of ever new human attribution of meaning, this surpassing of nature by human freedom is, according to the believer and the theist, only possible
on the basis of a fundamental trans-ascendance; that is to
say, secular transcendence is only possible through man's so-
called "vertical" transcendence, his constitutive dependence
on the absolutely transcendent: God.[5] Therefore as subjectivity or freedom man is fundamentally an orientation towards
the absolute subjectivity, God, the source from which he
draws his horizontally transcendent existence. What do this
finitude and creatureliness imply for the life of the man in
the world who acknowledges God? Therein we must distinguish two aspects.

God as the Transcendent Third in All Our Experiences with Fellow Human Beings in This World

Dr. Robinson's reaction against the God "up there" in favour
of a God "in depth" is understandable and legitimate. Indeed, the image is but a repetition of Augustine's "Deus
intimior intimo meo." "Height" and "depth" are both images. The notion of depth deserves preference from a certain
point of view, for as the ground of our being God is the
source of our existence, transcending through inwardness.[6] In

---

[5] It is not our intention to analyze critically the presence in man of this
natural moment of orientation to God (the so-called proof for the existence
of God). As a believer I here assume both the natural and the theologal
moment of our orientation to God, from which I wish, in confrontation
with the "horizontalism" of the radical attempt at secularization, to draw
the consequences for the concrete experiencing of Christianity. The fact that
this line of thought rejects the "proof" for the existence of God may well be
the source of the spirit and sense of direction of its attitude. This is a
further indication of why a well-constructed proof has an essentially religious
significance.

[6] This preference is at the same time somewhat relative, especially when

the depth of our personal existence we are continually given
to ourselves by God, so that proceeding from this freely given
freedom and thus from our security in God we ourselves
become the source of the human meaning of this world. In
so doing, God's absolute transcendence is affirmed via the ec-
static character of our existence; or, as one might say, through
the secular transcendence of man in the world, of which
God is precisely the absolute, all-supporting ground. In and
through our own existence, God bears witness to his existence. In this way we do not meet with God personally; we
"experience" God as the One who by definition surpasses all
our experience in an absolute way. Our existence, the contingency[7] of our personal existence with our fellow men, is
the source of our knowledge of God, because this ec-static
character is but the overflow into our existence of the very
mystery of God. This tells us that the affirmation of our ec-
static presence 'with fellow men in this world is co-relative
to the affirmation of the divine existence. We must therefore
say in the first instance that as the absolute ground of being
God is the transcendent Third in all our human experiences
and above all in our interpersonal relationships. We attain
God only in and through the intramundane, of whose being
he is the fountainhead; naturally, it is not in our power to
elude these relations. Under this aspect God is experienced
in and through our love towards our fellow men and the
world, realizing fully that we ourselves are not the ultimate

one supports it, as does Dr. Robinson, with arguments from "depth psychology." For that matter, to compare such a prereflective psychological depth
with metaphysical depth is misleading. It then becomes but a short step to
the statement that it is just the unconscious or depth-psychological that is
the actual ground of being of all our experiences (see, for example, *Rede en
religie in het Humanisme*, Amsterdam 1962, passim).

7 "Contingency" and "contingent" are philosophical terms, often rendered
as "accidental." The meaning is that, in and of itself, the creature has no
reason to exist and cannot itself explain its own existence: it is, and yet it
might (in and of itself) equally well not have been; in this sense it is
"accidental."

source of this human love and this secular involvement. Here the notions of "action" and "contemplation" sometimes play us false. Philosophical contemplation, which precisely explicitates the condition of the possibility of our secular relations, is not a detached experience apart from which there can be no talk of God. "Proving God"—i.e., accounting for God's existence—is conditioned in the first place by our very life in this world. Philosophical reflection does no more than illuminate its fundamental meaning. As Jean Delanglade has so eloquently and correctly said: "To affirm God's existence is not to undermine *active life* to the benefit of a *philosophical life,* which might be supposed to find its content and end in itself. In short, while it may be true that the affirmation of God is elicited by philosophy, this does not mean that existence is to be reduced to philosophy, or that philosophizing in order to establish this affirmation accomplishes in advance the task of living."[8] The affirmation of God is therefore not in the first place an object of contemplation but one which gives us responsibility for the world and our fellow men, one of living trust. One remembers Marx's acid comment that philosophers have done nothing beyond interpreting the world in diverse ways, while what really matters is its transformation. Affirming God's existence is a certain form of *Selbstverständnis* or self-interpretation, and it does not draw us out of this world. On the contrary: by this affirmation we fully engage ourselves in the secular. The affirmation of God points to a particular spirit with which we approach our fellow men and the world.

But this does not complete the picture. The preference we may give to the image of depth as opposed to that of height ("God up there, in the heavens") must not make us bypass God's personal transcendence. Doubtless, God's interiority to us—that is, our contingent existence—is the reason for us to

8 "(L'Affirmation de Dieu) n'est pas . . . le tâche de vivre." *Le problème de Dieu,* Paris 1960, p. 224.

affirm God's existence. But we cannot define God's divinity
as a transcendence-through-interiority. God is a reality, not
because we exist or because we engage in all sorts of secular
and interpersonal relations which require a metaphysical condition of possibility, even though for us existence in this
world is the only access to his reality. Even if God does only
make his existence evident to us via our existence—namely,
through an act in which he establishes our existence in love—
he nevertheless remains transcendent in this act. This is the
same as saying: God does not need us in order to be God. A
consequence of this is that we cannot avoid declaring God
to be a transcendent personal being and thus an absolute
person.

There is the real danger here that one might speak not
about God but only about man's inward orientation towards
"the absolute." The ec-static character or self-transcendence
of our existence cannot be the last word, it is but the pe-
nultimate. For the superabundance of being that there is in
man and the world, the dynamism of our existence which
through its contingency points objectively towards the Absolute—the reason why we affirm God's existence—is the repercussion of God's mystery in man and in the world. If we
stop at this ec-static depth-dynamism of our contingent, accidental existence without discovering therein an objective
perspective onto an absolute personal being, it is clear that
all "religious" life coincides with a "horizontal-ecstatic" attitude to life—namely, with encounter with one's fellow men
and involvement with the world. Heidegger has already
spoken of *Dasein* (his term for the human subject) as a *sich
vorweg* (a being which anticipates itself) in a purely "horizontal-ecstatic transcendence." Such a purely functional theology has Copernican consequences. For whatever God may
be in himself—if we may in this perspective already speak
of God as having a real independence of being—we experience our ec-stasis (according to this view), our standing out-

side ourselves, only with respect to the world and our fellow men. However much this may be the echo of the divine existence in our existence, yet we ourselves have only to do with our fellow men and the world, and we experience this secular and interpersonal existence as something supported by a transcendent Third—God, the great Unknown. Such a theology is purely an anthropology: a "theism" of human self-transcendence, i.e. of the giving of oneself to others, to one's fellow men.

Authentic theism, which sees our existence as a basic reference to the self-sustaining personal existence of an absolute Subject that is independent of our existence (independent, also, of our knowledge of God, although we can naturally affirm this only within a consciously immanent act)—this theism itself needs a certain demythologization. But to affirm that God is a personal being—and not just the "meaning of the depth of our existence"—though understanding personal being in a way completely different from personal existence as we experience it, is not the same thing as a negation of the personal nature of God. Because God goes beyond all human images and concepts and we must therefore abandon all our images of him, one by one, does not mean that our knowledge of God consists simply in the negation of our human representations, and is thus agnostic. The fact that we feel compelled to undertake these negations time and time again indicates that at the root of these denials lies a positive, if completely unexpressed, knowledge of what God really is. For on what grounds could we establish these negations if we did not transcend them?

It is because we know in an implicit way that God is God that we are able to deny all our created representations and refuse to apply them to God: otherwise we should be doing this without reason, blindly. Thus the positive knowledge of what God is, is to some extent expressed in these denials, though in an indirect way. "That which is denied gives us, in our transcendence thereof, a certain direction"[9]: that is to say, we transcend the inadequacy or limitation of our world and our existence, and thus of our representations and concepts, and we do this as "pointing" in the direction of reality, but in a manner that is not accessible to human expression. We have, in the line of the negative conceptual contents, a true-but-negative perspective of the very nature of God. We draw our natural knowledge of God's mysterious nature from the same source that yields us the affirmation of his existence.[10] We have naturally no other way, but this way leads to a *positive* knowledge in *conscious* ignorance.

The knowledge that God differs completely from the reality of our direct experiences, conscious ignorance, is thus the only knowledge that touches precisely that which is proper to God. But it is just this ignorance that draws its conscious quality from a positive-but-unexpressed moment of knowledge, of which we know that it is also valid as regards the absolutely transcendent God, without being able to make clear how it applies to him. Thus we call God a personal being by virtue of a *negative* knowledge which attains precisely what is proper to God (God is not a person in the way that man is a person). But this negative knowledge is sup-

[9] D. De Petter, *Over de grenzen en de waarde van het begrippelijke kennen. Kanttekeningen bij "Uber die Grenzen der Philosophie" van Dr. K. Oedingen,* in *Begrip en werkelijkheid,* Hilversum-Antwerp 1964, pp. 168–173; also E. Schillebeeckx, "What Is Theology?" in *Revelation and Theology* I, New York 1967, especially pp. 95ff.; and "The Non-Conceptual Intellectual Element in the Act of Faith: A Reaction," in *Revelation and Theology* II, New York 1968, pp. 30ff. and Appendix; J. Pieper, "L'élément négatif dans la philosophie de saint Thomas," in *DV* 20 (1951), 35–49.

[10] As Henri Bergson has said: "Who can fail to see that, if philosophy is the work of experience and reasoning, it must follow just the reverse method, question experience as to what it has to teach us of a Being Who transcends tangible reality as He transcends human consciousness, and so appreciate the nature of God by reasoning on the facts supplied by experience? The nature of God will thus appear in the very reasons we have for believing in His existence. . . ." *The Two Sources of Morality and Religion,* New York, Doubleday Anchor Book, p. 262.

ported by what is positively but not properly a moment of knowledge (namely, personal existence as we experience it), which gives the direction of our knowledge of God: God is a person, but not in the human manner of being a person.

Though we deny that these human concepts of existence apply as such to God, we nevertheless need them here. Despite our transcending denial of our human concepts to God through a projective or ecstatic act of knowledge, without these concepts we should not know the direction and meaning in which, owing to his inaccessibility, God's being is to be sought. In the last case the affirmation of God would be an agnostic one. And what would we then actually be contending, if we contended nothing, affirmed nothing meaningful or comprehensible? An intersubjectivity of grace with God would then be wholly devoid of meaning. Therefore we may legitimately say that God is a transcendent, personal Being, an independent being, an absolute, knowing and willing centre of action. We can say that he is a person, though we do not know the actual divine way in which this personal nature is realized. Deriving from our experience, the content of the concept "person" has thus the value of a *well-defined reference to the real* (God), which is neither thoroughly understood nor thoroughly mastered. The negation of creaturely modes of being gives us room for an unverbalized, unexpressed positive knowledge of God, which we might term a positive awareness of direction. God remains the impenetrable mystery, and yet we cannot speak here of agnosticism, of God as an x or "unknown number."[11]

11 This problem of the actual nature of our knowledge of God may seem academic, but it is nevertheless a matter of "to be or not to be" for religion. For if we know nothing positive about God, not even in an implicit manner, then the life of grace—which is nothing other than intersubjectivity with God—becomes, quite simply, meaningless and without content: people are not concerned about an unknown x, except out of mathematical interest (and in that case the x is ultimately determinable). Deism was at least consistent!

But by this affirmation we also transcend a purely horizontalizing conception of the affirmation of God's existence.
We must now investigate this.

Our "Standing Outside Ourself" Orientated
Towards the Reality of God as Lovable

The affirmation of God's existence, in which we become
conscious of the fact that he is the absolute ground of being
of all secular and interpersonal relations, is ultimately the
affirmation of a mystery of love and of absolutely unfathomable personal depth. For God is transcendent and independent in his act of establishing our existence; which is to say
that he does not need to create in order to be himself. When
he creates he can only do so out of pure, open-handed, free
and generous love, on the basis of a completely absolute subjectivity or freedom. Although the affirmation of God is itself
called forth in the first place by the necessity of affirming an
absolute condition of the possibility of our existence in this
world (and in this sense it is an element in our intramundane
experience), it comes down ultimately to the affirmation of
God as a mystery that can only be accepted in self-surrender.[12]
Moreover, this self-surrender does not take place only after
the proof of God's existence or the explicit justification
thereof. Trust in God is not the result of affirming God to
be a mystery, for if that were the case, then we should never
arrive at an affirmation of God's existence. Our mind's humble openness to reality as it reveals itself to us is already an
implicit trust in God, even before any explicit awareness of
his existence. But on the other hand, this openness becomes
formally a trust—one entrusts oneself only to a person—only

---

[12] See especially D. De Petter, *Het metafysisch karakter van het Gods-
bewijs en het hedendaagse denken*, in *Begrip en werkelijkheid*, Hilversum-
Antwerp 1964, pp. 150–167; J. Delanglade, *Le problème de Dieu*, pp. 182ff.,
and especially pp. 247ff. See also the foregoing chapter of this book.

with the affirmation of God. Only then does reality assume the pregnant significance of mystery: inaccessible by definition, because it refers to the mystery of God's absolute personality. Insofar as man and the world are a mystery in the strict sense of the word, they are the very mystery of God, seen from a creaturely, ex-centric viewpoint.

So it is that our life in the world requires—by virtue of a natural evidence (the very ground of our natural affirmation of God)—a surrender to God as absolute person, and this in principle before anything is said of revelation and grace. This demand for self-surrender, which is constitutive of man as such, breaks through the purely horizontally transcending mode of human existence in this world. God's essence transcends his "function" of being the absolute ground of our being: he is (independently of man and world) in and of himself an absolute, personal existence. He is lovable in and for himself and not only because it is he who establishes our existence, even though we do only draw knowledge of this absolute lovableness from our contingent existence in this world. But this also means that man cannot be satisfied by the affirmation that God is only the transcendent Third in our human relations. God is more than just the absolute ground of our being. We are aware of this precisely on the basis of our secular existence, and hence on the basis of our rationally tested knowledge of this ground of being, for the latter is completely absolute.

The consequences of this are enormous, and they shatter the vision of radical "horizontalism." When a horizontally transcendent or free being, such as man, arrives at the insight of God as the source of his human transcendence, it means that although by his bodiliness man remains firmly set within the limits of the universe, in his freedom, and thus as person, he nevertheless affirms, all along the line, an *immediate* relation to God; not only as to a transcendent Third in and underlying his orientation to man and world, but to the actual person of God. But he will naturally not be able to realize this immediate relationship with God, he will only be able to live it out in his interaction with the world of people and things. On the other hand, his natural orientation towards God is, as it were, a call that makes him long for a personal encounter or immediate intersubjectivity with God; not for a God who is experienced only as an absolute Third in human I-Thou relations, but for an immediate I-Thou relationship between God and man. Humanly speaking, this desire is as justified as it is powerless to attain its object. It is not naturally obtainable, because in and of himself man can open up this perspective of God only via the objective mediation of his secular and human relationships. And this, for its part (without grace), excludes per se intersubjectivity.

But it is just in the measure that he realizes what intersubjectivity is among human beings and recognizes that he is affirming God precisely as absolute person, that there arises in his relationships themselves the orientation towards an authentic intersubjectivity with God. Indeed, this intersubjectivity with God is already present in incipient form in the actual affirmation of God: in his secular and human relations man knows God to be intimately near as a Person who can only be approached in self-surrender, for he affirms God as the absolutely transcendent One without subjecting him to any limitations proportioned to human powers.

Human relationships provide him with the direction in which the desired vista of an intersubjectivity with God is presented. For considered anthropologically man is a being who becomes himself within his presence in and interaction with the world, and this means primarily in his presence among and interaction with fellow human beings. Man is a being who gains mature possession of himself in giving himself to others. Only in the act of self-donation to another person does a man arrive at self-possession. Being a person is self-possession in the gift of self to another person. The inward fulfillment and completion of personal existence lies in the intersubjectivity of I-thou relationships in the secular domain.

If man arrives at the justified realization that the absolute ground or condition of the possibility of his existence and of his human relationships is the absolute Person called God and herein recognizes God as an absolutely lovable person in, of and for himself, then he knows that the supreme fulfillment of himself as encounter-oriented person can only be in a reciprocity with God, in the intersubjectivity with this absolutely lovable Person who is the glowing hearth of man's life. But then he knows, at the same time, that here he is separated from this personal encounter with God by an absolute boundary: his contingent existence in the world. In point of fact man can only approach God via this human world, and thus not, from the human point of view, in a personally intersubjective intercourse. In concrete terms, that "grace presupposes nature" means: grace, or intersubjectivity with God, supposes a personal being which can only possess itself in giving itself away to the other, to a fellow person. Thus the "natural desire" for personal encounter with God himself emerges dynamically in concrete form out of human relationships experienced in the acknowledgment of God as the absolute Third. Hence the highest expression of the possibility of self-determination in and through the gift of oneself to the other lies in man's free response to God's gratuitous invitation to mutual love; that is, in the intersubjectivity between the human being and the infinite person of God which is effected by the power of grace.

The natural affirmation of God therefore comes down to a prototype of what Christians call faith, the surrender of faith. The existence of God is affirmed indirectly by natural evidence, but essentially as an incomprehensible mystery, which

we ourselves can never grasp and which can only be accepted
in self-transcendence and surrender.[13] There is present in
man himself, and thus on a human foundation, the demand
for a trusting assent to the mystery of God, and it is there in
principle even before this mystery addresses us freely in open
self-revelation. This prototype of faith is as yet not theologal
faith. It is true that in the factual order of salvation, in every
human confrontation with reality, we are faced with the God
of salvation, who offers his grace. In the concrete, surrender
to the mystery of God is an act of grace and of anonymous
theologal faith, which allows us to enter into intersubjectivity
with God. But this means that the natural evidence of the
prototype of this theologal surrender of faith is in the concrete no other than the *rational justification* of the act of
grace in which I surrender in pure, theologal faith to the God
of revelation. For this reason I can and must say that I cannot

13 All of this is already unthematically present in prereflective experience
(with all its consequences—religious expressions, rites, etc.—in which, indeed,
God's saving will is already active). The "proof" for the existence of God
only accounts for this orientation to the forum of human thought, inasmuch
as it lays bare its ontological foundation. It is only in thematic reflection that
prereflective thought comes to fruition and is at the same time critically
examined: because, even more than the "scholarly" affirmation of God, the
spontaneous affirmation of God (which in a hidden manner—at least when
considered essentially—follows the same path as the thematic affirmation of
God) will contain all sorts of elements that have no real validity. Thus in a
primitive conception of God, he will in fact function partly as a "long-stop,"
as Robinson puts it. This, however, does not alter the fact that the deep
in-tention (in the sense of intentional orientation, not that of inclination)
can be authentic, depending on the actual foundation of the affirmation of
God. To call such people "atheistic" is to go beyond all bounds and make
what is ultimately an essentialistic statement which attaches more value
to the conceptual realm than to the intended reality. On the other hand, this
shows the urgent need for a thematic, reasoned-out knowledge of God. For
what Christians often lack most, more than knowledge of their faith sometimes, is a true idea of God such as can be rationally attained by human
thought. A lack of this clear knowledge of God also threatens to distort their
understanding of the mysteries of salvation and their Christian life. In this
sense the "injection" being received by the faithful from contemporary
atheism can be beneficial to them.

give a rational account of what I believe; it is a question of trust in a self-revealing God. But I can personally and rationally account in the realm of my human thought for the fact that I believe (although this is purely an act of grace) and must do so if my faith is to grow into an authentically personal position in harmony with my life.

The proof of God's existence, i.e., the naturally justified certainty of the existence of God, through which I know myself to be called to give myself to this Mystery—this critical justification is not yet salvation for man. For in itself this self-donation comes up against an absolute limit. Seen in a purely natural way, which is to say: insofar as it relies on the indirect evidence of a rationally justified certainty, the entrusting of oneself to God has a completely different significance from that of theologal trust in God, at least when this is considered in itself. (However, it never appears alone, since it is an element in an integral religious act.) Naturally we can only speak about God's personal existence on the basis of our contingency. In other words, for us the existence of God, and the content of his Being, has no other ground except the contingency of our existence. Therefore I cannot naturally move outside this correlation between my contingent existence and God as the ground of my being, even though I know that God's nature transcends this correlation and thus possesses its own intradivine life, which completely eludes me, although it irresistibly fascinates me. In a strictly natural manner, this confidence in God coincides with the affirmation of God and thus with the postulation of the absolute condition of the possibility of my life with fellow human beings in this world. It is a trust, in grateful realization of our created status, in our personal involvement and responsibility in this world, above all for our fellow man. It is the realization that the goodness of these gifts of creation make me trust in this life. Naturally, I cannot trust in God "behind created reality." This trust is exercised by putting

my trust in my fellow men, in my faith in the humanizing
forces of mankind, all experienced in grateful, adoring realization that I am God's creation. For this reason natural trust
in God has in the first instance an *ethical* significance with
regard to fellow human beings. The affirmation of God cannot be separated from the human task of practising justice
and love in our human relations.[14]

And yet this is only part of the truth. As an inward demand
manifesting itself in the justified certainty of God's existence,
trust in God is certainly trust in a *Person*, in his reality as
absolute Origin or Freedom; a Person of whom we know that
he transcends the whole of creation, although by our natural
faculties we see this creative power only as it is expressed in
this natural world. In what else do we put our trust? In the
fact that God will not withdraw his creating hand from this
world, or in a reality still deeper? From this it is clear that
trust in God is concretely and in fact a surrender to the God
who has freely revealed himself as the God who saves. In
other words, it is the rational justification of my theologal
surrender in faith to God. But this implies the possibility of
a *natural* desire for a direct intersubjective relationship with
God, even though by definition this desire is incapable of
fulfillment. The whole bearing of this natural[15] trust in God

14 This was emphasized especially with regard to justice, under the clear
influence of his Jewish faith, by E. Levinas: *Totalité et Infini. Essai sur
l'extériorité*, The Hague 1961 (Phaenomenologica, n. 8), passim; e.g. "An act
of justice—the uprightness of face-to-face encounter—is needed for the
appearance of the opening which leads to God—and the 'vision' coincides
with this act of justice . . . apart from relationships with human beings
there can be no 'knowledge' of God" (p. 51); "Monotheism involves that
human relationship, that idea of the human race, which goes back to the
approach of the other in face-to-face encounter, in a dimension of depth, in
responsibility for oneself and the other person" (p. 190); "the miracle of creation consists in the creating of a moral being" (p. 61).

15 "Natural" is always to be understood as trust in God resting on a
rationally justified certainty of his existence.

is that it is a trust in the absolute, limitless personality of God, and by definition this includes man's openness to an eventual personal initiative on God's part: God is the power of an absolute beginning, a Being who can, insofar as his personhood is limitless, contain the wonder of the totally new. Indeed he is a Being who is this wonder in itself (the unfathomable richness of his nature: three Persons who—still more astonishing—wish to communicate themselves to us). Therefore natural trust in God, whether it is verbalized or not, whether expressed rightly, wrongly or imperfectly, is at its core the expression of a natural desire: "I seek your face, O Lord." It is an anticipatory preparation for contact with the astonishing, dynamic nature of the divine freedom of subjectivity.

The fact that, through his will to save us, God gives us our trust in him, even before we ourselves put our trust in him, does not lessen the importance of the above considerations in any way. For here it becomes evident that the concrete surrender of faith to God does not carelessly overlook the requirement of the "test of reason" (as the Humanists rightly demand). God himself affirms his existence through and in his creative activity, which bears witness in us to his divine existence. In the affirmation of God man arrives at the recognition of this divine self-affirmation. As lord of this world, man is the prophet of this "natural revelation": he interprets the eloquent signs of God's quasi-absent presence —a presence, that is, not in the manner of created reality (for we always experience that directly). Out of this there arises the intersubjective relationship with him, of person-to-person encounter. But as a finite being and by his bodiliness man is, as it were, bound to this world and to his fellow men by all the fibres of his being. Hence it is entirely feasible that the acknowledgment of God's existence should take the form of service of the God who is silent by personal devotion

to our fellow men and to the world; but for man considered
as a *person* it cannot be the last word. Man is aware of being
directly orientated in all things towards the person of God,
with an immediacy which he cannot by his own powers realize in personal intercourse even though he is conscious of
God as a living God. Man's meaningful but impotent existence, or reaching out, towards the reality of God as lovable
—that is, his capacity for grace—relativizes his human history in this world, for this history cannot contain the ultimate
meaning of his life. It takes its meaning continuously by reference to the suprahistorical mystery of God, the experience
of which he is capable of meriting. But man does not of
himself know whether or not this gift will be granted to him.

At the same time we have here an answer to the criticism
of "religion" as the product of a need for God. The act of
creation immerses us in a profane world, one which is by definition desacralized. It would be possible to conceive of religion as arising from the need for a being who would spring
to our aid as a *deus ex machina* should we fail (temporarily,
perhaps) in our secular achievements. But, as we have seen,
man, in being created, becomes aware of the fundamental
need of his being—namely his *metaphysical* need for God.
This need is not something deriving from the desacralized
world but belongs to him as a creature. And for this reason
Christian, theologal faith is not practicable without religion
(in this purified sense). Moreover, this need (rendered still
more acute by the concrete experience of our sinfulness) not
only makes itself felt in some special hidden sector of our life
but is, so to speak, present like breath in our whole being,
kindling a most disturbing restlessness when, through his
acknowledgment of God's existence, a man receives a glimpse
of God's inward lovableness which will prevent his ever again
being free of the longing "to see God." When a self-confessed
atheist like Simone de Beauvoir asks why God does not show

himself to everyone at least once, for a single instant, so that he could believe,[16] she is most assuredly turning reality upside down, but at the same time she betrays the fact that we cannot rid ourselves of the desire to see God. This "natural desire" belongs among the constitutive essential features of a human *Selbstverständnis* ("self-interpretation"), realizing itself by its own creaturely powers.

One sees where Salvation can be found, though without being able to take even one step towards it. However fair the view may be, man's own contingency and his corporeity constantly throw him back into the intramundane. But God transcends this contingency, and herein lies a promise for man. The person who takes seriously the affirmation of God as the transcendent Third in our human relationships can never consider this affirmation as the last word. The moment of natural orientation to God cannot simply coincide with the unconditional nature of the honour and respect due to one's fellow men. However much the ethical and the religious may have the same foundation, conscious relationship with God nevertheless surpasses the ethical: it lets us enter, in desire or in fact, into another world.[17]

16 See *Informations catholiques internationales* (Paris), December 15, 1958, p. 22.

17 Thus these two may be separated from each other even in explicit experience; an atheist can live a thoroughly ethical life. In our exposition we have passed over the matter of sin in man, as also the fact that there are people who do not feel that there is anything lacking in a life without religion and for whom "living without God" raises no problem. As I have already said, we are only concerned with the concrete experience of authentic Christianity. There remains just this: Bonhoeffer and Robinson repeatedly state that we could live equally well as human beings "even if God did not exist." How do they know this? "Living as if God did not exist" only means living "without religion," but not "without God." No man can exclude from his existence the objective, active fact that in Christ God effectively loves him to the end—even though he may deny this. Therefore this fact has an effect upon his life, whether he likes it or not. How can it then be contended that one can live equally well as a human being "without God"? What point of reference is one applying here?

THE OFFER OF SALVATION;
BEING-TOGETHER AND WORKING-TOGETHER
WITH GOD IN A REAL INTERSUBJECTIVITY
OF FAITH

It is because God wanted to admit man into the secret sphere
of his own life that he created him as a being who can become himself only by self-donation to others and who for this
very reason longs for personal encounter with God. This
desire is moreover both initiated and sustained by the gratuitous gift of God which draws to him the man whom he
wishes to liberate and save. No moment in the free activity
of man's life can be said to be purely "natural," as is evident
from what we have said above with regard to the constitution
of man's being. Yet his natural (as opposed to theologal) activity is nonetheless a real and indispensable element in an
authentically personal life of grace with God. We must now
analyze this intersubjective relationship with God, at least
from the standpoint of the problem posed: Is there an immediate personal intercourse with God which cannot be
reduced simply to love for one's fellow men and responsibility
for the humanization of the world?

Entry into Another World, the Sphere of Intimacy with God

In concrete fact religion—faith—is man's response to God;
for God was the first to speak. Even in the natural moment
of our concrete orientation towards God, namely in "religion," God himself, and not man, is the first to speak, even
if this is only through his act of creation, from which man
can learn if he knows how to interpret the contingency of his
own mundane existence as the reverse side of God's mystery.
But the theologal man-God relationship, which includes the

natural moment, is a response to God's act of grace. Revelation is the completely separate, personal gesture of the living God, who offers us "communion with himself": precisely that which we cannot attain by ourselves. In and through our reply to this offer we are taken up personally into a living communion with God, as his partners in our life. Holy Scripture expresses this in the homely terms of "dwelling with one another" in order to describe our intimacy with God by means of the intimacy of the personal relations in family life. Doubtless this implies a warning, for it would seem that intimacy with God can only be expressed by calling upon things and habits from the secular, human world with which we are already familiar. Thus we enter the intimacy of a new world, but still have to resort to our "old," familiar world in order to express in words this new sphere of life. Thus we have "intimacy," and yet a certain "strangeness"— from the very start it certainly seems to be a somewhat complex state of affairs.

It is already evident that there is immediate intersubjectivity with God: we have to do with the Father, the Son and the Holy Spirit, of whom our experience of contingency gives us not the faintest idea. In that case God must certainly have addressed us "person to person."[18] We now interact with

18 It is true that as "parole parlante" our affirmation of faith that God is Father, Son and Spirit also includes a reference to the once dead and now risen Christ, and to the outpouring of the Spirit over the Church by the glorified Christ. But from our faith we know that "Father, Son and Spirit" are not purely functional ideas (the so-called "salvation-history Trinity") but really refer, in a projective act of faith, to the inward and thus intra-divine independence of being of God as Trinity. The necessity of this affirmation (which is fundamental to our contention that there is present a real intersubjectivity with God) can only become manifest if we analyze the structure of faith. We cannot go into this thoroughly here, but we give the following brief note: the absolute in its totality is never directly presented in our natural human consciousness, it remains the horizon of our consciousness in-and-towards the world, the ungrasped background of our dialogue with man and the world. In contrast, in the self-revelation of God, and thus in our life of faith, the Absolute is given to us, as a mystery, in

God, just as we interact with human beings, in a familiar self-disclosure and real dialogue.

This means, first of all, that we have entered a "supernatural" order. What does this term "supernatural" mean? We have seen that the human person finds his or her most intimate self-fulfillment only in a real intersubjectivity with God, but that he or she is prevented from reaching God by an absolute boundary. This intersubjectivity with God, however much desired by human personal existence, lies ultimately beyond human power. But this means that man is a being who can find the ultimate meaning of his life *not in himself,* in the human, but only in the superhuman or more-than-human—in fact, in intimacy with God. The word "supernatural" means no more than this; it refers to a sphere of life which surpasses the human, though it is nevertheless the most intimate fulfillment of man. For this reason we cannot even say that a supernatural destination is necessary in life for the ultimate meaning of our human existence, for it transcends our human existence; we can only say that in order to live meaningfully in a personal way, man needs grace, but that his humanity cannot demand this of itself. This is to say nothing more nor less than that man cannot find in himself his definite goal. In other words, reciprocity with God is superhuman, and in this sense supernatural: God's pure grace. The fundamental astonishment and admiration evoked

---

direct communication, though thematically it is only *indirectly* ex-pressible. Thus although, owing to the fact that we are situated in history, there is a "development of dogma" in this area, that development is, by definition, of a completely different nature from that of the usual development of our human consciousness of truth. In faith the Absolute is no longer only "background" but becomes "foreground," though it can only be experienced in faith and thus in an indirect expression. This is inwardly qualified, however, by the *direct* givenness of the Absolute in his inner mystery. (It is just for this reason that the preservation in its purity of the eschatological content of faith ultimately requires the charismatic assistance of the ecclesiastical teaching authority, particularly because the Absolute is presented *otherwise* in the knowledge of faith than in our natural knowledge.)

by this is, in the first instance, not enchantment by the wonder that is man, but by the wonder that is God. The One who is independent in existence, who has no need of anyone in order to be fully that which he is, had already made himself God-for-us in and through his act of creation, and now in his love becomes more still, God-with-us. The wonder which is constituted by man insofar as he can find himself only beyond the boundaries of his human existence is only the reverse side, the creature's experience, of this divine wonder.

But from all this it is already clear how ambiguous it is to state that *Christian existence* (real personal communion of life with God) is an authentic *human existence.* For this intimacy with God is by definition not human but superhuman. It makes us into children of God. Our human existence is such that it will naturally find the most sublime fulfillment of its meaning therein: Christian existence is not an inhuman mode of existence, but an inward fulfillment of our human life in a transcendent—that is, a divine—manner. And this means that the intensification of our human life, as the repercussion of the life of grace on our humanity, becomes possible only on the basis of a sacrificial, radical going out from oneself, and it is thus only the resonance of a personal love for God. Hence entering into an intersubjective relationship with God, accepting grace, implies at the same time an essential shifting of our centre of life, for this intercourse by definition transcends the aims projected by human culture and the process of humanization: theologal (i.e., intrinsically supernatural) religion—in other words, intersubjectivity with God—is of its essence "not of this world"; it is not self-achievement. Theologal religion falls outside the autonomous *Selbstverständnis* (self-understanding) of man; the latter is only a *Vorverständnis* (precognition) of the former. It is grounded in an act of God, who brings into being the religious relationship of man to himself, and himself tells us how he would have us realize true religion.

Here we can no longer retain any of our own conceptions, as we still, in principle, might if we could simply proceed to our affirmation of God from the experience of our contingency. Here we stand in the presence of a revealed religion which God brings us (in Christ Jesus). In essence religion is thus no cultural act, but the surrender in faith to an act of God. This implies that in the act of accepting grace the essential thing is that man transcends his humanity, however true it may also be that this humanity is inwardly completed thereby. Here trust in God really becomes the embarkation upon a new adventure which falls quite outside the human project of life. God enters with man into a life of love, a life which surpasses all the tensions and expectations of man's design for humanization of the world and about which no meaningful thing can be said on the basis of this design. This is, if we wish to call things by their right names, in truth an entry into another world, not a human world but a divine world, in which, moreover, man no longer gives himself his determination in a continually re-assumed *relative* self-transcendence, but freely lets himself be determined by the God of salvation in an *absolute* self-transcendence which can therefore only be realized by grace.

Hence man is a "new creation," and thereby human life has by definition received an eschatological significance. In terms of salvation that which "makes whole" and definitively completes is God in his divine mode of being. Essentially God, and hence also God's spoken word, is a suprahistorical reality. Therefore that which makes man "whole" or completes him is his intersubjectivity with God the "healer." This is a suprahistorical and therefore an *eschatological* event. From this it follows that the secular is not in itself a sphere in which salvation can be found. The intramundane, be it involvement on behalf of one's fellow men or mastery over nature as a condition of the liberation of man, cannot in and of itself provide us with salvation, not even (in itself and on its own, at least) when all of this is experienced in creaturely dependence on God and in awareness of God as the transcendent Third. Salvation lies in God, approached as personal subject, a "Thou" in real intersubjectivity.

And yet God gives us salvation now, even if it is only as a beginning. This real intersubjectivity with God, which is already taking place in our secular history, therefore holds all sorts of implications, which we must consider.

Intersubjectivity with God in a Historical, Intramundane Form

(1) Intersubjectivity with God in confrontation with the history of salvation.

We have taken intersubjectivity as meaning the interpersonal relationship of two subjects who are attracted towards each other as subjects.[19] Presence is essential in this. This is expressed by the classical expression "sanctifying grace"; because, contrary to widespread opinion, sanctifying grace is the relation of reciprocity between God and man, in which God has the initiative. Since every action of God, including his action of grace, is divine it truly means that this grace-full reciprocity is a reality in man and thus involves an aspect of "created grace." But however important this latter moment may be, we are not actually concerned with it here. In a completely different context Heidegger has rightly said that we have a continual tendency towards "defining the nature and potentialities of a fish by the extent to which it is capable of living on dry land," outside its own element.[20]

---

[19] For the phenomenology of encounter see, among others: J. Buytendijk, *Phénoménologie de la rencontre*, Bruges 1952, and *Rencontre, Encounter, Begegnung* (Contributions . . . dédiées au prof. F. J. J. Buytendijk), Utrecht-Antwerp 1957. See also the literature under footnote 23, below.

[20] *Ueber dem Humanismus*, Frankfurt a. M. 1947, p. 6.

This admonition would be indispensable if one were feeling inclined to define created grace "outside its own element"— that is, in separation from the intersubjective relationship with God and from the theologal life. For in separation from its element the concept of created grace becomes internally contradictory and indeed unintelligible. How can something created be *as such* grace, since grace is God's absolute gift of himself to human beings? Since it is the actual reality of entrance into life in and with the God of salvation? In the theologal act of faith, hope and love the reciprocal relationship with God is completed.[21] The human (created) act of faith, love and hope, as an act of dialectic intercourse with God, itself becomes a grace.

A relationship of direct reciprocity with a God who is present to man is thus unmistakably an element in the life of grace: God addresses man personally, and man personally replies to God. But with all this we have indicated but one aspect of our experience of God, even though it is a fundamental and formal aspect. For God addresses a *human* subjectivity or freedom, a human "I." And this datum places immediate intercourse with God in a completely new perspective.

Some Anthropological Data. A human person is, after all, not a closed inwardness that subsequently incarnates himself in this world via bodiliness. He is an I-in-the-world; i.e., a spirit or person, to be sure, but in self-communication to the bodiliness which is thereby humanized and to a certain extent (and according to all types of gradation) "subjectivized."

21 See the pages on sanctifying grace and the theological virtues in E. Schillebeeckx, *Revelation and Theology* I, "The New Trends in Present-Day Dogmatic Theology," pp. 106ff., and especially p. 128. Regrettably, it is not within the scope of our present treatment to deal with the problem which has been raised in such a noteworthy way by Bultmann, that of the relation between the "personal relationship with God" and "scriptural and dogmatic affirmations" (the defined content of faith), even though this problem cuts deeply into the question under consideration here.

Therefore, insofar as it is humanized, the human body belongs to a human being's subjectivity, to his personhood. Since man is not a pure "I," not a pure spirit, but spirit that must live out its life in the body, he only becomes himself by going beyond himself. The human "I" is essentially in and with the things of the world. And so man gets a glimpse of his inwardness only when he looks towards the world of men and things, when he becomes engaged with people in this world. He is with himself, present to himself, a person, only when he is present to something else, and especially when he is present to someone else. Self-consciousness is then also the consciousness of an I-which-is-in-the-world, the consciousness of being present to things and primarily to fellow human beings. It is years since the Parisian school of psychologists made it clear that man becomes familiar with the world only via familiarity with his fellow human beings; in other words, that under a certain aspect the relation to one's fellow men is primary when compared with the relation to the world.[22] Under a certain aspect: because being-in-the-world makes it possible for man, as spirit in corporeity, as a being that expresses and reveals himself in corporeity, to be orientated towards the other, the fellow human being. For this reason the philosophical anthropologists rightly say that man becomes himself in a humanized world; which is to say: in the world inasmuch as it bears the traces of human presence. Human bodiliness, as visibility or the revelation of human inwardness, is therefore the necessary point of reference for all the personal activity of man.

The being-in-the-world of the subject through self-revelation in bodiliness is inextricably bound up with self-orientation towards our fellow human beings. In the encounters

22 See especially E. Wallon, *Les origines du caractère chez l'enfant*, Paris 1954; J. Piaget, *La naissance de l'intelligence chez l'enfant*, Neuchâtel 1947. These ideas have been subsequently developed further by the phenomenologists; see, for instance, R. Kwant, *Phenomenology of Language*, Pittsburgh, Duquesne University Press, 1965.

deriving from such orientation man becomes himself: this is the anthropological law of incarnation of his being. This does not mean that an act of the mind which has first been carried out internally afterwards expresses itself outwardly. Expression in bodiliness is a constitutive sign—that is, it is only in turning outwards towards our fellow men and the world that human inwardness determines—resolves—itself as completed personal activity. Inwardness is thus constructed in and from material of this world, and especially through authentic solidarity with other human beings.

In this way every conscious experience and personal activity of man has an unbreakable connection with the life of human beings lived in common in the world. Otherwise man remains a potentiality that is not capable of living as a person; his active life thus remains at a subhuman level; his "I" cannot attain its rightful place. As a law of man's being this will hold true of all his personal activity, even when this is a life of grace by which he enters into another world, life in union with God. But before analyzing this we must consider man's principal relationship, namely that with his fellow human beings, in a little more detail.[23]

If man becomes himself especially in and through human community, then authentic human life implies, purely anthropologically, contact with the material and verbal revelation of one's fellow man. For our fellow man's bodiliness is the manifestation of his inwardness, whereby I personally

[23] In addition to the literature already mentioned, for the philosophical psychology of humanity see especially A. De Waelhens, "Beschouwing over de historische ontwikkeling van de ervaring van het Alter-ego," in *TP* 13 (1951), 667–685; F. Buytendijk, *Het kennen van de innerlijkheid*, Nijmegen 1947; E. Levinas, *Totalité et Infini* (cited above); M. Chastaing, *L'existence d'autrui*, Paris 1951; L. Binswanger, *Grundformen und Erkenntnis menschlichen Daseins*, Zurich 1953[2]; M. Nédoncelle, *La reciprocité des consciences*, Paris n.d.; S. Strasser, "Het wezen van de mens," in *Annalen v. h. Thijmgenootschap* 46 (1958), 1–31; J. Arntz, *De liefde in de ontologie van J.-P. Sartre*, Nijmegen 1960; W. Luypen, *Existential Phenomenology*, Pittsburgh, Duquesne University Press, 1963.

encounter him, immediately and directly, without any sort of objectivized medium. It may still be vaguely and anonymously, but I nevertheless experience him directly as a personal revelation, because his body is the manifestation of his inwardness. On the other hand, he is a subjectivity or freedom that appears in corporeity, that expresses itself in alienation, thus in material which in itself is not human, but humanized through the self-revelation of the other person. My perception of this revelation of reality (which is my fellow man) is therefore, by definition, ambivalent and anonymous: on the one hand because bodily expression is the expression of a freedom (which is capable, therefore, of feigning), and on the other hand because this free self-disclosure is effected in a worldly material which, although it may lend itself to such a humanization, never adequately coincides with its freedom. In this way the emphasis will come to lie upon the side of the subject or inwardness, but not completely. Exteriorization continues to be characterized by an essential ambiguity. Only when the ambiguity and anonymity of this inwardness is removed by our fellow man's free, interpreting and clarifying communication (his "verbal revelation" or "revelation in word" to which we referred at the beginning of this paragraph) is it possible for us, in an act of trust in what he says, to call the "material revelation" he constitutes by its own proper name.

This must now be placed in the context of what we stated above about man's development into a person. If man becomes himself in interaction with his fellow men, his personal activity is achieved primarily in his perception of the reality which his fellow man reveals and in his listening surrender to the interpretation of this reality which this fellow man presents in the accompanying verbal revelation. Seen in a purely anthropological way, therefore, the completion of our human existence takes place above all within the sphere of "revelation" and "believing trust," which are both fundamental categories of our experience of human existence. Thus, when God reveals himself, the existential prefigurations needed in order to understand that revelation are already present in our life.

Inward Revelation and Salvation History. When the absolute person, God, reveals himself to man, to the human subjectivity of freedom, and this, naturally, in such a way that the divine revelation can be perceived by man, then God is addressing a human person. That is to say, he is not addressing a pure I or a pure spirit, but an I-in-the-world; man does not have any other I. But the consequence of this is that man can only listen to the revelation of God with a consciousness that is in, and present to, the world. However much man may be spirit—i. e., subjectivity—and thus capable of being addressed, he is this only in communicating himself to corporeity. He becomes himself in turning outwards and can become conscious of himself-as-inwardly-addressed-by-God only in and by the world and his fellow men. What is noteworthy here is that he will be able to find God only in God's inward, absolute and eschatological offering of himself (*locutio interna*) by going outwards: by going out into human history. Addressing human freedom as he does, the direct self-revelation of God—who is *intimior intimo meo* even in the offering of grace (*gratia interna*)—is, as revelation to a human being, at the same time and co-essentially a historical, "horizontal" expression of God. Were this not the case, there would be nothing for man to listen to (consciously and explicitly, at least).

When God speaks, he does so ultimately in order to be heard by man; and for this reason his spoken revelation cannot possibly reach our conscious inwardness in a purely internal, vertical manner. The vertical "inward invitation to believe" will necessarily be accompanied by a revelation in history, an "external revelation" with which "faith from hearing" will link up. In the human world one will be able to find a humanly perceptible, audible, tangible, visible form of God's expression in the words in which that expression is comprehensibly present to us. This does not mean to say that we compel God, if he wishes to speak to us, to speak in sacramental—i.e., historically palpable—forms. The fact itself of God's speaking, as speaking to *man*, essentially implies this mode of speech, because otherwise it could not reach secular man and would become meaningless.

As the movement from God's side drawing man into intersubjectivity with himself, revelation includes not only a moment of vertical "inward address" (inward because God, as God, addresses to us an invitation which reaches the very core of our freedom) but at the same time a moment of horizontal "address from without"—that is, from our human world (the *communicatio externa* of "public revelation"). This implies that God manifests himself in a supernatural way in the world of human relations and things and in the history of mankind which is its product. Just as man becomes himself in and through a secular sphere of human relations —i.e., only in a humanized world—even where that depth is concerned at which he can make the natural affirmation of God's existence—so he can come to himself at the depth at which he is inwardly addressed by God's love, drawing him, if he moves in a world that is not only a humanized world having a human history, but one having a salvation history. It is only in and through salvation history that man becomes himself in theologal intercourse with the living God.

In the continually self-incarnating existence of the human being who is inwardly addressed by grace it is possible to discern many elements. They are varied and interdependent. To start with, the individual human being comes into a world which has already made history; in the concrete, he enters a history of salvation in and by which his intimacy with God can be made capable of experience. On the other hand, he in his turn makes salvation (or perdition) history, since every free act which contributes to the making of history is (at least anonymously) made in confrontation with the living God of salvation, so that the (anonymous) acceptance or refusal of salvation is given concrete expression in history. For his action is carried out in and by intramundane material and in human fellowship. Furthermore, each human act by which man—expressing himself in the world—comes to himself is not only outward expression, but at the same time inward personal growth (constructive or destructive). Thus the religious man founds his life on a history of salvation that is, as it were, the sacramental cause of grace; he lives his life of grace in history, in the world of people and things which, in so doing, he himself helps to establish as sacrament of grace.

From what has so far been said it will be evident that the horizontal origin and source of the history of salvation is situated above all in human freedom, insofar as this freedom is inwardly touched by God's grace in an inexplicable manner. This contact of grace is expressed in history in human freedom which must grope its way forward towards what may sometimes prove to be a mistaken expression. Also the history of salvation begins in an obscurity which only gradually clears. God's offer of salvation continues with history and thus takes on ever clearer characteristics, until prophets can arise, by virtue of a stronger attraction of grace (*lumen propheticum*), to judge, in God's name (i.e. through the inward propulsion of this special attraction of grace), the value of history with respect to salvation or perdition.[24] In this manner the historically observable form of the revelation of reality—which is, as such, ambiguous—is clarified as revelation by the word of the prophet, so that therein the individ-

[24] See "Revelation, Scripture, Tradition and Teaching Authority," in Schillebeeckx, *Revelation and Theology* I, pp. 3ff.; also K. Rahner, *Weltgeschicte und Heilsgeschichte*, in *Schriften zur Theologie* 5, Einsiedeln 1962, pp. 115–135.

ual believer may personally discern the indistinct inward invitation from God.

Yet all of this is only a partial view of the reality of salvation. So far we have seen that the inward, unexpressed nucleus of grace ("verticality") is "horizontalized" in human history by human beings who have been touched by divine grace: human freedom, then, would be no more than the open window through which the supernatural enters our world in order to be further horizontalized in history by the operation of humanity's law of incarnation. It would be only *in the second place* (namely, as an *expression* of the freedom which is inwardly addressed by grace) that human history, in its turn, brought us to deepened intimacy with God. But there is more to the matter than this. Without wishing to appeal immediately to the real possibility of a divinely miraculous "intervention" in the world itself, we can and must nevertheless say that the external environment of man's life does not become an environment of grace because human freedom touched by grace expresses itself there. In actual fact our world also becomes the direct expression of God's saving will (and not only "via" human freedom).

God's act of creation, of which we can become conscious in and through our human, contingent existence in a contingent world, is, from his divine point of view, a personal act of love towards man. Man can arrive at this insight on the basis of his experience of existence, without being able of himself to reciprocate that divine, personal act of love. Yet herein lies a prefiguring of the personal communion of grace with God. We refer to the intercourse with the world and with our fellow men as the work of God's love, which is to say: an encounter with man and with the world, of which one knows that it is offered to us in a personal act of love by the creating God. But in the reciprocity of grace this gift of the world—and, above all, of our fellow men—receives a deepened meaning. In the loving gesture by which

God offers us living communion with him, his gift of the created world receives a deeper significance. The world, offered by God to man for humanization, is offered to him by the God of salvation. True, this does not change the inward profane structure of the world. Nevertheless, within the inward attraction of grace which takes hold of freedom, the created world (and in the first place this means our fellow men) is a reference not only to God's act of creation but also to his act of salvation. In this way the relation to one's fellow man in the world is brought under the light of salvation.

Hence the world, and in the first instance one's fellow man, appears as a *translation*—however weak, as yet—of God's inward address. Subsequently it appears as a medium in and through which man's attention is drawn explicitly towards the inward invitation of grace; and finally, as an *area* in which he gives his fundamental response (of refusal or of acceptance) to this divine appeal. And so, in countless mysterious ways, God's offer of salvation penetrates to human consciousness from within and from without. That offer permeates all man's experiences with something inexpressible, so that he can never, in any case, find peace in the purely intramundane; for even if he refuses, he cannot undo the fact that God loves him and in doing so never leaves him in peace.

Thus God's absolute self-offer of inward divine life goes together with the divine offer of an "external grace," and the latter is primarily one's fellow human being in the world and, therefore, in human history. For if, from an anthropological point of view, man is a person who only becomes himself in giving himself to his fellow man, then conscious entry into saving communion with God will also be accomplished only in the giving of oneself to one's fellow men, to fellow men who have come to be an objective reference to the saving will of God. But this means that the primary and fundamental sacramental form of grace is one's fellow man.

It means that human relationships in this world have a sacramental meaning: that of the offer of God's gift of salvation in a historical form. We can discern what this sacramentality consists in only by considering the sacramentality of our fellow man Jesus Christ.

(2) Intersubjectivity with God in the sacramental form of the man Jesus. In the man Jesus, God's saving will is completely revealed and realized in a historically perceptible form. The humanity of Jesus is a constitutive sign of God's offer of grace, because Christ is not only the person who, as man, reveals God's loving invitation to us, but at the same time the person who has accepted that offer of love from the Father as "man for us." As man he is the complete, historically perceptible form of grace.[25] It becomes apparent precisely in the encounter with him how "verticality" and "horizontality" are bound up with each other without any detriment to the *immediateness* of the free relationship with God. Because to encounter this man in faith (indeed, a human being must always be encountered "in faith") is to encounter immediately God himself; for this human being is the Son of God in person, and one does not meet a "human nature": one encounters a person. Hence, in Christ we do not first meet a man, then go on to a second stage and encounter God. Encountering the man Jesus in faith is real intersubjectivity with God, in spite of the "horizontalism" in the human appearance of Christ. This seems important to me, for we are quite ignorant about the possibility of a communication of grace without Christ.[26] But this also implies that God remains always absolutely transcendent, even *in* our intersubjectivity with him; even within this intimacy there remains the distance created by the divine holiness. We

25 Since this has already been thoroughly analyzed in another article (cf. "Die Heiligung des Namen Gottes durch die Menschenliebe Jesu des Christus," in: *Gott in Welt* [*Festschrift für Karl Rahner*] II, Freiburg 1964, pp. 43–91), the present exposition will be only brief and schematic.

26 *Ibid.*, especially pp. 73–79.

reach him immediately, and yet humanity, even when it is the humanity of the Son of God himself, is the sacramental and therefore "horizontal" form in which this reciprocity of grace first becomes capable of human experience.

Thus the implicit moment of inward contact with grace can be made thematically conscious only in a living contact with the man Jesus. The material and verbal revelation of Jesus, our fellow man, is the form in which the content of our intersubjectivity with God becomes thematic, the focus of our attention, and fully capable of being experienced by us.[27]

(3) Intersubjectivity with God in the perceptible form of the Church. Since the glorification of Christ our contact with our fellow man Christ, and thus with the human figure who makes the experience of encounter with God possible to us, perceptible, comes about in the Church. It is characteristic that baptism primarily incorporates us into the ecclesial people of God and, in doing just this, brings to life our communion in grace with God. Here also the "vertical" and "horizontal" moments intermingle with each other, without detracting from the immediateness and verticality of our encounter with God. The Church is the communal form, willed by Christ himself, in which we become acquainted

[27] Hence the central element of faith, "God's inward call," is itself also "horizontalized" in the man Jesus, who is thus the constitutive sign on the basis of which we surrender ourselves to the so-called "illumination of faith." Christ is the explicit motif of our act of faith precisely inasmuch as it is a theologal act. The same might be said of Christ in his Church. Furthermore, a more thorough analysis would be required of the way in which Bultmann's distinction between "historical fact" and "salvation fact" may be justified without our being able to clearly separate the two. The historical fact is attainable by what is called "objectivized knowledge"; the salvation fact can only be approached within intersubjectivity with God, but as objective content of this interpersonal relationship, not as creation of this faith. That which is visible of the salvific event in Christ and his Church can only be approached in faith because it is an eschatological reality appearing in its constitutive expression.

with the living God and by which the inward gift of grace is made accessible to our experience in and by a historically perceptible form. Of course, this is only possible if, on the basis of his definitive and thus eschatological act of redemption, Christ himself keeps this ecclesial community of salvation fundamentally holy and unassailable, standing firm in its confession of the Christ-revelation and in the diaconia of redemption. Now this is precisely what Catholic faith proposes. Hence growth in religious intercourse with God will go together with a personal growth in the already given religious community of human beings, the Church, and in the "objective spirit" of that Church: her cult, her sacraments, her preaching, her prayer, charitable activity, etc. In concrete terms, it is a question of a reacting, personal immersion of one's life in the already-existent community of grace, love, cult and prayer of the apostolic Church. Hereby grows that personal intimacy with God which in its turn fertilizes, enriches and activates the church community by virtue of Christ's continuing action of grace. The movement from without to within and from within to without this community of grace never ceases. Interiorization and exteriorization are inextricably bound up in this community (and this is typical especially of the smallest cell of the Church, Christian family life).

(4) Intersubjectivity with God in the perceptible form of human fellowship. From a consideration of Christ and his Church (and not without it) we may now understand how, even outside an historical confrontation with the man Jesus or with his Church, an authentic, though to a certain extent anonymous, intercourse with the living God becomes possible; namely, through human community: in unconditionally abandoning oneself to one's fellow men in disinterested love. But our fellow man is this only because of Christ, the sign of God's gracious will and activity. I hope to have

already shown elsewhere,[28] that man is created with an orientation towards Christ, and as such is given grace. In the concrete, man is a visible prototype of the man Jesus, although we understand this only from the Christ who appeared in history. Therefore, outside of an historical confrontation with Christ or with Christianity the sacramentality of human fellowship cannot be grasped in its real significance, and the possibility of experiencing this free communion with God in-and-by human fellowship remains unavoidably "nameless," vague and obscure. Every man is himself the administrator of this sacrament of human fellowship,[29] and every human being has a mandate to obtain for himself personally its gift of grace. "As you did it to one of the least of my brethren, you did it to me" (Mt. 25:40); "For I was hungry and you gave me food, I was thirsty and you gave me drink. I was a stranger and you welcomed me. . ." (25:35–36); "as you did it not to one of the least of these, you did it not to me" (25:45). In reality, disinterested love in human fellowship is implicitly a Christ-oriented attitude to life, and intimacy with God can be made capable of a conscious experience in and by concrete, historical human fellowship; that is, by approaching one's fellow man as "my neighbour." It was not without reason that Erasmus could write: "I could hardly refrain from saying, Saint Socrates, pray for us."[30] The relationship with God is always accomplished in and by a people of God, whether it be the as yet undifferentiated people of God we call mankind, or Israel—in which the Messianic mould of humanity became

[28] "Die Heiligung des Namen Gottes durch die Menschenliebe Jesu des Christus."

[29] The mediaevals would have said "sacramentum naturae," though perhaps with a somewhat narrowed perspective. Pursuing the sense of what has been said above, we might do better to call the human community of persons—created in orientation to Christ—the prototype of the Church: the Church in the making.

[30] *Erasmi Rot. Colloquia,* Leiden 1666, p. 145.

increasingly clear—or whether it be, in sharply defined characteristics, the people of God redeemed and constituted as a church by Christ. Intimacy with the living God builds up fellowship, and, on the other hand, this is brought about by God himself precisely in and for a community of human beings.

The existence of the sacramental form of the humanity of Jesus, the Christ, does not mean that this general sacramentality of human community is thereby done away with or only, as it were, transferred to the "formal structures" of the visible Church. On the contrary, it is precisely through the historical appearance of the man Jesus that now, in and because of the Christ who has already appeared, the sacramental power of grace in human community can be experienced in its full force. Hence the general sacramentality of human community is only made concrete in the community which we call the Church. And the seven sacraments, preaching, cult, government (etc.) of the Church are but the high points of the crystallization of this involvement with one's fellow men. From this it is evident that here and now it will be possible to experience intimacy with God in the familiar milieu of the Church only if the human love of this Church becomes concretely visible and palpable in that community, and does not remain limited to those few peaks at which Christ presents his grace in a concentrated manner (in fact these are independent of the personal goodness and holiness of the administrator). If the latter were the case, these peaks would in fact only constitute a few bright spots in a cold domain devoid of real human community and personal effort on behalf of fellow human beings. The tendency towards secularization is also an indictment of us all in that we have been too economical and sparing in showing the world that real and authentic human love by which intimacy with God must grow.

The Reality of Personal Intimacy with God

We began the second part of this section with the affirmation
of authentic intersubjectivity with God. Gradually we came
to realize that the "verticality" of this personal communion
with God is bound up with the "horizontality" of our human
life. In this concluding part we must find out whether this
so-called "verticality" is nevertheless ultimately real.

The working of God's grace, as a divine and hence absolute
act on which our personal communion with him rests, always takes hold of one from the "intimius intimo meo," from
one's innermost depths. The immediacy of this action cannot
be added onto or placed alongside the mediated activity,
whether that of the humanity of Jesus, or the saving action
of the Church's sacraments, or of human community in this
world. The "horizontality" of the offer of grace is always an
explicitation of what takes place in a hidden and in itself
incomprehensible manner inwardly, through the absoluteness
of God's action of grace, which vertically grasps our spirit.
"Vertical" means: in and based upon the transcendent interiority of God within our person. In other words, if, with
Greek patristics and Western theology since Thomas
Aquinas, one rightly posits in the action of grace (conceived
of in a non-physical way) the so-called "instrumental causality
of salvation" of Christ and the sacraments (as the crystallization of what takes place in a less concentrated way in all our
human and secular relations), then this does not invalidate
the Augustinian notion according to which only God can
directly and inwardly grasp the spirit ("Deus illapsivus in
animam"). From God's point of view the action of salvation
is "unmediated" in all aspects, it works vertically in our
spirit "and" (the following must not be taken as something
added) at the same time horizontally in the history of salvation. Thus it becomes possible for us to experience God's
inward invitation consciously in and by the "contribution"

from the outside. At the same time, God himself "horizon-talizes" his immediateness in this world: in the man Jesus, the Church and the community of humanity as a whole as a prototype of Christ and his Church, as also via the humanized world as the dwelling place and living environment of human beings.

Furthermore, all forms of "horizontally" mediated actions of salvation draw their actual saving significance from the "horizontal" appearance in this world of the man Jesus, the Son of God in person. Because all grace is a saving act of *Christ*—the "horizontalized," personal grace of God in this world—we can no longer conceive of any grace which does not come upon us from the horizontal level of our lives. However obvious it may now have become that human com-munity remains the fundamental sacrament, it will—because of its sacramentality—have to point towards Christ. No one will deny that unconditional love for one's fellow men is real Christianity, even when someone remains outside the Church or does not acknowledge Christ. The question, how-ever, is whether this is the only way in which the Christian himself is called upon to love God. But for the Christian this would mean a return to the pre-Christian stage of anonymous sacramentality in the community of mankind as a whole. Does not the sacramentality of "pre-" or "extra-Christian" human community draw the whole of its meaning from its objective reference towards and longing for the man Jesus, the Christ? Can we, after the centuries of longing for the Christ, turn our backs on him when he has as last appeared? Doubtless this has been done, but it was the summit of man-kind's sinfulness.

Therefore the solidarity of mankind does not have the last word; this is reserved for consciously experienced human communion with Christ and, therein, intersubjectivity with the living God. It is only in the express encounter with Christ in his Church that the completely perceptible form of

our Christian existence is possible. But that Church needs
to be a truly habitable abode, and it is part of her mandate
to bring this about differently in each different age. A complete relationship with God is experienced in an explicitly
Christian and ecclesial form. And it is just for this reason
that, however bound up it is with our everyday cares and
tasks and the whole of our intramundane activity, in and by
which we grow in intimacy with God, our Christian life also
has a separate, sacral sphere, set apart from secular history
and culture: a domain in which we pray and are simply together with God in Christ. There silence has a place. Seen
anthropologically, silence is a moment in conversation or
social intercourse; it has no actual meaning in and for itself,
it is only a factor in human community and social intercourse. There silence is needed in order to make interpersonal contact human and to keep it so; in order to humanize
it. Silence personalizes speech, and without it a dialogue
would be impossible. But in a revealed religion silence-with-
God has a *value in itself* and not only as a factor in our
dealings with fellow human beings: this is so precisely because God is what he is, God. To fail to appreciate simple
passive communion with God as the Beloved is to take away
the very core of Christianity.

Certainly our whole existence in this world of people and
things penetrates even into this form of communion with
God, and as something belonging to it essentially, not merely
as distraction in prayer. We cannot tell God that we love him,
or at least that we are continually trying to love him more,
other than in words, ideas and images which we borrow from
our secular human world. Moreover, this intercourse is not
individualism, for our prayer would be insincere—not
prayer at all—were we to pray: "Our Father . . ." and to fail
to remember the kingdom of God and our fellow men in
saying this prayer. Being a Christian is not just being united
with God in the perceptible form of Christ in his Church, it

is also *co-operation, working together* with the living God, with the Father who is "working still" (Jn. 5:17), both in the Church and in the world. The religious attitude to life is primarily a personal intercourse with God, but with the living God who is also the creator of the people and things he offers to us to humanize. Therefore the relation to one's fellow man and to the world is not only cultural but also religious. Love of God neither can nor may be separated from human love. Christian love of one's neighbour means that we, God and I together, love *my* neighbour. Whereas in the case of natural human love God is only the silently present, transcendent Third, my *caritas* towards my fellow men is just as much love, but a human love in experienced loving communion with God. And thus the Christian loves his fellow man with the same love with which he loves God and with the same love with which he and his fellow man are loved by God.

Prayer in interaction with one's fellow men, *contemplativus in actione,* is a deeply Christian reality, but to be honest, it is cut off from its true source if it is not accompanied by moments of purely passive communion with God. Even the epitome of prayer in action, Christ himself, saw the necessity for us of regularly going into our room and shutting the door, in order to pray undisturbed. If the modern tendency towards "horizontalized" Christianity ignores this essential element of Christianity, then in its heart it will have cut itself off from the Christianity of Christ (and I know of no other), and human community will ultimately be the greatest sufferer. For it is only from Christ that one learns what "being human for others" actually means (although secular and human experience will teach us how we should bring human community into being in particular situations). One can always argue for something which one would like to consider proven by means of a few scriptural texts, on the condition that a number of other scriptural texts are ignored.

Certainly, the biblical *agape* means, especially for St. John, the love of God for man and the love of man for his fellow man. There is nothing about an *agape* of man for God; but this is for the simple reason that man's relation to God is expressed by another typical word: *pistis,* the unconditional surrender to God in faith. It is St. John himself who clearly brings forth the image of God "pitching his tent" among us, dwelling with us. In one's place of residence one is really at home, from there one goes out into the world. Reflecting on the unconditional nature of Christian self-transcendence and the intrinsic value of communion with God, I am reminded of a Dutch proverb originating in an area of rivers and canals in which the pride of a sailor in his ship did not absorb the independence of his nature: "One hand for the ship, one hand for oneself." But Christianity asks us to yield to it this free hand as well, in order to put our whole trust in God. It asks us to forfeit our life for the Other.

On the other hand we ought not to forget the insight that our secular intersubjectivity with God can only be achieved in faith. For that reason there is no true experience of God, not even in this real reciprocity with God. God's witness to himself is experienced in ourselves, i.e., in the experience of our existence. In the final analysis we are able to experience only our existence, which is personally addressed by God. We are personally united to God only in faith, i.e., in the surrender to the unseen and unexperienced. (This is perhaps the central insight of Dr. Robinson.) We experience grace in the experience of our humanity. We experience an impulsion that we know we cannot elicit or explain ourselves. God is known only in signs; in the case of natural knowledge he is known by means of the objective mediation of creation; in the case of faith and intersubjectivity with God, by means of the subjective mediation of the attraction of grace.

This immediate, intimate and reciprocal presence remains

one that can be approached only in faith. It is for this reason that our intimacy with God is of itself eschatologically orientated towards the beatific vision through the intuitive encounter with the glorified Jesus in heaven. On earth it can be realized only in the sacramental encounter with the man Jesus in Scripture and the Church, or outside Christianity in a hidden way in our fellow men. Nevertheless this personal relationship with God must still be called direct. It can develop into an interior life of mysticism, where it is a dark knowledge experienced as alienation. For the believer who has entered this sphere of the divine influence and is ruled by it, this state will become his crucifixion. But the genuineness of our personal relationship with God will have to be constantly measured by the authenticity of our love of other human beings and by our use of the forms which have traditionally served as channels of this relationship: the hearing of God's word in Scripture and the reception of the sacraments.

But there again, the test of the authenticity of the spiritual experience deriving from these particular forms willed by Christ himself, the "sacrament of the Church," will be the sincerity of our human solidarity, our love for our fellow men. Hence there is in our world a *sacral* sphere and equally a *secular* sphere of life, so far as our intimacy with God is concerned. In all that man does he is either working out his salvation through openness to God and neighbour or bringing about his damnation by shutting himself off from love. We must be with God not only in church, in prayer, in the sacraments, in the reading of Scripture—in other words, in the sacral forms of religion—but equally in secular relationships, in our daily tasks, in our interaction with fellow human beings. And then we may say that various types of Christian life are possible: some people will experience the growth of their intimacy with God above all in the sacral forms; others, on the contrary, will do so more easily in the world of concrete life: in "secular holiness." But the question here is one of emphasis: if the accent on either element of a full Christian life is lost, our experience will lose its authenticity. Thus within Christianity it is possible to distinguish two radical types: that of the Christian in the world and that of one who has "renounced marriage for the sake of the kingdom of God"; the secular experience of Christian life and the sacral experience of the same Christianity. A radical break between the two will certainly kill religion, on the one hand because religion is not a separate world beside our human world and on the other because it is nevertheless an authentic being-together and working-together with God himself, the superhistorical and supersecular, absolute reality. The foundation on whose basis horizontality can be joined with verticality into a living unity within human experience itself is, it seems to me, precisely the theistic moment of our natural orientation towards the completely-Absolute, a moment that is made explicit in the so-called proof for God's existence. A typical feature of the one-sidedness of the exclusive horizontalization of Christianity in certain secularizing tendencies appears to me to be the continually recurring contention that a natural "proof of God's existence" is impossible. It is precisely because fideism radically separates intramundane reality from God that in the long run the intramundane either becomes "Godless" or is melted down with the religious, and then we get—in modern wrapping, perhaps—either the typical experience of "eighteenth century" atheism, at least in the form of an agnosticism, or a "secular religion" in a complete horizontalization, like the model already proposed by Feuerbach.

CONCLUSION

In conclusion I should like to show, by means of a concrete example—namely, the sacrament of penance—how the "horizontalizing tendency" produces a gain on the one hand, but brings about a definite loss on the other.

In former times it often happened that when someone had, for instance, sinned seriously against brotherly love, then repented and gone to confession, he did not think it necessary afterwards to settle the quarrel with his neighbour in person. Today, on the contrary, when we realize our lack of love, we approach our fellow man and set things right with him. This is a gain, because it is genuine, but unfortunately we often experience no need to "set things right with God" in confession. For isn't everything right with God when I have undone all that I did in sinning?

Now it is true that, from a purely theistic point of view, one can contend that however much sin may be sin against God, even though committed by using secular "material," I can only give God satisfaction where God was affected, namely in his creature: in myself and in my fellow man. For God himself remains transcendent, even with respect to our sins. Seen purely theistically, a sinful act can be revoked by the will itself, namely through a new self-determination. Entering once more into love for one's neighbour undoes the sin, even from a theistic viewpoint—i.e., with respect to God. But this is an abstraction, because in the concrete order of life sin against one's fellow man also destroys personal intersubjectivity with God. From our human point of view a renewed self-determination, by which we might set in order our quarrel with our fellow man, cannot lead us once more into intimacy with God; for this a purely redemptive act of God's own free grace is needed. Grace itself is the principle of our repentance and renewed self-determination. Now it is certainly true that this grace is not exclusively attached to the sacrament of confession, but is already at work precisely in the act by which I set everything right with my fellow man. But this is not all. For our sin touched not only our fellow man and, in him,

his and our absolute ground of being, God; it also affected
our intimacy with God, which, however much it may be
interiorized in our relationship with our fellow human being, is a value in itself. The question must be settled not only
with one's fellow man but also in a personal dialogue with
God.

Now I am quite aware of the fact that this conversation
with God is experienced in the fundamental sacrament of
human community, and not in a purely inward solitude with
God. Fundamentally, our repentant re-entry into communion
with God can only be made through the fellow human being
against whom we have sinned. But as we have said, this
human community draws the whole of its sacramental value
from its orientation towards Christ (concretely in the
Church). In itself human community is not an adequate sign
of God's wish for reconciliation; its constitutive sign is the
personal encounter with the man Jesus, and that in the form
proper to the experience of this mystery of Christ; namely,
the Church in her salvific form of confession. Thus reconciliation with our fellow man refers us inwardly to the explicit encounter with Christ in his Church. The completion
of what has been set right in the presacramental encounter
with our fellow man is therefore to be found in the sacramental encounter with Christ himself, in confession. The
repairing of our human relationships can of course take
place equally well before or after confession, but in either
case it belongs essentially to the integral sign of confession
as reconciliation with Christ and with one's neighbour. Only
thus are both evangelical purity and human authenticity
fully realized.

From this example it is clear how greater authenticity has
rightly been attained through frank recognition of human
community as the sacramental field of experience of our
personal communion with God. But, on the other hand, the
example also reveals that modern man is showing a tendency

to set up as independent that very sacramentality of human community, to disjoin it from Christ, from whose humanity it draws its sacramental value. In other words: there is a greater solicitude for human authenticity, but a weakening solicitude for loyalty to the gospel. Or, to put it differently and perhaps more accurately; a tendency to remain in a merely implicit and anonymous Christianity. (Whence, rightly, the great sympathy towards world religions and other philosophies of life, and the recognition of an implicit Christianity therein.) Now I know full well that implicit and explicit Christianity are substantially identical. And the whole question is ultimately about authentic Christianity. This is why a non-Christian (someone who stands outside historical confrontation with Christ or his Church) can in the end be more authentically Christian than an ecclesial Christian. But the historical fact of the personal appearance of Christ, who still lives, gives to the conscious experience of the mystery of Christ living in the Church in her Scripture, in her dogma, her sacraments and preaching, a complete, objective form. And it is from this form, as Christ willed, that Christian life can develop to its highest level and become capable of human, connatural experience. To deny the latter is to deny the sacramentality of horizontal human community. But on the other hand such a denial is implicitly contradicted by the sincerity and authenticity with which a person unconditionally abandons himself to his fellow men. And so hope continues to live in the human heart. The urge to horizontalize is in fact a desire to see the Church of Christ as an authentic community of love!

5 Dialogue with God and Christian Secularity

"I praise thee, for thou art fearful and wonderful. Wonderful are thy works! Thou knowest me right well. . . ." (Ps. 139 [140]: 14)

Introduction

In a moment of deep existential experience Ernest Psichari wrote: "J'ai la permission formidable d'être un homme."[1]

Human existence is something granted, it is a grace: an overwhelming grace. I am given the chance to be a human being. To our present-day world, with its feeling rather for the abandonment, the *Verfallenheit* and "situatedness" of human existence, this pronouncement is somewhat jarring. It reminds us of the biblical idea of our fortunes being dependent on God's grace: "Upon thee was I cast from my birth" or, as the Vulgate more evocatively puts it: "Towards you I was cast."[2] Yet it is precisely this very psalm which sees our relationship with God against a background of the darkest abandonment: it begins with the words: "My God, my God, why hast thou forsaken me?" In Scripture man is seen as a being whose life is fraught with immense perils from without and from within, but who is yet held firmly in happy security by God.

[1] *Voyage du centurion*, Paris 1931, p. 175.
[2] Ps. 22(21):10.

During these days of study the enormous reality constituted by man is being examined from various points of view. It has been left to this introduction to present a general orientation, without going into the biblical and secular views of man which will be developed in other conferences: it must therefore remain general, but its approach is formally theological. Proceeding from a faith that is perhaps still anonymous and vague, we are attempting to reach a stronger and more personal faith: for it is in this that the mediating function of theological reflection consists.

Thus our purpose is quite different from that of a related congress on "Man" held at Louvain and Brussels in connection with the World Fair of 1958 by the Philosophical Society and the Conference on Thomistic Philosophy. We may—in a certain sense we must—take as a theoretical presupposition for this theological reflection on faith the philosophical and phenomenological ideas developed there by such eminent professors as S. Strasser, A. Dondeyne, A. van Melsen, A. de Waelhens and L. de Raeymaeker; but this will be a basic supposition only, for however much philosophical anthropology may logically precede theological anthropology, the Christian consideration of man follows quite a different path, for faith is an existential attitude in the immediate relationship to God. Theological investigation concerning man's essence means asking what man is and what he becomes through entering into dialogue with God.

Here we can leave aside whatever philosophy may tell us concerning this. Theologically, it is certain that man becomes himself only in moving outwards from his own centre of life towards God. Or to express this in another way, in a deeper introversion, so as to press on in grace through the most profound depths of his subjectivity to God; more accurately, to experience personally God's presence within him. But we are now immediately aware that in speaking theologically about self-transcendence we have made a certain presupposition: we have mentioned the "self," "man," before he has even come to himself via his relationship with God. We have already used a certain concept—namely, "man"—and now we are asking what this being is and becomes through his relationship with God. Thus a relatively independent, for the moment let us say a *philosophical,* view of man is already supposed before we begin our *theological* reflection upon this reality. Now it is true that even this provisional view of man is not neutral from a religious point of view. For either we have already, as our starting point, taken into account religion or atheism as a twofold, real datum of human experience, or we have left this phenomenon aside. But to take the latter course would be to produce an abstraction which, even though of the methodological sort, would nevertheless involve the singling out of certain data from a general human experience of life that is possibly far richer in content. From this taken in itself, then, we must reach a twofold conclusion. We must conclude that the concept of man as a being who finds himself in the world without having asked to be there, in this world in which he is able, freely and responsibly, to construct his own existence through his bodiliness and in community with others—this concept may well be a true concept of man, capable of yielding fundamental insights concerning him as *ein Wesen de Möglichkeit* (a being of possibilities). But we must also conclude that such a view tells us nothing about the ultimate and total potential of this being: the potential whereby he becomes himself only in personal communion with the living God.

This concept of man as a personal subject whose essence it is to be, or to construct himself in freedom by giving meaning to a world of people and things, is one which we shall assume from the outset as a forward-looking, open-ended definition of man in which believers and non-believers alike can find a common ground for dialogue. The opposition in views between the partners in the dialogue—the believers and the non-believers—does not then consist in a denial by the believers of the possibilities of which the non-believers speak; rather it consists in the fact that the believer is taking into account possibilities which give an entirely new significance to the intramundane possibilities with which the non-believer is concerned: the ultimate possibilities implied by a fundamental relationship with God. For being-in-and-present-to-the-world takes on a completely different meaning if a man experiences this presence in the world and in history not as an isolated individual—that is, in a radical personal loneliness which persists even in face of the fact that personal existence is co-existence—but as a dwelling in and with the living God in the historical situation of this world. And then the question becomes urgent as to whether an adequate definition of man can ultimately be given without making any reference to his relationship with God, which he can freely assent to or freely deny. In the final analysis the definition of man is *vocational:* he is defined by God's call.

However the matter may appear from a philosophical point of view, it is certain that the theological definition of man is gained precisely from this existential relationship of man to the living God, and that it is just this existential relationship that at the same time reveals the profound meaning of human existence in this world. Using a scriptural term (which originally had quite a different orientation), Christian tradition has summed up this theological conception of man in the expression *imago Dei:* man is the image of God.

It is our intention to discover what God in his grace intends for man by considering the living reality of divine Providence. What does the Word of God say about man? *How does God see man?* That God sees man does not mean simply that he knows what man is making of his life here below. On the contrary, it is the gaze of one who is personally

interested, who calls us to salvation and participates with us
in a personal, creative and sanctifying way: he is involved in
the fortunes of man (so much so indeed that in the *theo-*
phania of the man Jesus he personally devotes himself in
solidarity with human beings to the formation and construction of the "essence" of man in himself). For this reason, the
question as to the meaning of human life coincides with that
regarding divine Providence. But not in the sense with which
this word is used by Rudolf Bultmann, who identifies theology, discourse on God, with a Christian anthropology. Even
though we can only speak about God on the basis of our
relationship with him, especially insofar as it has been made
manifest in the man Jesus, our affirmations concerning God
are nevertheless no mere anthropological affirmations; they
are not just things said about man, but things also said about
God himself. Having set up this condition in advance we
cannot approach man's essence better than by doing so
through reflection on divine Providence.

THE MYSTERY OF GOD AS THE CENTRE OF
MAN'S ESSENCE

Theological Definition of Man

We describe the human person, according to his horizontal
dimensions, as a being who must define himself in and
towards this world in community with his fellow men
through the exercise of his freedom. Thus, from a theological
point of view (thereby bringing in the vertical but all-com-
prehending dimension) we could describe him as a free being
who must define himself in and towards the world in dialogue with God. Though it originated in an atheistic climate,
the modern definition of man is more open to his theological
description than the closed Aristotelian definition (which
Aquinas had already reinterpreted in a more open-ended

way). Man is a being with a superhuman or supernatural potentiality. The definition of man will only be seen clearly
when we consider him in the light of the dogma of creation
and salvation; that is to say, in terms of his whole experience
of existence, which includes a salvation history.

The dogma of creation (supported by our own experience
of our contingency) informs us that, in spite of his bodiliness
and his essential involvement in this world, man comes from
the hand of God as a person and therefore under all aspects
possesses an immediate relationship to God which calls him
forth as a person—a situated freedom—into existence. Man
belongs "first" to God and only secondly to himself. He exists
for God. This is his metaphysical and moral significance. The
relationship with God is not something added, it is constitutive of man. This means not only that I have been called
into existence by God, it means at the same time that I continually receive my being from him; that I really am myself
and yet am completely and thoroughly in and of him, as
much in my thought and desire as in my essential bodiliness
in this world. I discover myself in this mysterious condition
which I cannot change: I am really myself in and of this
world, becoming myself more and more therein, and yet at
the same time created, even to the most delicate fibres of my
being; completely of God, from whom I borrow myself and
by whom I am continually given to myself. I am myself in
dependence on God: the more I am God's, the more I become myself in transcending myself. In this constitutive relationship to God, who is a mystery, I am a mystery. The whole
crux of my definition is precisely the mystery of God. The
essence of man can only be defined in correlation with God.

This immediate relation to God is given even before I take
it up in freedom. It belongs to the "existential" aspect of my
being, which I have to take up in freedom and to which I
have to give room in the exercising of my freedom. I am
orientated towards God, and he turns towards me even before

I enter into personal relation with him. To express this in philosophical terms: the relation with God which I constitute as spirit in essential incarnation first exists in the modality of "essence" and only subsequently in that of freedom and "essentialization," through which I give myself my determination.

The paradox in this created condition of the human person is that its natural recognition coincides with an affirmation, critically founded in this world, of security of life in the personal mystery of God, whom we nevertheless cannot encounter in this world by our own powers. Orientation towards God, standing in function of God, man cannot of himself realize this immediate relationship with God as such. He stands attuned to the mystery of the living God but powerless to respond to it. His very essence is a request for self-transcendence, a demand to rise above himself, to step outside himself and into communion with God. But it is precisely this essence, this definition of man, that he himself cannot realize, except in and through a completely new and free initiative of God, who calls theologal intersubjectivity into life through his grace. In concrete fact man is a being who does not hold the personal meaning of his existence within himself, and cannot realize it of himself. It is only in God-given love, through which he goes out of himself towards God, that man finds the personal fulfillment of his life, his true essence. Only then does he know that this possibility is his true definition.

In the light of this relation to the living God, the creator and giver of salvation, the horizontal definition of man as a person in essential incarnation—according to which personhood is primary and being incarnate, although co-essential, only secondary—takes on a more intimate significance. The theological definition of man's personhood is his theologal intimacy with God; man is primarily a dialogue with God. The theological definition of his essential incarnation or dialogue with the world then becomes the following: in his intimacy with God man approaches the world and his fellow men. This religious relationship, though primarily orientated towards God, also includes the essential incarnation of man; nevertheless, the latter, although co-essential, is a "secondary" aspect of religious life and of the definition of man. In this way the profane is taken up in the relationship with God, which is constitutive of the theological definition of man. And this shows us why man may not simply absorb himself in his intramundane task, which becomes personally meaningful only in the context of his theologal relationship with God: wrested out of it, his dialogue with the world has only a limited intelligibility and meaning; it does not have a *personal* meaning. Without this man as a person, though certainly not inconceivable, is ultimately a concept devoid of meaning: in such a case he could be evaluated only as an element contributing to the development of culture and the elevation of mankind and then, having served his purpose, passing into anonymity except for a brief survival in the memory of the living. The *personal* meaning of his life would thus be put in question.

Therefore, if we wish to approach man theologically as a situated freedom, we must consider him in his intersubjectivity with God and situate in it his dialogue with the world. If we then see divine Providence as an encounter between divine freedom and human freedom, it will become apparent how God wishes to bring the human person via his history-making freedom to the deepest meaning of human life: primarily to encounter with God and in the second place to life in union with God in this world of people and things.

Dialogue with God, Man's Primary Task in Life

The primary concern of God is directed towards bringing man to self-transcendence, in which he goes out of himself in loving communion with God. An experience of existence that is taken up in a personal and collective salvation history allows us to penetrate this reality in the light of faith.

God is a being who is so interested in our lives that our own hearts must urge us to interest ourselves in him. God never gives up. He fights for us and sometimes against us, but always in order to gain us. He searches for us, and cannot reach us as long as we have not found him. For this he must set heaven and earth in motion; he gives and takes away, raises us up and lets us fall again. He gives us delight and joy, then grief and setbacks; he gives sickness and health, exuberant spring and autumnal calm. He turns us about, spins us; spurs us on to the triumph of generous action and then, as it were, lets us go and we fall, through our own weakness, into sin . . . all of this so that the living God may ultimately penetrate in and through our love for him. Thus, from a superficial point of view, we all receive plenty of misfortune during our lives: God is continually giving us gifts, but one by one he takes them back again. Then we receive something new, but it does not last long, or again life itself cancels out its benefits. It can happen that we become tired of this incessant buffeting, close our hearts off from life and mourn it as a vale of tears. But it is also quite possible that these continual vicissitudes—this achievement and deprivation, this switching on and off of fortune and adversity—may teach us to look beyond all these gifts in order ultimately to discover the love-sick Giver who is trying to gain our heart. God's love pulls and tugs and shakes at our daily life until we raise our tired eyes, which are continually fixed on earthly things, and make them look deeper, beyond the changes in our lives, to the living God, who is trying in and through all these events to gain our hearts. He finds no satisfaction in making things difficult for us, nor does he regret the liberality of his gifts of good days in our lives, nor grudge us the pleasure we take in them. But above all this and through all of it he wishes that our hearts, excited by earthly joys and softened by disappointments, should ultimately realize that our life is greater than this secular universe and that there is a God of love who wishes to encounter us and enter into personal relationship with us. "If one does not find God in the vicissitudes of life," says Newman, "where, then, will one find him?" Our God is someone living, who understands the art of love well enough to disappear now and again only to reappear before we grow too tired in seeking him.

Thus what God really aims at in his providential guidance of our lives is that we should be brought to intimacy with him; not coercively and unwillingly, but freely and out of love. This is the most profound mystery of our life: personal relationship with God, and it is such that there is action and reaction between God and ourself, true reciprocity in freedom and love. Even in God reciprocity is real, though in a divine manner. We distort the interpersonal relationship between man and God by conceiving too statically of the "over-determined" and all-determining reality that is God, and by denying real reciprocity as possible to him. From the experiences of believers, above all from those of the saints, the opposite would seem to be the case. This much is certain: we have no clear idea of the divine dimensions of the concepts by which we designate God's qualities. The divinely unique nature of God's immutability and independence with respect to our human interventions and initiatives escapes us and can surprise us again and again. Thus we know, for example, that God is one and not many, and as believers we must fully preserve this strict monotheism. But the actual divine manner of being one escapes us, till revelation gives us the added surprise that this oneness is none other than Trinity. Such is also the case with our insight that God is almighty, irresistible and good. There must be no tampering with this insight; it is not contradicted by revelation. But we have no representation of the actual divine modality of this omnipotence and goodness. We are given a glimpse of it in a surprising way: in the impotence of the cross this omnipotence is shown to us and in the loss and sacrificial abandonment represented by that cross we get a hint of the mode of goodness proper to God. And ultimately this is how God's sovereign independence stands with regard to human interventions, with his immutability and freedom from contingency. Although we cannot dispute this immutability, its actual divine modality escapes us. But from a life in which religion is lived, above all from the answers to our prayers, we know that this independence offers us a full range of surprises and that God really takes his creatures' wishes into consideration. There is clearly an action and reaction between God and man, and that is the essence of personal community. In terms of intersubjectivity rather than merely in a language of imagery, we may contend that God freely allows himself to be influenced by men and reacts to them, but this in a divinely transcendent manner which, nevertheless, does not destroy the reciprocity of intersubjectivity, but makes it a mystery. This mystery is withheld from our earthly view and loses itself in the living God's transcendence of definition. Hence man's life with his God is a truly intersubjective life: theologal intersubjectivity, I-Thou existence (which is called "sanctifying grace"[3]). These intersubjective relations constitute the very heart of human life. They have value in themselves and not only insofar as they are of use in intramundane endeavour.[4]

The nature of this intimacy with God, which is the primary task of human life, can be seen in more detail by con-

[3] With all the ontological implications that this grace contains for man as a *creature*.

[4] It becomes all the more important to note this inasmuch as the present tendency of not a few is to take another direction, with the consequence that the relationship with God which is experienced for itself (e.g. in contemplative religious life) is called into question, and is in practice not appreciated or is at least distorted.

sidering the man Jesus. In and through Christ, God the Father
has also become, in the force of "the Spirit of sonship," truly
our Father, so that we are taken up into the special providential relationship which exists between God the Father and
the incarnate Son. God's personal care for us is a fatherly
solicitude, not just the concern of a great ruler of the world
who controls everything. In the East, at the time of Christ,
the word "Father" had a stronger meaning than our present-
day family idea of a father. It was not lacking in tenderness,
but above all it expressed the competent, authoritative, all-
arranging care and leadership of someone to whom thanks
are due for everything. The "Father" was the unconditionally
acknowledged and trusted holder of authority in the Jewish
family. The attitude among the Jewish people of a son
towards his father was, especially at the time of Christ,
an attitude of obedient veneration: the father's will determined everything in a Jewish household, which was also
called the "father's house." The sons were really "about their
father's business": they worked at his business and remained
in his home. It was proverbially true that between father and
son "all that is mine is yours" and "the son is with the father." The parable of the prodigal son provides a very good
sketch of Jewish family life.[5] From this parable it is evident
that sin is always a break with the Father: leaving your Father's house, his home, to serve yourself and be your own
master, using what has been received from the Father, hence
at his cost. And conversion consists in returning home, entering once more into working partnership with the Father.

Faith in God's paternal guidance essentially underlies the
all-determining motto "the will of the Father," obedient love.
Open contradiction of the Father in a Jewish family was
simply unthinkable. When Christ speaks of the "will of the
Father," if we are to grasp the real meaning of this, we must

---

[5] See especially Lk. 15:31; applied by St. John to the relationship of Christ
to his Father: for example, Jn. 8:35; 16:15; 17:10; 14:2.

situate it in the father-son relations which the Jews to whom
Christ was speaking knew in their own families, and which
Jesus himself experienced with regard to Joseph (so that
Scripture says: "He was subject to them"). This was not just
a passive obedience. For just as the Jewish father could give
his son a mission, so that he went forth in his father's name
actively and with full initiative, so also "the Father who is
in heaven" gives us instructions which we, in childlike sub-
missiveness, must actively carry out.

And yet Christ gave this obedient trust in God's fatherly
solicitude a note of tenderness and intimacy: he called God
"Abba," a word that was never applied to God by the Jews;
they would have thought it far too familiar. For like the
Greek child's "pappa," "abba" was the Jewish child's first
attempt to speak, the first baby sound (already filled with
childlike feeling) which was his word for "father."[6] In this
way Christ added to the element of sacred respect in the
Father-Son relationship a note of intimate tenderness, a childlike need for help.

That we are children of God is the deepest significance of
our being made in his image and it is also the fundamental
theological definition of man: a definition that is ultimately
still in the making and which is only accomplished through
truly intimate intercourse with the living God.

From our being children of God it follows that man's
supernatural-social dimension, namely human relations on
the basis of *caritas*, are part of the essence of man. The child
of God exists essentially in a family context, the context of
the Mystical Body. Community-building brotherly love (*caritas*) is the penetration of our intimacy with God into human
relations. Therefore Christian brotherly love is essentially a
religious event, a religious task, and not simply "morality."

----

6 "Ab" means "father." In English too, we find that words for parents, such
as "dad, daddy, dadda, mommy, papa, mama," originated in babies' first attempts to speak.

It is never secular, however much it may be embodied in the reality that constitutes this world. Brotherly love means being oneself for others in orientation towards God. This is the ultimate theological definition of man.

Dialogue with the World within the Immediate Relationship with God

We have already spoken earlier in an oblique way about man's dialogue with the world, but only insofar as God wishes to draw man's attention to his offer of grace by means of man's changing confrontation with this world. Seen thus, human dialogue with the world is the way in which God attempts to gain man for himself through the circumstances of human life.[7] Thus the intramundane is already a dialectic element in this divine interplay of love, an element contributing towards theologal intersubjectivity.

We must now investigate the meaning proper to this dialogue with the world within the dialogue with God. For it is part of the factual essence of man that he participates in a dialogue with the world of people and things in which he stands. God calls on us to actively contribute meaning with respect to this world and to do so on the basis of our experience of God, which is not only a partial aspect of our human life but an integral attitude to life which also comprehends our being-in-this-world. For human freedom, which is personally addressed by God, is also a culture-creating freedom. We Christians tend rather easily to leave the ordering of temporal society to the non-believer. We forget that the so-called profane, the acknowledgment of mundane reality, is

---

7 We have borrowed this dimension of the history-making dialogue with the world from "The Search for the Living God" (see above, Chapter 2), in which, however, attention was directed to the people of God as such and not directly to God's interactions with the individual person. Nevertheless, the same principles hold in each case: God wishes to have the individual man and mankind for himself.

only one part of a total religious attitude to life. Laicization
or secularization is in itself an intra-Christian and intra-
ecclesial event, an event within the life of the people of God.
These are ambiguous words. But their meaning lies in this,
that within his dialogue with the living God the believer
comes to the recognition of secular reality as calling for his
commitment to its tasks. In this way Christian "laicization"
is completely different from atheistic laicism, which experiences secular reality as its only horizon in life. Seen objectively, exclusively secular or atheistic laicization is an *hairesis*,
a tearing away of profane or secular reality from the whole
into which it fits, the existential relationship of faith with
the living God. Only outside this connection is secular reality
"profaned." For, although the intramundane possesses independence to a certain extent, through which it has of itself
a certain intelligibility, it remains a question whether this
secularity (in which the personal essence of man finds himself) can find a complete intelligibility *within its own boundaries*. The secular point of view is always circumscribed by
temporality, and it is valid only when it remains open to the
higher whole into which it is integrated in God's plan.

With regard to God, *coram Deo*, man will take up his
personal responsibility in secular history together with God.
On this level he lives out his immediate, intersubjective relations with God in the secular sphere, which has its own structure and immediate meaning. Although they are situated on
completely different levels, the supernatural or religious and
the intramundane or secular dimensions are not without influence on each other: despite the fact that the secular has a
certain autonomy in its own sphere, dialogue with the world
becomes a moment in our dialogue with God. The value and
significance of secular life in itself remains untouched within
the consciously experienced relationship with God. But all
this calls for clarification.

(a) In itself this dialogue with the world runs according to a secular law of reality. In this sense we may really speak of a secular dimension of the task of human life. To be sure, this secular element is only human when it is given its place in the actual plan of a human person. It is a question of the achievement of authentically human values which, as such, are realized *diesseitig,* in this life, by the power of human capacities. On this level one meets general aspects of human life which are in no sense the exclusive property of Christianity and in which believer and atheist co-operate: the humanization of the world and of man. In its inward structure this task is therefore non-Christian; that is, not supernatural but purely and simply human. This whole area has an autonomous human value and its own sphere of activity in which anyone who is sensitive to general human values can participate. On this level the Christian can claim nothing as exclusively his own.

If we wish to talk about the Christianization of this intramundane task of life or of the "profane," we must definitely begin by recognizing the secular character of this calling. It is, of course, true that man is affected in his humanity by the repercussions of sin, and that sensitivity to general human values has received a blow thereby. Personal communion with the living God will give us a particular sensitivity towards human values. Thus the christianization of the intramundane task of life may certainly be considered a restoration of general human values. Nevertheless, these remain truly human values, so that we do not leave the intramundane point of view hereby; in themselves they remain recognizable by man as man, independent of his theologal experience of God. This situation means only that under this aspect personal communion with God has a remedial significance even with regard to intramundane reality; in other words that, at least in principle, humanism and the secular stand their best chance within personal communion with God. But on the other hand it must be admitted that however much commun-

ion of grace with God may make us more sensitive towards
recognizing general human values, it does not of itself, as
Professor R. C. Kwant has rightly pointed out,[8] make us
concretely aware of given historical facts: for instance, of particular examples of deficiencies in the humanization process.
Hence Christians may be late in recognizing the necessity for
structural reform as the condition of a more personalized
existence for the worker—or later, at any rate, than non-
believers. But under this aspect, Christianizing our secular
undertakings amounts to no more than fully recognizing human reality and human values as such. This is not specifically
Christianization, except in a supplementary sense.

(b) However, for the person living in communion with
God through grace—that is, man as we defined him theologically—this means that the secular sphere or lay task in life
does not involve *laicism:* in this world the secular becomes a
mode of incarnation, of personal communion with God, the
taking up of the intramundane into our theologal relationship with God; and from God's side it becomes a thematic
appeal. With God, and supported by his security in God, man
stands in the midst of the secular world, which thus becomes
the free space in which, as a child of God, he takes an active
role in creating culture. Although remaining of this world,
this reality becomes a moment in his presence with God, and
thus the secular is present with God. Although the distinction
between the secular and the sacral remains, the two spheres
form real aspects of human presence with God. Being-in-this-
world is a part of man's total religious existence.

In this way there is also a Christian "laicization,"[9] which is
completely distinct from atheistic laicism—with which, more-

8 "Het doel van het bedrijfsapostolaat," in *Sociale Wetenschappen* 1 (1958),
162–183.

9 Here we are thinking especially of the scriptural "laos," the people of
God. The lay state is a positive form of existence within the Church, although formally distinguished therein from the clerical state. The differential
task of the layman relates partly to the intramundane plan of life.

over (taking into account a prudential assessment of the
historical context), a co-operative dialogue is possible on this,
its own level. As believers we live with God in this world,
which we construct into a home worthy of human habitation
in which, moreover, the incarnation of our personal communion with God is expressed. This expression takes place in
the secular order itself; non-believers work at it too, from an
exclusively secular standpoint, but on a common basis. In
this way the biblical theme that the world is for man and
man for God is given its ultimate significance. Were we to
express this in classical terminology, we should say that the
finis operis, the aim proper to the activity of secular life, is
immediately intramundane. It is the humanization of man
through humanization of the world, the construction of an
earthly home for the glory of man. But men are there for
God: the personal meaning of life is superhuman, non-intra-
mundane, and cannot be gained on the basis of man's own
human and mundane powers. Only in a self-transcending act
can man receive the personal meaning of his life as a grace
from the hand of God. This means that human dialogue with
the world finds its ultimate sense only within the religious
attitude to life. The "intrinsic aim" of the intramundane is
orientated via man towards the *Eschaton.* To contend that
this introduces into the question only an extrinsic, supplementary end to man's activity (*finis operantis*) seems to me a
failure to grasp the full implications of this fact. For the
secular world has a meaning only inasmuch as it constitutes
a *demand for meaning* over and against which man appears
as a *giver of meaning:* man grants to it its human meaning.
Because man's bodiliness relates him essentially and inextricably with this secular world, the ordering of the secular towards personal community with God, a relation not of necessity so far as the secular in itself is concerned, becomes of
necessity owing to the orientation of the secular towards man.
In virtue of the complementarity which exists between man

and the world the destination of man living in dialogue with God may to some extent be termed the "proper end" of the secular itself. Hence the Christianization of work and of secular undertakings means giving full value to the secular —that is, fully recognizing the reality of the world, but as part of the integral communion of life with God. It means standing with God in the world.

In this manner the secular task of giving meaning becomes the embodiment of authentic love of God and authentic love of mankind: concrete charity or a theologal approach to existence. In and through the faithful, the secular task becomes an expression of God's redemptive love for humanity in the historically visible form of secular readiness to serve mankind. For it is a partnership in the creative activity of the God who saves, and not only in that of an abstract "creator God." Hence the intramundane order of life differs considerably, according to whether it is the incarnation of the man who is in communion with God or of one whose life is attuned exclusively to an intramundane wavelength. The two forms differ, even though, so far as their structure in itself is concerned, they are subject to the same laws. We might say as a rough comparison to illustrate this point that an animal and a human being each have a face, but we should only speak of a facial expression, the reflection of a deeper sphere of life, in the case of man. In the secular sphere we cannot speak of monopolies by Christianity, nor, on the other hand, by exclusively secular humanity. The secular task is an appeal directed to man as such, and anyone sensitive to human reality can participate in it. The man bound in grace to God is still a citizen of this secular home: he may not permit this to be taken over by a purely intramundane mankind. Both stand on their own ground; neither the believer nor the atheist is an outsider here.[10] Though one cannot exclude the

10 Note that we are speaking here of the secular task of Christians, not of the Church as such; this latter has only—directly, at least—a supramundane

possibility that non-believers will now and then achieve most in this sphere, nevertheless, when seen in its entirety, a secular ordering of life, achieved apart from communion with the living God, will not infrequently become rather the empirical manifestation of a break with Life. In spite of a few "epoch-making" high points of secular success, in the long run the results of sin will show themselves in distortions of what is authentically human. Here the secular task of the Christian has a redemptive meaning, in the deeper sense of that term: the Christian layman redeems the secular not only through his communion in grace with God as something extra, which might be conceived as rather like the icing on a cake; he redeems the secular from within his historical situation and within its own limits through the finality of grace. But this grace cannot be termed extrinsic to the personal meaning of the life of man, who is essentially rooted in this world.

However, the fact that the secular order of life becomes the embodiment of the personal life of the man who is taken up into personal communion with God means that this same secular order is taken up into the mystery of man insofar as he is integrally orientated towards the divine mystery. In this orientation lies the innermost definition of the humanity of man, even of his humanity as a being-in-the-world. Hence the ultimate significance of the secular merges, by virtue of its human character, into the mystery of the order of grace. Because of the communion of the human person with the living God, this secular reality brought into being by man carries within it a claim to glorification, along with man, at the end of time. In its secularity it therefore transcends the purely *diesseitige*. For this being-in-the-world is in the concrete a life of faith, and thus the Christian, while standing in the world in the midst of the same human reality as the non-

---

mission, which equally holds secular consequences. The Christian himself, the *laikos*, however, has a task which is also secular.

believer, knows by faith that this standing-in-the-world is a
moment in a personal relationship between a God who loves,
gives, and calls and a humanity that loves, is called and re-
sponds. It is this faith itself which is the highest element of an
authentically human existence, and precisely because of this
it is the foundation of the only true "Christian humanism."

The way in which this secular reality, humanized over the
course of time, is extended into eternity is ultimately a mystery of which we can construct no positive representations.
We know only that in intimacy with God everything human
becomes and will always remain important, and that ultimately, in the new heaven and the new earth, the intramundane order of life will be the harmonious expression of the
personal communion of mankind with almighty God in
Christ, the Lord. But this harmony is thus also a grace, and
no human achievement, though human acts are not extrinsic
to it.

From all this it follows that integral humanism is itself a
grace, and that secular humanism stands within the continual
possibility of *sacrifice.* "Seek first his kingdom and his right-
eousness, and all these things shall be yours as well." This
brings us to the idea of a *kenosis* in the life of the believer.

THE HUMILIATION AND EXALTATION OF
CHRIST, PROTOTYPE OF MANKIND

Christ came to restore our relationship and dialogue with the
living God, and in so doing, without paying explicit attention
to it,[11] he restored the Christian meaning of the secular and

11 We must insist upon this point: not infrequently one finds dogmatists
who, in support of theses which they already hold, appeal to some or other
scriptural text which is to provide a scriptural basis for "Christian humanism." We may not lose sight of the difference in point of view between the
Old and New Testaments. The fundamental optimism concerning creation of
the Old Testament (which continues to constitute part of revelation) is not
rejected by the New Testament, but hidden beneath a moral-religious view

of the intramundane task of life. Through the redemption the world too is liberated from its unredeemed state, and can once more become the expression of, and at the same time a disposition towards, a harmoniously experienced personal communion with God. Yet the redemption leaves its mark not only on the life of grace with God, the ultimate meaning of human life, but also on the intramundane task as an incarnation of this communion of grace. Like Christ, mankind goes through a "kenosis" in the world on its way to heavenly glorification.

This kenotic situation of a mankind on pilgrimage brings us back to the existential *Verfallenheit* and abandonment with which this conference started. And yet there is a world of difference between the kenoticism of Christian life and the tragic, lost state of an exclusively secular humanity. The profane *Sein zum Tode* (being unto death) means the absence of redemption, while kenotic existence, though it can be no less tragic, is a redeemed existence: it is redemption from that lost state which can, in Christ, be made a sign of the security of our life in God. However far we may be able to journey with unbelievers along the way of the secular, undergoing with them the human experience of existence, we cannot follow them into the unredeemed state itself. The Christian's *présence au monde* is always a presence founded on the redemption, and thus in and with the living God, a redeeming presence. Not only, therefore, can we not go with them into sinful situations (as Coccioli's "priests of the poor" wish to do), but even the most miserable situations of human

---

of life which is caught up with the opposition between the state of perdition and that of salvation, between death and life, sin and redemption. The New Testament world-view is formally *soteriological*. The experience of the meaninglessness of human existence apart from Christ does not involve pessimism with regard to creation. Thus the optimism of the New Testament is also formally a soteriological optimism. The intramundane implications of this will only gradually find expression over the course of time—in this respect there is a "development of dogma."

abandonment will be experienced inwardly in a different way by believers—not in less pain or tension, but in company with God who gives joy to our youth. Everything becomes (this is what we try to realize, at least) the expression of child-like dependence on the living God, the primary task of human life: self-transcendence, love. All of this does not make the dialogue of Christians with the world less authentic or less intense, but brings it into immediate relationship with God. Nor can the partial failures of secular tasks have the same significance for them that they must necessarily have in an exclusively secular world. That a particular undertaking is a fiasco cannot separate us from the living God. On the contrary, failure can become an incarnation of our personal communion with God. Only within this communion is *kenosis* spoken of.

The kenotic condition of Christian life produces a certain ambiguity, introduces a problematic element into the secular order. For the secular also enters into the mystery of the redemption brought by Christ. Both success and failure in the domain of secular reality can be the expression of a personal communion with the living God: by his success the Christian may be brought closer to God, or in spite of misfortune he adheres to him. Hence the urgent task of redeeming the secular order remains, in its inward reality, unaffected by either. Yet failure on the part of Christian humanism may sometimes be interpreted as a blessing. Considered in terms of the one thing necessary, even a general collapse of the structures we have raised in the world may not in the final analysis involve the destruction of anything vital; for since our humanism has reference to the end of time all our successes in this world must be evaluated eschatologically. It is in this sense that existential atheism is fundamentally different from Christian secularity. Existentialism, Sartre claims, is a humanism because it makes man mindful of the fact that it is in a condition of abandonment that he will decide for

himself.[12] We, on the contrary, believe that in the personal
loneliness in which we exercise our freedom we are securely
held in the embrace of God and that it is in partnership with
the living God that we enter dialogue with the world. Christ
says that he is never alone, for his Father is always with him.
These words utter the deepest meaning of human reality in
this world, but it is a reality which we can approach only in
faith: the affirmation that human life has a personal meaning
can only be the product of faith. Hence even the meaning of
the secular order of life can ultimately be approached only
in faith, since man as a person is a living mystery whose
meaning will be revealed only in the future. The king of
creation is a simple child of God: this childlike relationship
to the living God effects a shifting of the centre of human
life, putting it outside man. Man becomes fully human only
when he is not *only* human, for by his definition he transcends the purely human. Christ, therefore, is the real definition of man, and we can realize the fullness of our humanity
only through the bond of grace with Christ, the Son of Man.
The essence of man is not a datum, not something already
given, but something to be achieved in grace. By transcending
our humanity we shall permit ourselves to be human.[13]

---

12 *L'existentialisme est un humanisme,* Paris 1946, p. 94.
13 This at the same time is at the centre of the eschatological mystery of
heaven and hell.

6 God's Good Guidance of Life

C. S. Lewis once remarked wryly that many people take the view of God which an airman takes of his parachute—he always keeps it on hand in case of need but hopes he will never have to use it. For many, faith in Providence has unmistakably become a faith in the last resort. A sick man, for instance, when he has consulted all the specialists without finding a cure, turns to God. God becomes the super-specialist. Julian Huxley—a self-professed unbeliever—says, in this connection, that when a Christian thinks of God as his "father," the image he has before him is of a grandfather—a "bonpapa" who behaves as if he were blind to the evil in life and had as his only concern the desire to make everything on earth pleasant and easy for us. When someone becomes seriously ill, his spontaneous reaction is never to say, "That's really providential!" but if he narrowly avoids an accident in crossing the street, then that is just what he does say. Popular faith spontaneously thinks of Providence in connection with escapes from accidents, misfortune, suffering and all that threatens earthly well-being. Or (though this is in fact the same sort of thing) when someone has an enormous piece of good fortune, such as winning a football pool. Faith in Providence seems to work in one direction for these people: for them it is Providence only "if it turns out all right for us."

Others see Providence as a sort of fate controlling their lives. If someone in the family dies, these are sure to say, "It had to be: it was God's will." Certainly this can have an authentically Christian meaning, but in itself it is unchristian, and often so is the emotional atmosphere from which this kind of consolation and resignation stems. It sounds so matter-of-fact, as if an impersonal authority ruled over our lives like a fate. No feeling of the solicitude of a personal God; no idea of a loving, even if incomprehensible, gesture from a God who invites us, who wishes to say something completely personal to us.

There are yet others who "practise abandonment." After all, they say, the world is evil and wicked, so while everything here becomes more and more confused, let us Christians patiently make sure of "saving our souls." They forget that faith in Providence also asks us not to leave the world as it is, that we are called to renew the face of the earth. Faith in Providence is not simply a "respectful attitude"; sometimes it may call for great courage.

It is these one-sided or false conceptions of faith in Providence that force us to ask plainly: What, in actual fact, do we mean by faith in God's providential guidance of our lives? We have seen from the Old and New Testaments that what is related there is completely different from the banal notions we have been discussing.

TRUST IN THE LIVING GOD, WHO IS PERSONALLY CONCERNED ABOUT OUR LIVES

Religion, faith in God, is never the first datum for us to consider in this connection, for religion and faith are a reply, the second word: the first is spoken by God himself. Revelation, upon which the whole of our concrete faith is founded, is the completely personal gesture of God by which he, as it were, steps outside himself to encounter us with the offer of his love; that is to say, with an offer of "communion with him," of a love that only reaches fulfillment in our reciprocal love. It is through this personal relationship to God, a rela-

tionship of child to Father, of a child that grows in Christ to
the full measure of humanity, that we stand in the grace
which sanctifies us. In a somewhat careless way we say that we
have sanctifying grace. In reality there is more to it than
this: we are personally taken up into communion of life with
God; we live, we are and we move to the rhythm of the
divine life. We abide in God as in our own home. This is a
matter of quite special, personal relations between God and
us. Attracted by this divine offer of love, which we can accept
only in faith, in the hopeful trust that his initiative of love
will henceforth reach our life in a personal way, we go out of
ourselves into this community of love, by virtue of the love
of God, which is granted to us in Christ in the joyful outpouring of his Holy Spirit.

It is only within this personal community of life and love
that it becomes possible to understand what Providence is
and what believing in Providence means. But because this
personal relationship between God and myself—together
with many others—is from our side grounded in faith, we
can only speak and think about this watchful care that is
divine Providence in terms coming from our human experience of the watchful care of fellow human beings for us.
Therefore what we say explicitly about divine Providence
contains a reference to our ordinary human experience on a
natural level, in which we have received the watchful care
of a mother or father or friend. Through our natural orientation towards the Absolute, towards God, on whom we nevertheless can never lay any claim, we project this experience
of watchful human care onto him—onto God, whom we have
learned to know from creation and in our lives as a God of
love. This vista which our experience of human providence
opens up onto divine Providence becomes lost to sight
beyond the horizon. Yet there is here a reference to a further
possibility, the possibility of a personal, free God. Finally,
then, we see how this divine possibility (for which the heart

of every religious man, and more explicitly of God's people, Israel, is already prepared) is realized in the man Jesus: in Jesus Christ the meaning, the content of the act of divine Providence, is shown and realized. From human experience and from the historical fact of Christ (with the whole of salvation history contained in it) we can begin to understand something of what takes place in faith between God and myself, and in the whole of human history, if through God's generosity we truly come to dwell with him and there take part in living a communion with him.

We can consider only briefly here the experience of the human concern which one man may have for another. We have all experienced it in one way or another. It is the sort of real concern which a fellow man has for us, not just a foolish kind of sympathetic condescension. In him we feel a respect for us as a person; he affirms me in my uniqueness and in my unique value. He helps me to become myself; he lets me be what I am and tries to give room for growth to the good in me. All this takes place within a personal relationship of love and trust, yes, in one of conversation, of action and reaction. And the other person does not act thus towards me just on one occasion, but continually. There is, as it were, "planning" behind it: not cold calculation, but planning born of solicitude and love, a planning which does not begin by sketching general schemes of action, going on to specific detail later. It is more of a "loyalty to the other person" through all his changing circumstances of life. This loyalty is unassailable, though it reveals itself differently according to whether I am ill, or tired, or get into financial difficulties, or feel the rub of heavy psychological or intellectual problems. This planning is, so to speak, made "in collaboration" with myself through the inventiveness of love. But though this is all a question of love, that love is not blind, it is clear-sighted. Sometimes we ourselves do not understand the true meaning of another's watchful care: he may even seem hard-hearted. But we have confidence in him, knowing that he has our well-being at heart.

It is only on the basis of this experience that in talking of God's Providence we can express something of this divine reality within the obscure experience of our faith. Of course this method falls short seriously. Where could one find a man who unites all these splendid characteristics of unceasing loyalty and watchful care for us? And, apart from that, every human being is finite and limited just as we ourselves are; and he, the other, also has need of a providence in his life. We all stand here on earth in need of help, never able to survey our whole lives, unable of ourselves to penetrate the deepest meaning of a single fact of any human life. We help each other as blind men help each other: we get along somehow. And ultimately some other person will be able to advise us: he may even be able to strengthen us, if he himself embodies in his life what he tries to bring out in us, or through us. But all the same I am free; I stand alone, apart from him. At the heart of my freedom, at the very source from which my personal actions must rise, I stand absolutely alone. Here no human being at all can help me.

But if I know that a God created me, gave me life, and that this can only have been done out of love, because God does not need me for his own fulfillment, then the idea of Providence, of his watchful care, acquires a startling, wholly unexpected, meaning in the very person of God. For I know that God's creative act is meaningless if it is not a purely generous act of love for a personal being who can at least aspire to a realization of that love. And then, at the same time, I know that my whole life is supported by a personal love. For the whole of this life is purely creaturely. Nowhere do I escape this act of creation: not in my desires, nor in my thoughts and action, nor in my corporeity and my constant immersion in ready-made situations. God's love is active through all of this. The whole of life becomes a kaleidoscope:

whatever I see therein, however much the figures and formations may change, it always reflects God's creating love. Of course in our enormous freedom we can play aimlessly with these reflections, or we can ultimately come to understand them at least in part. But nothing is an obstacle to God, who is the power of an absolute beginning, capable, in his continuing work of creation, of making all things new—except when we obstinately continue to refuse his love.

All this, however, is still in the abstract. The living God is not only Creator, he did not make us primarily to carry out a human project in this world under his loving supervision. He created us ultimately in order that we might enter into a communion of life with him. He placed us in the world, not so as to leave us there, satisfied, as creatures, with just his creative love. He placed us there with the further plan that we should come to live in his Son, Jesus, who became the Christ, so that with and in his Son we should be able to make our home with him. Thus God's creative act of love becomes a love which personally invites us to direct mutual love, so that in everything we may experience life on earth "as partners"—that is, God and I in a community of many. Hereby divine Providence acquires a deeper dimension, it realizes in a divine manner the watchful care which we learn to know in our human relationships. And this is an everyday event, between God and ourselves, who stand in the midst of the world.

But what happens in the obscurity of faith has, as it were, already been made clear to us by God in the man Jesus, the concrete form of God's Providence. For in Christ God not only revealed his love for this man Jesus, and therein his love for all of us; he revealed at the same time, in this same man, how a person who trusts in divine Providence lives his life. Religion, as a dialogue between God and man, receives its concrete, unique form in Christ. In this man we see revealed what God, in his watchful care, actually has in mind for us; and at the same time, how a human being must respond to this watchful care of God's. All of this was accomplished through the whole of Jesus' life, but his death and resurrection are the summits in this manifestation of God's watchful care and of Jesus' inexhaustible and unshakable trust.

Through faith and baptism we are taken up into the providential relations between Christ the Son and the Father. Just as the Father personally devoted himself to the life of the man Jesus, so he does now with regard to each of us. And just as Christ put his trust in his Father's guidance to the end, so we receive with our baptism the mandate to put complete trust in God's guidance of our life. And this trust, like Christ's, includes two aspects: on one side, the *personal intimacy of community with God,* who is personally concerned about us throughout our life—the characteristics borrowed from human solicitude give but a weak idea of the divine way of being with us and caring for us; and on the other side, the *mission* which we have to fulfill, in the Church as much as in the world; for by our entry into Christ we are not only the "object" of divine providential care but at the same time enter into this divine concern for our fellow men. We become, as St. Paul says, God's "co-workers" in the redemption of the world.

THE INTENTION OF GOD'S PERSONAL, WATCHFUL CONCERN

This belief in divine Providence does not mean belief in a sort of world-wide industrial management. It concerns a wise love which aims at man's good, at his happiness and well-being. Belief in this Providence is the belief of a free human being in the living free person of God. Just as God in his Providence treats us as free persons and not as subdivisions of a great, precisely structured universe, so we, believing in divine Providence, must accept God's freedom, which is a "divine" freedom: transcendent, reaching beyond any human capacity of comprehension.

But again, in all this we must have a correct notion of what God has in mind with regard to our personal good and salvation. For it is towards this that his watchful care is directed. Man's salvation lies in communion of life with God together with other human beings. In the concrete, Providence is a concern for salvation: it is the divine, active, loving concern for the only necessary thing in our life, after which, as Christ tells us, all the rest is given as something extra, an overflow of love. From this it is also clear that bourgeois, banal conceptions of Providence have nothing to do with authentic faith. This also means that the temporal sphere, for which God is certainly concerned in his providence as an object of his watchful care, can never provide the ultimate meaning of life. For with an exclusively secular expectation we could easily be bitterly disappointed in Providence, for the simple reason that no such providence exists with regard to the things of this world. Providence embraces higher perspectives: "Your Father knows that you need all these things. Instead, seek his kingdom, and these things shall be yours *as well*" (Lk. 12:30, 31).

Hence there is a definite direction in God's guidance of life, in his love towards us, through which he orientates his solicitous presence with us towards our salvation: to our communion of life with him. This he does with respect for our freedom; a respect which is not human but divinely creative. This means that God values our voluntary acceptance of this communion of life. Thus the loving care of his Providence aims at the freely accepted community of love of man with God. God's deepest concern is not as to whether we in fact do this or that, but as to whether we do this or that freely, out of love. This is to say that he aims at our personality, precisely at that original centre of man from which the person germinates and matures into a living subjectivity that God can treat as a person. In order to bring us weak, struggling humans to that community of love, God has often to accompany us on detours: one direction with one person, another with the next, but in one way or another he must shatter the illusion of our intramundane self-sufficiency, so that we may go out of ourselves to encounter him and the world of people and things in confidence. Such a guidance of life sets every secular, bourgeois conception of Providence on its head. God "hinders" us in our secular illusions. This was expressed beautifully by St. Augustine, who could well speak from experience: "God wishes to give us something, but cannot, because he sees that our hands are already full"; we no longer have our hands empty to receive his gift, we are greedily clasping something else in them. Which is why God's guidance of life, and thus his love, can take this form of removing everything we hold in our hands in order to give us what we need above all: himself. "Oportet ut exinaniaris quo plenus es, ut possis impleri quo inanis es"; Augustine, who so readily puts his playful love of verbal expression into the service of his witness of faith, had personally experienced this: "You must be emptied of that which fills you, in order to be filled with that of which you are empty." It is only a truly religious man who can believe in Providence, can know how to give a place to Providence in his life. Belief in Providence is in the last analysis a religious act, not a technical calculation on the level of the flourishing secular existence. And yet this attitude of faith penetrates to the smallest details of the secular necessities of life—but I do not wish to go into that yet.

How in fact does this watchful care of God function in our lives? In order to understand this we must be quite clear what a man actually is. The technical term which defines him in modern philosophy is "a situated freedom." This means that our freedom is not creative freedom but one only able to clarify and assign meaning to the situations in which it finds itself from moment to moment. We find ourselves in a world we did not make; our life begins at a particular historical point not of our choosing; and all through life we are continually confronted with all sorts of facts and situations which are already established before we, as free beings, encounter them. When we consider that both our situations and our freedom are equally creations of God, and in addition that in our situations we free human beings are called by God to a personal communion of life with him, then our freedom and also the situations in which we find ourselves will come to be seen in a completely different light: they acquire the significance of a moment of conversation which constitutes an element in our personal relationship with God. From God's standpoint these situations have meaning: they are the thematic content of God's personal invitation, which he addresses to my freedom. Taken up into the salvation perspective from which the watchful concern of God continually addresses me personally through grace, these situations themselves become a grace—an "external grace," we might say—which gives me the first signs of the direction within which God wishes me to experience communion of life with him here and now. All these nonvoluntary factors of our human life: naturally determined events, what is termed "luck," historical cycles (in which man's free posture is "objectivized," when the results of what men have freely done are seen apart from individual actions and encountered as hard facts), accidents, suffering, death, and so on—all these factors are seen as the secular appearance and embodiment, the concrete form, in which God's personal concern for our salvation shows us what our task in life is from day to day.

And this external divine indication of our concrete tasks is accompanied by the inward attraction of God's grace, a grace which invites us and at the same time gives our love the power to respond to what God's love asks of us. These two forms of grace are linked: the situation—or external grace— is, as it were, the "exteriority" of the clearly oriented content in inward grace. Here faith in Providence coincides with what we call Christian conscience. This conscience or faith in Providence is the realization that we are personally addressed by the God who loves us, in and through the situaations in which we find ourselves. In conscience I experience myself, with respect to a particular situation, as responsible for the task to which God is calling me; in and through this act of conscience I personally take part in the history of mankind, in relation to God; I put my trust in God. Hence I freely participate in history and in giving it the very direction in which God is leading the world of people and things.

From this it is sufficiently clear that believing in divine Providence does not mean a particular kind of passivity; on the contrary, it involves the most intense personal activity in which we are nevertheless aware that we are not alone but are guided and sustained by a solicitude which sees further than our short-sighted eyes. Faith in Providence therefore includes an element of acceptance and an element of personal effort, and something which arises freshly out of our own personality. The person who believes in Providence accepts the circumstances of life which are independent of this free will, a point in which we are often found lacking. We set ourselves against the unavoidable facts of our humanity, our mere humanity, with all that this includes in the way of ambiguous situations. We forget that these are precisely the ways which Providence itself has established so that we may be able to realize our calling concretely within these given limits. Instead we constantly show a tendency to seek it outside these limits. We compare ourselves with others who do not have such a difficult temperament as we do, or who are healthier than we are, or possess more intelligence or skill. In so doing we are forgetting that God's calling with regard to us can only be realized within the limits he personally defines for us. Thus in the very first place my faith in Providence must include a believing, humble acceptance of the circumstances of life in which I am involved independently of my free will. It must include a realization that these situations, with their external, apparently impersonal and arbitrary form, nevertheless give some indication of the love which is active in directing my life towards what must ultimately bring me salvation.

But faith in this divine watchful care is not only an actively personal acceptance of the unavoidable circumstances of life. It is also a belief in the divine mandate to alter these situations ourselves insofar as they are subject to our free will, and in so doing to change the face of the earth. This is all the more urgently necessary because the world in which we live remains under the influence of our historical sinfulness, which is embodied in the whole great weight of humanly wrought problems in the world which make changing the world so difficult. Not only does life in the world not show the face of God; it is a fertile soil for sin, needing, as it were, to be decontaminated. And herewith we have an indictment of the false faith in Providence of those who in the face of their own blunders and neglect call for a suffering surrender to God from others, or of people who refuse to consider any demand for more justice on earth—in social, political or national-cultural spheres—appealing instead to trust in divine Providence. The same accusations weigh against those who think that "the good Lord" will cure their moral faults and sanctify them against, and in spite of, their own aims. But faith in Providence is, on the contrary, the trustful awareness that God is personally at work in one's own effort and application, in self-training and self-formation, and that, along with the sincerity of this effort which is supported by him, God really helps us and corrects the shortcomings that continually impede all our efforts. Thus if we go ahead bravely, faith in Providence will remove every worry which disquiets us. It is precisely our situated freedom and the fact that God's appeal becomes thematic through it that result in our having an inalienable responsibility, but only within a sphere defined by God himself. This implies that however much we may have the fate of the world at heart, we have a real and active concern for it only as it touches our own limited situation (apart from the prayer and sacrifice that reach beyond this). This way of seeing the matter removes the tension one finds in people who try to measure up to what is really a divine and thus universal providence and thus are distressed when they realize their impotence, which leads them to anger at the unwillingness of those who oppose their ambitious efforts to play Providence. Each of us receives in our own situation only a portion of responsibility, given according to God's free generosity. We must not want to do everything on our own; what is asked of us is that we be able to trust in the vocational responsibility of our fellow humans, and above all in the fact that, even when our sincere efforts somehow go astray, "God will provide" (Gen. 22:8). It is only in this perspective, in which it has become clear to us that Providence does not make us inactive, that the depth of the words of Scripture becomes apparent: "Cast all your anxieties on him, for he cares about you" (1 Pet. 5:7).

PROVIDENCE AND ANSWERS TO PRAYER

Faith in Providence is faith in the fact that we have hazardous tasks to achieve in the world, which we accept courageously, with trust in God's watchful care. Thus this faith does not exclude human initiative but includes it, as much in the sacral-religious sphere as in the sphere of our secular activity. It is faith in our being associated with the creative and saving activity of the living God.

It is just this realization which acquires its most profound significance in prayer and answers to prayer. In prayer we personally turn towards divine Providence, whether in connection with our religious life and that of others, or with the secular necessities of life and the future of our secular system. In supplication we call upon God's providential guidance and affirm our trust therein, not only by surrender but by taking initiatives ourselves and laying them before God.

An example may be of use in making this clear. Someone who is dear to me, my mother perhaps, is seriously ill. Faith in Providence means more than mere acceptance of this; I resign myself to the fact—which is to say, I accept this aspect of God's Providence as it involves me personally. But it can also mean my taking the initiative of asking in supplicatory prayer that this situation may change. That he hears prayer has meaning within the sphere of our personal intimacy with God. From a purely intramundane point of view, prayer for the healing of my mother seems useless— as if there might be a means apart from the medical help we call in, by which she could be cured. Prayer and answers to prayer belong entirely to the religious level. We live in God and with God: this is our grace and our nobility. Thus we can turn to him, as Christ did, because the Father takes delight therein: "This is my beloved Son, in whom I am well pleased." So we speak with God, even about the so-called banal, everyday things. About my mother's illness. But why tell God about this? Doesn't he know that she is ill? He knows it very well; he himself willed or permitted it. But why and how can I then ask him for her recovery? Can I persuade God to change his mind? Or is he using subtle tactics: permitting my mother's illness so that I will pray and he can then answer my prayer and cure her? That seems overcomplicated, inauthentic. No, the heart of the matter cannot lie there. Nor is it at all certain that we shall ever be able to discover God's actual mode of action while we are on earth. This divine modality of existence escapes us completely. We have to cling to a few perspectives established by our faith in God and by the experience of the saints here on earth—above all that of Christ himself, even though we do not see everything clearly. After all our deep reflection, the solution is only to be found in unconditional surrender to the personal mystery of God, of whom we at least know that he has entered into authentically intimate relations with us.

Reciprocity in love means action and reaction. Our God is not a God of the same type as the Greek god who constitutes the origin of human love for him but does not love mankind in return. When we read in the Old Testament of Yahweh being known as a mighty warrior who fights hostile powers for his chosen people (Ex. 15:3–6), as a "roaring lion" (Hos. 11:10), and as a leopard lurking by the wayside (Hos. 13:7) who "sets his eyes upon the sinner for evil and not for good" (Amos 9:4) and grasps him with his hand (Amos 9:2); as a jealous God (Ex. 20:5; Deut. 5:9), who calls (Lev. 1:1), listens to the people (Ex. 16:12) and laughs (Ps. 2:4); who is happy and rejoices at human generosity (Is. 60) and then again threatens and punishes (Is. 16:13), or looks with disapproval on human doings (Gen. 6:6; Lev. 20:23), and yet continues to aim at human salvation (Gen. 8:21, 22)—when we read all this, we certainly realize that it is imagery, human representation; but representation of living reality in God, a reality which escapes our representational capacity. These images suggest to us that God occupies himself with human life as a living person devoting himself to our human and religious existence in this world.

The unique manner of God's reaction to man escapes us. We know that he is not changeable: to dispute this would cause internal damage to the image of God. But we do not actually know the unique mode of this immutability, and the history of salvation offers us so many surprises that we may not in any case identify it with an immovable immutability on earthly lines. The dialogue between God and man is not pretence, but a living reality. It is of the very essence of grace that God should really take man into consideration. God listens to man; otherwise all prayer would be meaningless. But God's listening is, after all, not human listening: here our secular conceptions of reciprocity or mutual relationship fall short. It is impossible that there should be something that is completely intelligible in and of itself anywhere in the world, even in a free human act: in everything God remains the deepest source. Not only my capacity to perform a free action, but the very origin of my free action, the pure initiative of my free "I," considered more deeply, arises from God. It is impossible for us to conceive of the action and reaction which exists between God and man as being the same as that between two created free persons. Our free initiative draws on the absolute initiative of God, which always comes first. Not in time, for God is not measured by time: it is not as if chronologically, before we began our prayer of supplication, God had already set up a strategic plan to permit my mother's illness to elicit my prayer. Once the world exists, eternity is, so to speak, a depth-dimension of that world, but this means that in my mother's actually being ill and in my actual praying God is truly God; he is a living Someone with whom, moreover, I have personal contact. But in all this God is absolute freedom, the eternal and complete Self-determination without which nothing can happen on earth.

God therefore really answers my prayer. But he gives this answer in an intramundane form of appearance, in and through the cosmic process (whether or not deterministically governed in itself)—for example, when we pray to God for good weather—through the normal course of history (as when we ask God to preserve us from war), through what we call "chance," and finally, by way of (regular) exception, through a miracle. All these objective forms have reference as such only to relations between human beings, but they acquire a completely different meaning for those who stand in a personal relationship with God.

Hence, in the hearing of prayer there are always two dimensions. First: the actual nucleus, the religious situation of petition and answer within the personal relations between God and man. I prayed to God for my mother's recovery. God answered me: she is well. Herein is accomplished the second dimension of this hearing, which I would call the technical aspect; that is, the secular form in which God gives his answer. Seen technically, the recovery of my mother, for which I prayed to God, was the effect of successful medical treatment. Seen in a religious perspective (i.e., for me in my personal relation to God, which is a reality) it is his answer to my request. For God's providential guidance of life comprehends, in a creative way, the whole causal relation between "medical help" and "recovery." Thus in the concrete, full reality, the recovery can only be understood as the fruit of my faith and hope in God's Providence. This connection does not stand outside God's creative influence, and the living God makes it into a moment of conversation, a detail in my prayersful, personal intimacy with him.

From a purely intramundane point of view my prayer was of no use: no mysterious influence went out from my prayer to the sick person, as if my prayer were an element that could be added to the means of cure and the doctor's help. And does not this mean that my mother would have recovered if I had not prayed?

This consideration is an abstraction. It argues on the presupposition that outside the visible there is no reality. The question as to what would have happened if this or that had not happened is a question without content, a fiction, to which the imagination can provide an abundance of answers. The Creator, without whom no secular event can occur, is in truth none other than the Living Person with whom I intimately interact through grace. In point of fact the secular connection between "medical help" and "recovery" is supported by the creator-God, by him who is at the same time my God, God who listens to my prayer. In and through this earthly connection the creator-God, my God, gives his affirmative answer to my request. In this way the whole of creation and of the plan of salvation (in which I, too, exist in personal interaction with the living God) is concerned in every secular event. If my mother does not recover, although I prayed, then God has still answered me: he has said "No." Then I know that in not curing her, he had something personal to say to me, something which I must take into account. Thus the hearing of prayer acquires meaning only within personal dialogue with God: this is the very essence of prayer.

It is for precisely this reason that prayer for temporal things seems to me incomprehensible from a purely natural point of view. Based on such a point of view more and more voices are being raised to declare, against the whole of tradition, that supplicatory prayer for temporal things is senseless. The Church thinks otherwise about this, because she experiences the reality of God not in a merely natural way, but supernaturally, in a religious way. And indeed, Christ's promise is at the origin of this religious manner of seeing things. God is not only "the Creator." He who in Christ became our Father has in the resurrection made Christ Lord over the material world. On these grounds we know that the Father wishes in Christ to put his dominion over material things into the service of those who enter the sonship of God and believe that Christ, who is "Lord," is also Lord of the material creation. The person who seeks first the kingdom of God and believes in the reign of God, who came "amongst us" in Christ, receives everything else from God, if he asks for it in faith (Mt. 6:33). We can turn as children to the Father, with the sure knowledge that according to God's promise the Father will take account of our believing prayer. Herein is revealed the overwhelming fact that the

whole of our life, down to its smallest details, is an object of
the Father's providential concern. Those who would remove
supplicatory prayer for temporal things from our personal
relationship with God are really acting as if he had not
created the world; or, to put it differently: as if the world
as it actually is no longer interested him. But if the God
with whom we personally interact is the creator God who
takes a personal interest in all that goes on in this world,
and if this world in which we are deeply involved also interests us intensely, then it is obvious that in our encounter
of prayer with this living God we shall spontaneously talk
about these things, which interest him as intensely as they
do us. Naturally, we are sometimes short-sighted in this; we
show great concern for the unimportant aspects of this world,
forgetting more important "temporal matters"—for instance,
international relations, the future of our secular world, the
new cultures being formed in the world at present—these
are just as important as good weather, or rain, for the fruits
of the earth. Not that it is wrong to pray for these, but
eliminating prayer for other "temporal matters" which are
more important than our daily bread even from a worldly
point of view, as if God held them unimportant—that is
wrong!

But do not most of our prayers remain unanswered? And
did not Christ, without adding any of the conditions thought
up later by our moralists, explicitly say: Ask and it will be
given to you? This is what Christ said, and in an absolute
way, without conditions. And we see in the lives of the
saints, those beloved children of God, that they were given
whatever they asked. God complies, it seems, with their least
important wishes—brings down snow in fair weather, for
instance, because a little girl, St. Thérèse, entering the con-
vent all in white, thought it would be such a nice idea if
everything else was white too!

The fact that such things occur so often in the case of the

saints should make us reflect. It gives us a better understanding of the meaning of prayer. God unconditionally hears the prayer of his beloved children. This means that reciprocity of love is an astonishing reality with God. He actually spoils some of his human children—after all, he is free in his love. In prayer we accept God's love and at the same time all the consequences of the freedom of that love. But the fact that answers to prayer occur more frequently in the case of his beloved ones makes us suspect that the nature of personal intimacy with God makes a great difference. These are people who have grown to be completely and utterly at one with their beloved God. The whole of their being is in sympathy with God, so that the desires that rise from their hearts also, so to speak, touch the heart of God, and so come from his heart too, and then the result is unfailing. Through love one sees things differently. For the newly-wed couple the sky is a different blue, or rather only now do they see how blue the sky is. What may be considered romantic on the human level becomes reality on the divine level. For the person who lives in intimate intercourse with God the renewal of the world is an authentic reality. Such a person really sees things differently from the exclusively worldly man, and thus his wishes and desires become different. In the clumsiness of our own prayer we can feel this now and again. We feel we should certainly like to see something accomplished, but when we come to stand before the face of God in prayer, we suddenly feel that the request is not worth making—all at once, in the nearness of God, we see our silly request in its true proportion and lose interest in it. In other cases, on the contrary, the experience of the nearness of God strengthens us in a particular desire, which we then direct to him in a burning prayer of supplication. The believer is, in some sort, experiencing what is in God's mind.

With us all of this is a long and even laborious process; with the saints it is a matter of course. The sifting of their desires occurs spontaneously: they live unceasingly in the presence of God, and thus they experience not only their minds coinciding with God's but also God's mind coinciding with theirs. All our prayers too are listened to and heard by God, but because of our unholiness, our failure to sense the personal direction which God's providential guidance intends for us, we just go on with our own wishing and desiring, and then God's personal reply is often "No!" It is only because of our unholiness that moralists have had to formulate conditions in connection with the hearing of prayer! For in truth, how often, when we pray for temporal things, is it not a question of temporal things in themselves? But the temporal simply does not exist for God in this way! Even with the saints it may still be a question of temporal things, but they see these in the dynamism in which they are bound to the living God: they receive the temporal as a gift from their Beloved, and this is the whole crux of the matter. It is in this that the personalism of every gift consists. The person who sees a present simply as an object and does not advert to the personal gesture of the donor stands completely outside any I-Thou relationship, and it is only in this that a gift has meaning. Pascal says somewhere: "tout ce qui n'est pas le fin, en est le figure." The gift of a temporal good only acquires its full meaning in personal community with the intention of the giver. Often enough God, as far as our practical attitude is concerned, is merely a cause, someone who can make something happen. I cannot see, however, how supplicatory prayer can acquire any meaning at all in a purely "cause-effect" relationship. Prayer only makes sense within the personal communion of grace with God, and this living communion may perhaps comprise God's omni-causation (God's action outside the godhead is always a "creating out of nothing"), but it nevertheless reaches further. Here lies the reason why on the one hand some people cannot understand the meaning of prayer for temporal things and why others are so often disappointed in their "supplicatory prayer" for such temporal things!

There are, of course, other aspects attached to the problem concerning supplicatory prayer. We not infrequently ask God for escape from difficulties which are entirely our own fault, or which we at least got into against our better judgment. So God must now clear things up for us! And this he sometimes does, for his mercy knows no bounds. But this is not the ordinary atmosphere in which we go to God; especially when our hearts have arrived at a recognition of their own guilt. And even though Christ himself said that every prayer is heard, it is evident from the life of Jesus himself, in particular his cry to the Father in Gethsemane, that God is always greater than our prayer of supplication; there must be moments in life when we really seem to be abandoned by God: moments in which he seems to work alone, apart from our prayer. Then we can only say "Not my will, but your will be done." It would seem that every human being, even the saints, the beloved of God, must, like his "well beloved Son," undergo this supreme moment of self-emptying as the ultimate experience of God's divine nature. It is here that every analogy with the relationship of one human being with another falls short of reality. Only the Infinite is sufficient here; only by virtue of the Infinite One and his power is this experience within the capacity of the human heart. This is why it is only beyond the boundaries of death, when we are disengaged from all temporal reality on earth, that the deepest meaning of supplicatory prayer can be understood. Our fulfilled communion with God will make us the possessors of a glorified world: we shall live in "God's world," the world which he has prepared for those who love him.

The fact that God is personally concerned about us is summed up in Holy Scripture in incomparable words which, because we know them so well, we often fail to grasp in their most profound, overwhelming significance: "In this the love

of God was made manifest among us, that God sent his only
Son into the world" (1 Jn. 4:9). Of this Son it was said: "In
the days of his flesh, Jesus offered up prayers and supplica-
tions, with loud cries and tears, to him who was able to save
him from death, and he was heard for his godly fear"[1] (Heb.
5:7). But heard . . . through the boundaries of death!

---

[1] *Eulabeia,* "godly fear," signifies the religious experience of the *tre-
mendum,* of the majesty and transcendence of God. This basic category of
religious experience must not be lost from sight in the life of grace, seen
as reciprocity between God and us and thus by analogy with human "encounter." It places the emphasis upon the "wholly other" in this encounter
with the living God, with respect to which all human phenomenology falls
short. It may be noted that the other translation: "He was freed from his
fear," instead of "for his godly fear" has less likelihood of being the correct
one.

7 The God of Love
and the Moral Norms
of Human Action

Introduction

Under the above title we have combined three contributions dealing with the ethical assessment of our human life. It may be that the ethical order is immediately and completely explicable on the basis of man himself. The ethical appreciation of life of Humanists, for example, demonstrates that even without religious faith an ethical attitude towards life can give it a profound meaning. In *Les Mouches*, Jean-Paul Sartre has one of his characters say that justice is a human affair and he has no need of a God to instruct him with regard to it. Nevertheless the intramundane, ethical point of view can be deepened by the recognition of man's created status and the acceptance of grace in faith. The immediate foundation of the moral order is the value of the human person, but this value is seen as wholly inviolable only when man is acknowledged to be a creature of God—and, yes, a child of God. Then an offence against human community is deepened into an offence against God's act of creation and salvation. That the ethical is something which must be *made* by man in his historicity is a fact that is grounded, not immediately, but without doubt ultimately, in his metaphysical

257

condition and in his situation of salvation. Here we are not in the first place concerned with the secular establishment of ethics, but with its relation to God, our Creator and Saviour.

THE "NATURAL LAW" AND THE CHRISTIAN ORDER OF SALVATION

Vocation, Design for Living and Ethos

Man's original choices and the fundamental design of his life are inspired in the ethically good person by reality which addresses him as an absolute value, inviting him to take up an attitude to life of willingness and loving service. But this reality falls under the mercy of God's grace. What all this means in practice must now be investigated in some detail.

"The life of a person is not a datum, a ready-made reality, complete as it stands; on the contrary, it is a destination, a history in which chance is always playing a part. The life of a person is not something capable of being composed in analytical language; it is a trial, the point of departure for manifold realizations. One must live life, fulfill it as a task."[1] Such is the description of human life given from a purely human point of view, by G. Gusdorf, and we can certainly say that this is a conception which is generally accepted nowadays. A human being is not a tree or an animal, unaware of any future or any vocation. These lower forms of life are placed in an environment from which they receive stimuli to which their structures react in a predetermined way. Man, by contrast, is a being who lives a self-questioning, searching existence. He must take his life into his own hands and seek

---

[1] "La vie personnelle n'est pas un donné, une réalité prête, achevée une fois pour toutes, mais une destinée, une histoire où des chances se trouvent sans cesse en jeu. La vie personnelle n'est pas un discours, que le langage de l'analyse pourrait transcrire tel quel, mais une épreuve, le point de départ des réalisations multiples. Un devoir être. . . ." (*La découverte de soi*, Paris 1948, p. 500.)

its meaning. His life in, and in relation to, the world flowers in a view of the world and of life. He discovers values which appeal to him; values which cast their spell over him and for which he finds life worth living. In the measure that he lives in an authentically human way, and does not just let life take its course with him, he lives for, and on the basis of, values which he freely accepts as norms because he sees that in themselves they are worthy of humble devotion. Gradually he forms his own value system in which diverse values each receive their place, higher or lower. Insofar as he lives in an authentically human way, man designs his own plan of life, a scheme of values in whose light he can meet the situations that confront him. In this light he can act meaningfully in this world on the basis of a "prognosticated and therefore challenging future."[2] In our plan for living we project our expectations in regard to life. To be sure, we can do this arbitrarily; but we can, must, and are permitted to do it on the basis of a patient attentiveness with regard to the values which make their appeal to us from objective reality. And so man determines the course of his own life, amidst the many contingencies which surround him and from which he cannot escape. His plan for living is not merely the result of intellectual considerations concerning it but is based on a conviction, a basic intention, and thus also a basic attitude; and at the same time it is charged with emotion.

Even from a secular point of view we could term this plan which governs all the domains of life a "vocation," our actual calling in life, just because, and insofar as, man establishes this project in accordance with the appeal of objective values. For, although we can indeed accept and assent to the absolute validity of these values without having an express awareness of the living God, their absolute validity cannot be maintained in the face of reflective experience

2 This forceful expression comes from F. Polak, *De toekomst is verleden tijd*, 2d abridged ed., Zeist 1958, p. 22.

unless within this experience the infinite appeal of God as worthy of all love is also experienced in a living manner. It is by reason of this theistic background to our human plan of values that we may truly call it response to a calling. Only a person can call us by our name; a thing cannot, nor, even, a "great organization." To be sure, our fellow man is also an invitation to us, and for this reason even the person with only an intramundane orientation can conceive of his life as a calling. But the force of this invitation can never be absolute, so far as reflection is concerned, unless the absoluteness of God is at the same time implicitly affirmed. Thus the insistent force of a calling always comes, even if anonymously, from God's lovableness and irresistible attraction. Vocation demands a "personal identification" of the one calling on the part of the person called. It is only when we have identified the divine person that the appeal of values becomes an authentically personal calling. To be aware that one is called is to refuse to consider life and the world as a massive, impersonal event. God gives me my life in order that, living in his love, I may give a positive meaning to it. For man life itself is a vocation. It is God who appeals to us via the appeal of values. Thus the unselfish life project that respects reality is the intramundane form of "faith" in God's call. This fundamental design for living is the heart of the response to God's call. Vocation and design for living are the divine and human sides of one and the same psychological, deeply human reality, which embraces a free but objectively ordered image of the future and at the same time declares an expectation and sincere intention with regard to it.

But all of this is still abstract. The appeal of values, as an "oblique" self-testimony and self-affirmation of God, takes place in a world in which God personally encounters us in generous love. God is not merely the foundation of all human values. He is not only sovereignly free in his establishment of the attraction of these values, so that man is induced to gaze longingly towards the silent mystery of God; he has also revealed himself to us as a value: he is the God of salvation, who summons us in grace to a personal communion of life with himself. The call proceeds directly from God. This means not only that God's supereminent value addresses itself inwardly to our sense of value by the stirring of his grace, but, at the same time, that the history in which we are situated is so led and directed by the God of grace, that—in its secular aspects—it tells us more than it could of itself. This may seem like an abstraction, but it ceases to be so when life is really lived. Secular matters and history become signs pointing to God only when we have first experienced them in their own particular value. In this way the situations of life in which we continually find ourselves become part of a conversation in our personal relationships to God. From God's point of view these situations have meaning: they are the thematic content of his personal appeal to my freedom.

Taken up into the perspective of salvation from which God's watchful care continually addresses my personal freedom through grace, these "secular" situations themselves become a grace, an "external grace" in which there is already present an outline of the direction within which God wishes me to experience, here and now, communion of life with him. All these real factors are the appearance and embodiment, the concrete form, in which the divine solicitude shows me my tasks from day to day. God's inward invitation of grace and the external situations of life are linked: the secular situation is, so to speak, the "exterior" of the inward grace. It is because of man's ability to give his life a direction only by giving meaning to the situation in which he stands—in other words, through the fact that for man the world constitutes the only path to any sort of explicit knowledge—that he is able to become aware of God's call only insofar as it manifests itself in this world. A purely "inward initiative" from God that is not also "embodied" in history is uni-

maginable and would completely break the structure of our
human existence. God's grace always becomes known in and
according to the form of our human mode of being. This is
why the calling of Israel's great prophets was never exclusively "inward"; the inner call was combined with an
invitation from the historical circumstances in which the
prophet lived, and through which he could interpret its
meaning. History itself posed a question to the prophet. The
religious man in the grip of God's grace cannot but interpret
this question as an offer from the living God, of whose quiet
prompting he becomes expressly aware in and through such
difficult situations in his life.

God, then, makes use of natural, intramundane factors, but
in such a way that these "secular" events become the expression of his free generosity, his offer of grace, inviting us to
give them a religious meaning. It is at the great crossroads
of life that the divine intention of salvation becomes discernible in secular events for those who open themselves to God
in prayer. At times this has distinct emotional overtones. It
is a matter of conversation, in acts rather than words, between God and man, in which the world and history are, as
it were, slipped in by God between him and us as the *translation* of his inward discourse; as the *medium*, moreover, in
and through which man becomes aware of this inward communication; and, finally, as *space* in which he can put into
action his living response to that invitation. Thus we may
say that it is precisely in and through the world and history
that the believer becomes expressly aware of the concrete
content of God's inward call.

Therefore we cannot explain vocation on the one hand by
a divine decree and on the other by a free choice of man, for
it lies between the two. It is the immediate effect on man of
the God who calls and the recognition by man that he is
being called by God.

This is, then, the real, inviting attraction of the vocational

motif which brings about an affective, appropriating movement within me. It is this which causes me to decide that the
profession or work which I have considered, or which was
suggested for me by social, psychological or family circumstances, will be right for me. It is a question of experiencing
the "suitability for me" of this reality. What I experience is
therefore the attraction of this value, and in this attraction
lies the invitation of God. Hence this divine invitation, personally directed to me, heard and appreciated by me, is the
actual and only formal vocational motif. It is all of this
which constitutes the reality of being called and of knowing
oneself to be called.

This grace-full awareness is thus the experience of vocation. In this God is, so to speak, working alone. But this
experience of the invitation must be freely and positively
accepted. It demands our decision to take up this calling:
only in our free conscious action does the vocation come to
its first realization. Invited purely by grace, the person called
now proceeds, through the power of grace, to co-operate with
grace. In this way, in reply to God's grace, man gives a clearly
defined direction to his life; he makes the divine calling his
own, so that this becomes a free choice, an autonomous self-
determination, and not the blind acceptance of what "another" has decided for him. It is on the basis of his own
personal experience of value that he makes his choice, and at
the same time it is authentic obedience in faith to the living
God. The "external" precept is interiorized in a grace-filled
experience of value.

This approach clarifies our notion of ethics and the concept of "natural law." The latter is nothing but the categorical requirement that goes forth from a reality which
presents itself to me as a subject. When one person encounters another, immediate, absolute moral requirements
come into being. If in this a man is conscious of the created
status of everything which presents itself to him, and of him-

self as the creature to whom it is presented, then he will
know that the appearance of another person in his life is a
divine invitation to acknowledge and evaluate that person
in his subjectivity, conditioned as he is by all his concrete
situations. This freedom, which is ethically determined by
this other person and ultimately by his creaturely condition,
is from the outset a grace-filled freedom. It is a question of
the influence of grace upon our ethically-ordered freedom.
What does this involve?

In general it means that ethically ordered human existence
enters into a real, personal communion with the living God,
even though this may turn out eventually to take the form of
a refusal. This has inescapable consequences for our awareness of ethical values.

God's communication—both as conversation and as revelation which makes claims upon us—is immediate and direct
and no longer via created values in which God's value is also
experienced. Here it is a question of reciprocal communication between persons, even though this reciprocity is only
achieved under the veil of faith and even though the content
of this invitation is, moreover, expressed only in the forms
of our secular humanity. In the concrete existence of our life
in the world we are attracted to Love by an inward, con-
fusedly conscious stirring of grace. And the actual content
of that Love is expressed from without, which is to say, in
the concrete history of mankind, by that same God of love.

Considered in its essence, the content of this divine invitation is an invitation to personal communion of life with the
absolutely Holy. It is a direct, inward self-revelation of God's
holiness. This inward invitation to goodness is not formally
the same as the invitation we experience via our appreciation
of the created reality in which we stand. Ethically speaking,
"absolute norms" signify that which for man as man can lead
to an authentically human fulfillment of life. Evangelically
speaking—that is, from the point of view of our grace in

Christ—"absolute norms" signify an authentically Christian fulfillment of life for the human being conscious of God's love. By reason of the mysterious character of our Christian existence, the precise content of this fulfillment is ultimately revealed and secretly communicated by God himself. This communication takes place in an obscure and, as it were, inexplicit way through the "inward address" (*locutio interna*) of grace; it takes place externally through what is called "public revelation" (*fides ex auditu*), and this latter occurs ultimately through the man Jesus, who, prefigured before his coming in the religion of mankind and specifically in that of Israel, now lives on amongst us in his Church.

There are, therefore, two complementary facets of revelation (which we are now considering from the ethical point of view): the inward pressure of grace, urging us towards the love which is forgetful of self; and the exterior commands and prohibitions which the Church's proclamation of the gospel puts before us as law. Through its connection with my personal conscience which is addressed by grace, a divine command or prohibition presented by the Church becomes a divine invitation and an ethical imperative for me. Via my conscience, which is addressed by grace, general commandments thus acquire a personal character, while, reciprocally, conscience obtains an explicit content from these commandments. The inward attraction of grace and the external commandment or prohibition are each a grace. There is no duplication of grace, but through the interaction of the two grace receives its visible form; it becomes incarnate.

The inward summons to love cannot, therefore, be separated from the ethical directions given by the Church. It is not just a matter of "love," but a matter of a love directed by God. To my personal question to God, "What must I do?" I receive a personal reply in the moral commands and prohibitions which Scripture holds up to us through the Church. The commands furnish us with the explicit content of what

inward grace itself already suggests to us in an obscure
manner: the "mores," the way of life, the morals of the
Children of God in Christ Jesus.

Our task now becomes that of determining more accurately
in what this evangelical morality precisely consists. Are there
supernatural moral norms separate and distinct from the
natural moral norms? To put this a little differently: Do we
not stand, *prima facie* at least, before a double morality? On
the one hand, there would be the absolute norms which we
are able in principle to see as operative from our human,
objectively directed evaluation of the person—the so-called
natural law. And on the other hand there would be the
absolute requirements which are implicit in our condition
of grace; that is to say, the absolute ethical implications of
our new kind of existence which is a personal communion
of life with God, the Holy One—implications which, because
they are sealed within the mystery of a saving reality, can be
explicitated only through our reflections in faith in union
with the Church of Christ.

The Ethic of Grace

We shall now investigate the content of God's revealed
ethical requirements. The ethical requirements of life, insofar as they are immediately revealed in the precise sense
(*credible per se*) and can thus be approached only in a supernatural act of faith, fall into the following two groups:

a. *The requirements of sanctifying grace,* namely the requirements of life in intersubjectivity with God, the inviolable demands of life in union with God. These are primarily
the consequences of faith, hope and love. The core of supernatural, evangelical morality is thus the Christian life of
grace itself, with its divine virtues: life in an I-Thou relationship with God in Christ together with other human beings
in this world. The supernatural, ethical life is thus a theo-

logal, religious life. And so a fundamental constituent of Christian moral obligation is the absolute requirement of experiencing one's human existence in faith as a life of hope and love, of love for God and one's fellow men. These are the first truly supernatural, absolute norms which for the Christian contain the meaning of an authentically Christian fulfillment of life. They form the core and at the same time the mystery of Christian moral life.

b. *The requirements of the sacramentality of this grace.* Grace comes to us visibly, and according to God's economy of salvation, the visibility he wills for grace is that of the man Jesus and his Church. In actual fact, this means a theologal life of grace based on our profession of faith in Christ within the manifest mystery that is the Church of Christ on earth. Theologal life together with the implications of the sacramental Church of Christ is the new element of the Christian ethic compared with a humanly justified and thus natural ethic. Hence the evangelical ethic relies upon the absolute requirements of the reality of grace in which we stand and on the "Mystery of the Church." The positive ecclesiastical laws, the commandments and prohibitions,[3] are therefore a saving-historical embodiment of a divine command of salvation in Christ—that is, of the divinely willed sacrament that the Church constitutes as visible manifestation of the Christian norms of life. Thus in their ethical application or obligation ecclesiastical commands or prohibitions bind us in conscience, although their concrete form may vary or even be changed according to historical circumstances. One example by way of illustration: the eucharistic celebration is a Christian moral obligation for every baptized believer because of his membership of the eucharistic community. The

[3] Here we are only talking about the ecclesiastical commandments and prohibitions, which (at least implicitly) refer to revelation and the natural law, not about positive ecclesiastical laws, which can be changed as regards their content and are only obligatory on the grounds of the prudent organization of the Church.

Church has specified the general Christian obligation in the command to attend Mass each Sunday. Granted the administrative power given to the Church by Christ, the reason for this ethical obligation comes fundamentally from the very structure of the sacramental Church: Christian life is eucharistic life. The Church might equally well have obliged us to attend a monthly, yearly or Thursday celebration of the eucharist, or have given no explicit command at all. But the absolute obligation of celebrating the eucharist would still be implied in our membership in the eucharistic community.[4] It is only those whose Christian experience and love are weak who really feel this obligation (inward requirement of love) as a command imposed purely from without.

In the first place, therefore, Christian moral law is determined in content by the requirements of theologal life and the implications of the sacramentality of this life of grace in ecclesial life. All of this forms the *revealed* ethic. What place do so-called natural norms or "natural law" occupy with respect to these revealed ethical norms? We may describe the significance of natural law within the Christian attitude to life in analytical terms, as follows:

Ethical Norms: Humanity

Evangelical Morality "Presupposes" the Natural Law. Man is the subject of grace. If this "life of grace" is formally in-

4 In every command of the Church in connection with the ethic of grace and its sacramental implications one also hears the natural law to some extent. The obligation from natural law to worship the Creator (worship, moreover, which includes a positive but impotent desire for personal communion with God) has been made concrete by Christ in his redemptive sacrifice on the cross and in the founding of the eucharistic community of the Church. The ecclesiastical obligation to celebrate the eucharist is therefore an ethical requirement of Christ and of the Church, but it ultimately traces its origin to a natural ethical requirement. Thus the ethic of grace is an inward, though transcendent, fulfillment of a positive but impotent self-transcendence of natural law.

tersubjectivity between God and man it presupposes, by definition, two partners who enter through grace into a personal communion of life with each other. Grace thus presupposes man as a person, as an incarnate person living in a world of people and things. For openness to grace (*capacitas Dei*) lies in the fact that man is a being able to fulfill himself in self-donation to others; this is the essence of the human person, upon whom the so-called natural law is founded. Through grace man becomes himself through giving himself to his personal God.

Grace, Christianity, thus essentially implies a doctrine concerning man's values, in both his personal and social dimensions. And precisely because the message of salvation is offered to human beings, it is essential that it be accepted in freedom. Man's situated and norm-governed freedom (in which the whole of natural law is implicit) is therefore more than just the object of human, philosophical reflection; it is, with all its implications, ultimately a *preambulum,* a starting point, for faith and Christian love. It is precisely for this reason that faith takes this situated and norm-governed freedom under its protection; for without freedom this faith destroys itself. And, because natural law is a "starting point" it comes, in the interest of faith, under the protection of the Mystery of the Church. In protecting the treasure of faith, the Church also has the right to instruct us concerning the value of the person and those values which constitute the person: the fundamental values of human life. Therefore, while at the same time transcending it, Christian morality implies that which is called natural law as the indispensable basis of the Christian view of life. The Church is also the protector of natural law for the sake of the ethic of grace.

The Natural Law Is a Christian Law. But natural law is not only a starting point, a *preambulum.* Considered in itself, it is the mediate self-testimony of God as the Holy One; mediate since the immediate appearance of my fellow man

to me as a subject becomes for me a divine invitation and
demand, for this encounter is founded in God's created act.
The acceptance of natural moral norms is (at least implicitly)
an oblique acknowledgment of God's holy will. In and through
grace we now enter into a personal relationship with God.
Personal communion with God involves a personal contact
with this holy will of his; it is also intimacy of will with the
living God. Therefore man's community of grace with God,
the Senior Member in this community, implies the opening
of man's will to that of God. It makes no difference to the
moral attitude of the believer whether God reveals his will
directly or indirectly via his creatures: in both cases the believer is concerned with the personal will of the Beloved.

In this sense the whole of natural law is taken up into the
evangelical ethic, although it is not in itself revealed, in the
strict sense of that term.[5] As the mediate self-testimony of
God, who now directs himself to me in personal dialogue as
the God of salvation, natural law is assumed into God's
gracious, saving revelation to us. Even though it is by way
of faith, through grace we come into direct contact with this
personal will and love of God, which lie at the source of
creaturely values (which, as it were, can only point "from
afar" to this personal love). In grace we have direct experience of the source of the absolute validity of natural law.
In the life of faith we therefore personally confront God's
holy will, which as human beings we have only acknowledged
via natural law and thus only to a certain degree. The holi-

___

[5] This must not be wrongly understood: God's holy will concerning the life
and fortune of man is certainly revealed (thus also as regards what we call
the content of natural law), but the natural law as such cannot be revealed,
because the idea of it excludes saving revelation by definition. For "natural
law" is the holy will of God insofar as this shines through in our evaluation
of created reality; in other words, in the appearance of man as subject.
However, the revelation of the same holy will of God is his *direct* self-
manifestation. In faith we attain the content of natural law under a different
formal aspect.

ness or inviolability of God, which is the ultimate ground of the obligatory value of natural law, becomes clearer to us in this communion of grace. We approach it personally, and thus not merely indirectly, although the explicit content only shows forth in the experience of human existence. The content of natural law thus becomes a subordinate part of the requirements of our intimacy with the Holy One. Natural law, the content of an intramundane evaluation, becomes for the believer the joint-content of the personal grace-full invitation of God's holy will.

Natural law is therefore in fact a Christian ethical norm of life. In a personal gesture of grace, God makes me recognize my fellow man as a person. In concrete fact, we may even say that Christianity is the only domain available for the natural law to exist in. Morality is involved wherever man as man is involved. This moral event is also a Christian event (of acceptance or refusal), for in his moral freedom man is confronted with revelation. The natural, morally ordered act is acknowledged and preserved in its intrinsic structure by grace. At the same time it has a salvific significance for the whole of human life confronted by grace, even though this may be in an anonymous way. As partial content of a Christian totality—namely, the personally experienced holy will of God—the natural law contains (in being concretely experienced) an objective and inward reference to the Christian totality. Where and insofar as we make a total pronouncement on human existence in and through our free actions, we do this in a Christian way, whether in acceptance or rejection. Therefore we prefer not to speak of a "taking up" of the natural law into Christianity. On the contrary, natural law by itself is an *hairesis,* an excision from Christianity—partial Christianity. This cutting off of natural law from the Christian totality is possible to a certain extent on the level of reflection, because within the Christian ethic of grace natural law has in itself an intrinsic structure. It is a presupposition of the subject of grace, which is human existence. It is precisely for this reason that an agnostic or an atheist can confront human life in a moral way. God makes his holy will known to us in a partial and incipient way, in and through the "natural law," but in a complete way only in and through grace and the history of salvation. In both cases it is a question of the "revelation" of God's personal holiness, though the mode of revelation differs.

The exact content of natural law is not altered in Christianity, but it acquires a deepened significance in the reciprocal love between God and us. The so-called natural virtues, which are the consequence of our response to natural moral norms (i.e., the visible acknowledgment of the theistically orientated personal value of man), are now supported by the ethic of grace, by the theologal realization of ourselves as sons of God and of the calling of all men to that sonship. In this way natural moral norms become qualitatively different. They become the embodiment (in interhuman and secular relations) of our believing, hoping and living intimacy with the living God, an intramundane incarnation of the life of grace. At the same time they serve and further theologal life itself (within the ethic of grace).

A personal life of faith can hardly do without the help of the experience of natural values, because the natural law is not revealed but already present as part of God's creative act, so that in principle the importance of this human value-experience can be grasped naturally. Grace does not replace nature.

The Ethic of Grace, Ultimate Meaning of Natural Law. We have not yet finished with this particular subject. It becomes clear to us, in the light of faith, that the personal meaning of human life can only lie in the personal religious communion of man with God. Although God is not obliged to give grace, we must not imagine it as something given "afterwards" to a being which otherwise might by its natural powers attain its own fulfillment. Hence, though there is in man a natural domain with its own consistent spheres, one cannot say that man is consistent and complete in himself within the boundaries of his human life. For he is willed by God in such a way that the gift of grace signifies for his actual humanity a transcendent yet inner fulfillment. Therefore there can be neither Christian nor even theistic support for radical secularization. In discussion on the meaning of human life, a natural answer can never be definitive. This should be borne in mind, not only by the philosopher, but especially by the psychologist and phenomenologist.

All of this points to the fact that purely human reflection on natural law will be to a great extent "incomplete." Natural ethics must leave questions regarding the ultimate destination of man's life in great part unsolved. If one does not accept a supernatural perspective of life, if one therefore considers human thought as the final authority, then one can only exalt the incomplete insights proper to philosophy or natural ethics into definitive pronouncements, instead of leaving them "open" to transcendent completion in our sonship of God. And so the whole of natural ethics seems problematical, even without the consideration of man's sinfulness, which hampers and unavoidably blunts the natural recognition of ethical values (this aspect demands a further analysis, which we must omit here).

The consequence of all this is to confirm the insight that it is only possible to speak, in the concrete at least, of natural law within the perspective of grace. Moreover, this natural law, though possessing a certain consistency, can ultimately have its full inward significance clarified only within religious communion with God. The inviolability of the human person, for example, takes on a completely different meaning according to whether we approach it atheistically or theistically or, the final possibility, on the basis of our communion with the living God in love for our fellow human beings.

The conclusion is therefore clear: natural law as such is not revealed. Natural ethical norms are the real implications of our created personal existence together with others in this world, implications of the subject of grace. Hence they are in principle accessible to man as man, intrinsically capable, therefore, of rational justification. But what has been revealed is God's holy will, and thus also the ultimate meaning of this natural ethic. This ultimate meaning is not extrinsic to natural law but intrinsic: it is an intrinsic but transcendent fulfillment of what natural law itself asks but cannot fulfill. Compared with natural law, the grace of revelation and the theologal ethic is a confirmation and a new enlightenment, and thereby at the same time a stimulus for the created and unaided (as such) natural awareness of value, which grows only gradually. Furthermore, it is also a remedy for our sinfulness and the confusion in our conscience. And finally, it is the ultimate meaning of natural law which is needed to make the latter fully significant in a personal way. Thus Christian and professed non-Christian alike have an obligation to feel and test their way in seeking out natural law in the ever new situations of life. To this self-discovery of norms revelation gives (within the Church's life of grace) the religious, theologal orientation which is their due. That is to say, what man discovers by way of absolute norms on the basis of his human experience must be experienced by him as a child of God—on the basis of his human experience of communion with Christ. But through this personal experience of God's holy will he finds himself in a condition best suited to apprehend the content of natural law. In addition, he lives in a church community in which the collective life of grace and believing reflection thereon make awareness of the content of natural law grow so that it can be explicitly formulated by the ecclesiastical teaching authority even before the individual believer has been able to arrive at a personally justified experience of value. Thus, via the sacrament constituted by the Church, the man who truly believes and knows himself to be a living member of the church community is in his free action concretely faced by the holy will of God, as it concerns him personally, even when his natural sensitivity to value (and hence to the natural law) is in some respects inadequate. Hence he is not faced with a general, abstract norm presented by the Church, but stands before the personal holiness of God, which teaches him clearly, by visible and audible ecclesial grace, what is the content of that inner grace which is as yet undetected by him. But this also means that such an ethical action can only be accomplished in the darkness of faith (such a situation is then ethically meaningful only when the Church has made a pronouncement with all her apostolic authority).

An application to married life may help to give these general insights concrete shape.

Having followed the above considerations, the reader will see that there is no supernatural ethic of marriage "beyond" a natural ethic of marriage. In itself marriage is a human reality in a theistic and religious perspective.[6] The Christian ethical norms of married life are the natural ethical norms of life, but taken up into the theologal life of the Mystery of the Church. This means that apart from the new element constituted by the sacramental ethic of grace, the Church does not impose one single new ethical norm regarding married life.

Perhaps an example will make this clearer. It is impossible, for instance, that contraceptive techniques should be natu-

---

[6] This in no sense means that marriage can appear as a purely human reality. In the first place, the purely human involves (as a formal idea) a positive though impotent openness towards the living God. But, furthermore, every human, moral reality stands within the concrete, if perhaps anonymous, invitation of God's saving love, to which man can reply by accepting or by refusing. An opposition of "natural" and "religious" marriage is completely impossible.

rally justifiable, yet forbidden by the Church, and thus to the faithful. If they are not permitted for the faithful, then this must also be the case from the natural ethical point of view. And if they are allowed by the natural ethic, they must also be permissible for the faithful. The laws of marriage are not altered by their subsumption into the evangelical ethic, only deepened by theologal life. Furthermore, the ultimate meaning of marriage can only be disclosed from revelation, which means that an intrinsically justified ethic of marriage cannot be the last word concerning that state. Thus, although the reality of marriage and the ethics which belong to it according to its own nature remain unaltered in Christianity they are nevertheless taken up into a higher totality which includes Christian virginity for the sake of the kingdom of God; hence, though not changed, they are relativized. Christian virginity, a corollary of Christian "self-emptying," is a datum of revelation; that is, it is implicit as a potentiality in the sacrificing love which belongs to the ethic of grace. It tells us something about the ultimate meaning of marriage, something that is not given to us in or on the basis of natural law. The ethically new aspect of Christianity regarding marriage therefore lies, not in new "ethical" norms, but solely in the taking up of these natural ethical norms into theologal life within the visible sphere of the sacramental Church. The possibility and factual necessity of sacrifice implied in the realization of all natural ethical values and therefore in fulfillment of human life is transfigured in the life of grace into a redemptive sacrifice, in union with the Lord who died and is now glorified.

Moreover, in virginity for the sake of the coming kingdom, this loving sacrifice can be freely accepted as a life project. It is precisely on the basis of this theologal meaning that the Church can (under a certain aspect) grasp the real natural ethical significance of marriage more easily and can, living from her mystery of grace and her feeling for the

Christian's sonship of God, more easily pronounce upon the natural ethical norms of marriage than can even a sincere man whose only basis is his "natural" experience of life (although, as I have said, this is never purely natural). Obviously, these ecclesiastical pronouncements concerning natural ethical norms of marriage must also be internally justified by theology, otherwise there arises an unavoidable tension between the obedience of faith and the personal insight of conscience. But, on the other hand, ecclesiastical pronouncements do not depend (directly, at least) on this argumentation but upon the sense of faith of the Church concerning the reality of salvation, which intrinsically transcends natural law. When we say that the Church recognizes the content of natural law more easily by reason of her life of grace, this must be seen not so much in a point by point historical manner as in a dynamic way. In fact the ecclesiastical hierarchy judges not only on the grounds of the ecclesial life of grace, but also from a particular historical situation and the current state of its theology. And there can be elements here which hinder the recognition of new aspects, aspects which have perhaps already been positively evaluated by non-Christians. This indicates that even the presentations of the pastoral teaching office of the Church are partly dependent on the strong natural experience of value, present or absent as the case may be.

In concrete Christian morality there are therefore aspects which, though already elucidated by the Church, could in any case be reasonably justified by us in principle (in conjunction with a natural awareness of values) and must be so justified, if faith is to be incorporated in our personal lives in a human manner. And on the other hand, there are aspects which exclusively derive from and depend upon our divine sonship, and therefore belong completely to the sector of mystery. Consequently these can be approached only in faith, and the theological justification that can be given for them is

ultimately no more than a supporting argument. Furthermore, these two aspects are not to be distinguished as two
categories lying side by side: the mystery of grace flows
throughout the whole of our human existence, so that the
very last foothold for our conviction concerning particular
ethical values is always the life of grace, faith, and thus ultimately the ecclesiastical teaching authority. In our trust in the
power of grace, which is to say, in the power of God's personal
love which transfigures our human powers, we know in addition that what he asks of us in love is never impossible. Thanks
to grace, which makes us free, we are capable of obedience
to that to which we are bound. Thus, for me, ecclesiastical
pronouncements concerning natural ethical norms (e.g. that
the essence of marriage or of the project of marriage does not
admit deliberate exclusion of children) are clearly an invitation from God to accept with believing obedience this requirement of life which will give me freedom and happiness.
And at the same time they are an invitation to me to form
my own conscience and thus to interiorize this norm in a
personally reasoned experience of value. Under the insistence
of the inward attraction of grace the Christian conscience
searches for the expression of something it has not itself been
able to see, but whose explicit content the Church formu-
lates. It may result in the poorest achievements, but the believer nevertheless wishes in all sincerity to grow towards the
concrete form of God's holy and sanctifying will. The growth
of this sincere basic intention is the growth, through weakness and repentance, to holiness.

Because of the concrete existential unity of "nature" and
"supernature," and because of the fact that we are, in a natural way, already discovering the so-called absolute norms as
the hidden face of a personal God, we can now understand
from the revelation of God in Christ that the concrete ethical
norm of human fulfillment of life is the man of grace and
love, Christ Jesus. In his historical, human form the man

Jesus is not only the appearance amongst us of the unassailable holiness of the God to be loved, which addresses us with its absolute sovereign value; at the same time he is, in that same humanity, the absolute realization of moral and religious life, the totally adequate ethical response to the living God's absolute summons to holiness. In Jesus the absolute ethical norm is realized in the most sublime freedom. His life portrays what our moral life ought to be. And at the same time this very person is the power on which we draw in order to remain loyal to the ideal of moral and religious perfection. In this way the living person of Christ is—as Holy Scripture shows him in his role of obedient servant and in the consecration of his obedient love, his glorification—both ethical norm for us and the mirror of every moral, religious realization. And finally, a force: for he not only shows us how we must act, he also brings it about, in and through us, by the grace of his Spirit: "We are enlightened from without by the law as to what God urges us to do through the inward stirring of his grace."[7] Conversely: in order that we might be able to realize the ethic of grace presented by the gospel and by the Church and the natural law implied therein, Christ gave his life in sacrifice. Through the victorious grace of this loving sacrifice we are able to keep the "commandments and prohibitions." "He who loves me, keeps my commandments." Love ready to make sacrifices is the secret of morality.

THE DEBATE CONCERNING SITUATION ETHICS

Global Definition

"Situation ethics" is a philosophical and theological conception of the moral law, in which the basic element appears as the notion that the content of what is morally good or bad

---

[7] *ST* II–II, q. 44, a. 8, s. c.: see also I–II, q. 106, a. 1, ad 2.

is ultimately not determined by general abstract norms—
which might hold without exception for all human beings—
but solely by the actual situation with which one is confronted in an existential context. The proponents of situation
ethics (the situationists, as we shall call them) are of the
opinion that since the situation, in all its aspects and its
existential totality, is unique to each human being, unre-
peatable, and therefore not susceptible to generalization, general norms have absolutely no normative value, or at least no
absolute normative value.

The central idea of these ethical and moral theological
currents in contemporary ethics is without doubt the notion
of the "situation." The difficulty is that situation ethics has
not yet defined clearly what is meant by this term, and that
not all situationists define a "situation" in the same way;
indeed, the idea even varies in its use by a single writer.
Nevertheless, it is possible to give a reasonably precise sketch
of certain characteristics of this situation concept that are
common to all its users. "Situation" says something concerning the intrinsically human mode of existence; it is an
anthropological concept that also defines the essence of man.
The situation is the concrete resultant of all spatio-temporal
factors in which the personal freedom of man is involved. It
refers to the corporeity of the human person and all that ís
involved therewith—being-in-the-world—but this is actually
different for each and every person. The freedom which man
is, is co-essentially a freedom situated in this world, so that
there is no such thing as "human nature *in vacuo*," but only
this personal freedom in *this* situation.

Several writers go further and make a distinction between
"elements of the situation" and "situational elements": the
former are susceptible of generalization (every human being
is in the world), the latter are completely unique, completely
individual and personal. Others distinguish between "objective" and "subjective" situations (or *situation donnée* and

situation vécue). The "given situation" is the totality of the elements of the situation insofar as they in fact influence my total "I." Insofar as this influence is consciously experienced, one speaks of a *situation vécue*.

Among other moments of the situation, mention is made of geophysical elements (variations of climate, season, day or night, etc.), bio-psychosomatic elements (sex, age, constitution, temperament, etc.), cultural elements (education, intelligence, religion, housing, etc.), social elements (family, race, people, nation, living environment, social class, etc.), historical elements (a man's personal past),[8] moral elements (sensitivity to moral values, strongly differentiated in purity, depth, intensity, and extension; the emotional or rational tone of moral awareness, etc.), saving-historical elements (under this heading some authors range the giving of grace, the condition of original sin, the fact of redemption, vocation and selection, the degree of infused theologal virtues, the relationship to the Church, to the local church community, to other religions, etc.).

All these elements of the situation are to a great extent identical (at least from a material viewpoint) with classical moral theology's "circumstances of the human act." But the actual point of view from which situation ethics considers them is formally different: it considers them as the foundation of *objective norm-giving*, and not merely as mitigating or aggravating influences upon the subjective observance of general and abstract objective norms. In the past it did in fact go unnoticed that such differences give rise, for example, to obligations proper to men and obligations proper to women. They establish an intrinsic and adapted rule of behaviour. Various characteristics of the situation are thus given: (1) Its "factuality." This is to say that a situation

8 See G. Gusdorf, *Traité de l'existence morale*, Paris 1949, pp. 9–10: "Horizon intérieur de chaque homme, style de vie qui exerce son influence sur les plus secrètes de nos certitudes immédiates."

unavoidably imposes itself upon every human being and is, moreover, not made by him, or at least not directly. Before a man can freely take a stand he is already influenced by his situation; he takes his stand in circumstances which he experiences as "already there." No man can act outside an "objective situation." (2) "Unicity." A situation holds only for one person, and only occurs once in the course of any one person's life. (3) "Mutability." This characteristic follows immediately from the second: a situation is subject to continual change; man has no "immutable nature" but a nature-in-historicity, which means that growth and change belong to his very essence. (4) The "ethical invitation and claim" proceeding from the situation. A situation is an appeal to the person, a value appeal, and, for believers, a loving call from God addressed to their freedom, which summons them to an attribution of meaning to their situation. In this way the situation itself is the objective ethical norm.

Situation ethics can be formulated more clearly against the background of this central concept of the situation. In contrast with the Sartrian ethical view (cf. the works of J.-P. Sartre, S. de Beauvoir, F. Jeanson), in which all objective norms seem to be denied as soon as freedom enters in, the non-atheistic situationists accept the validity of an objective norm. However, they deny the validity of abstract general norms for the concrete person; or if they go so far as to accept them, then there are certain exceptional situations in which a man cannot and may not take them into account. In exchange for these general norms they propose the situation as the only objective moral norm, which is thus concretely individual by definition. This concrete norm is experienced in personal confrontation with the situation, which means for the believer that it occurs through an immediate experiential contact with the situation as the form of grace-full confrontation with the living God. It follows from this, so they believe, that there are no immutable, absolute norms:

ethical norms are historically conditioned and alter with an evolving mankind. As far as their flexibility is concerned, moreover, they must not be seen so much as a "categorical imperative" or a "must" but rather as an invitation and appeal. For all these reasons moral norms cannot be presented from without by someone (whether or not in the name of the Church) as commands or prohibitions. The authentic moral norm must be discovered from within as a personal "victory" of the situated subject. It is the fruit of a deep, maturing experience of life.

It is therefore unfair to contend that situation ethics wishes to deny objective moral norm-giving and to reduce the whole of morality to a matter of arbitrary personal choice of conscience, as is contended in articles by overenthusiastic supporters or by staunch adversaries of situation ethics. On the contrary, the chief concern of situation ethics is precisely with the objective norm of morality. It is not directly interested in personal conscience as such, which is considered as the ultimate subjective norm of morality in traditional morals. For situation ethics, just as for traditional morals, a human act is good or bad according to whether it conforms to or deviates from the objective norms of morality. That which is "new" and "proper to" the so-called "New Morality" lies in its interpretation of the essence of objective norms of morality. Certainly, in its most extreme, atheistic form, situation ethics recognizes only conscience as the norm of morality (a morality without norms), but in general non-atheistic situation ethics it is formally a question of that to which the judgment of conscience has to conform—namely, an objective norm. Conscience itself is regulated by a norm, and it is that norm which one wishes to trace. According to the situationists the normative value of each personal judgment is to be found in concrete reality. Thus the situation ethics of believers tries to apprehend exactly what God's will is for me here and now: "It is in our conscience that God invites us to take a moral decision concerning that appeal of his which is found objectively formulated in the situation."[9]

The "newness" of situation ethics lies in the fact that it does not see the objective norm of conscience in abstract norms which hold in the same way for all men, but in concrete norms, namely the concrete situation, in which one is involved in an *einmalige* manner. For the person in question this is the objective norm according to which he must regulate his behaviour, and this situation is for him the revelation of God's will insofar as it concerns him. The "morality of abstract norms" is charged by the situation ethic of believers with a distortion of the moral sense, with hypocrisy, rigidity, scrupulosity and laxity, and finally with rash judgment regarding fellow human beings. All sorts of historical causes have combined in bringing about the rise of situation ethics, but it is above all a critique of a purely conceptualistic view of human thought. It is from this that it borrows its core of truth, which often deteriorates into a declaration of the invalidity of all conceptual moments in human knowledge. But in doing this it falls into relativism.

The Three Directions in Situation Ethics

At the moment situation ethics is more of an empirical tendency which is seeking to formulate itself than a systematically worked-out theory. Even to divide it into some of its main directions is already to resort to bold simplification. As is often the case in a period of cultural change, it is more a matter of a diffuse mental atmosphere (which here and there achieves systematic expression) than of a clearly formulated system. The developing system is much more a schema-

---

[9] "C'est dans la conscience que Dieu nous invite à prendre une décision morale concernant l'appel de Dieu qui se trouve *formulé objectivement* dans la *situation*"; J. Fuchs, "Morale théologique et moral de situation," *NRT* 86 (1954), 1085.

tic, as yet vague, reflection on what human beings with all kinds of views about life do in fact reveal in their ethical attitude to life: "Here laws can bring no solution, each person's conscience must judge for itself"—as one so often hears said in daily life. One finds here the expression of some sort of situation ethic. "Situation ethic" is furthermore a term capable of embracing widely varying contents. What is more, writers whose thought leads them in the direction of situation ethics come from various ideological positions.

Even so, it is possible to recognize some three currents in situation ethics: French existentialism; the situationism of Protestantism (mainly German); and, finally, the moderate situationism of some Catholic theologians. Extreme situationism is, as we have said, orientated in a fundamentally different way according to whether an agnostic or atheistic view of life is involved (e.g., the atheistic existentialism of Sartre, Simone de Beauvoir, Jeanson) or a theistic, religious view (especially Geisebach, Brunner and Thielicke, but the view of G. Gusdorf and the "existentialism" of Karl Jaspers and Gabriel Marcel can be placed within the same trend). We may describe these "three directions" in more detail by mentioning some of their fundamental characteristics.

The Atheistic and Theistic "Existentialist Directions." The atheistic form of situation ethics proceeds from the basic affirmation of man's total, unbounded freedom. The only moral obligation is the development of one's freedom: the freedom with which I realize myself is the only moral criterion of a human act. Certainly, this freedom is necessarily situated, but the only important thing is that man should freely engage himself in every situation. This freedom is the only real value. It is not *what* I do that is ethically relevant, but the intensity of the freedom with which I do it. Sartre speaks in this sense of "une morale de l'authenticité." Norms for moral life come neither from God (who does not exist), nor from so-called "human nature," for man is not a nature but a freedom; that is, an indetermination which is required to determine itself in freely choosing a position; every man is to find and determine his own norms.

Theistic existentialism reasons to a considerable extent on the basis of the same anthropological insights but with the difference that man, who is freedom—that is to say, a capacity for determining himself—must achieve this self-determination in the light of objective values insofar as his conscience can appreciate them. Morality is therefore a question of faithfulness to reality, which can only be approached by concrete existential contact and not through abstract ideas. Nor can any invitation at all proceed from abstract norms; an invitation comes from reality itself, and in this connection man is not just passively receptive but a giver of meaning and establisher of value.[10]

Protestant Situation Ethics. This direction is naturally religious. Man stands in a situation which must be evaluated as a summons from God. But he must decipher God's will in this situation. General norms may perhaps be useful, but they do not excuse man from a personal decision of conscience. No law, no authority, no Church, can reveal to my conscience what in this situation is God's will for me. This judgment of conscience is regulated by nothing more than the "situation-as-revelation-of-God's-will," and this personal revelation can now and again clash with what are termed the "general abstract norms" of natural law or positive divine law.

This direction coincides with the previous direction in this,

[10] Relevant literature besides the work of J.-P. Sartre: S. de Beauvoir, *The Ethics of Ambiguity,* New York 1962; F. Jeanson, *Le problème morale et la pensée de Sartre,* Paris 1947; from the theistic viewpoint: G. Gusdorf, *Traité de l'existence morale,* Paris 1949; L. Jaspers, *Der Begriff der menschlichen Situation in der Existenzphilosophie von Karl Jaspers,* Würzburg 1936; F. Peccorini Letona, *Gabriel Marcel y la ética de la situación,* in *Crisis* 5 (1958), 165–189; R. Troisfontaines, *De l'existence à l'être,* Namen 1953.

that there are no general abstract norms. As such it belongs to "extreme situationism."[11]

The Moderate Situationism of Some Catholic Writers. Some Catholic writers have attempted to integrate the core of truth enclosed in situation ethics into Catholic morals, but few attempts have reached the stage of synthesis. One can point out Steinbückel and Schüler, and the occasional studies of J. Fuchs, K. Rahner and G. De Brie.

Their work is characterized by adhesion to a "general human nature" and to a "generally valid natural law" founded thereon. Yet the "general essence" of humanity and each man's concrete individuality permeate one another completely. There can be no contradiction between the two. The so-called natural law rests upon the essence of humanity, with its orientation to value; the concrete, original realization of natural law rests upon individuality. By virtue of his "human nature" every man, in whatever situation, is bound to the natural law. There is no situation imaginable in which man may act against the negative norms (prohibitions) of natural law: these hold in an absolute manner. The case is different with respect to the positive norms (or commands). The plurality of values makes it impossible for us to live up to all positive prescriptions at every moment of our life. In its positive commands natural law requires only that we should not in principle deny certain values. One cannot, for example, exercise punitive justice and forgivingness at the same time, but ethics asks us to throw overboard in principle

11 Relevant literature: E. Brunner, *Das Gebot und die Ordnungen. Entwurf einer protestantisch-theologischen Ethik,* Tübingen 1932; F. Gogarten, *Politische Ethik,* Jena 1936; E. Grisebach, *Gegenwart. Eine kritische Ethik,* Halle 1928; H. Thielicke, *Theologische Ethik,* 1, Tübingen 1951; H. van Oyen, *Christelijke Ethika,* The Hague 1946, and *Evangelische Ethik* 1, Basel 1952; G. Brillenburg-Wurth, *Christelijke zedeleer,* Groningen 1954; L. de Jong, *Karl Barth als ethicus,* in *NTT* 7 (1952–53), 19–43; F. Ebert, *Das christliche Ethos,* Tübingen 1949.

neither justice nor mercy. Which of the many, simultaneously unrealizable values one should choose, and how one should realize it, are matters which depend upon each individual's personal judgment of conscience in his particular situation. In this domain no general, abstract norms hold.

Thus this situationism attempts to safeguard the absolute validity of general norms and to make a plea for the situational moments of our existence for which there can be no absolute norms. Thus God makes his will known in a two-fold manner: by way of general orientations, through his laws —natural law and saving revelation, these being entrusted to the ecclesiastical teaching authority for interpretation, and, since these general orientations will not always suffice, through the inward action of grace. This inward grace is directed towards the interpretation of the concrete situations of life which constitute an appeal to man.[12]

Causes of These Tendencies

A number of causes have been at work in bringing about the rise of situation ethics. Here we should like to mention some of those which are more clearly distinguishable.

In the first place one can point to present-day conditions of life. In our time it is more difficult than ever before to know what one ought to do. The enormous complexity and obscurity of economic and commercial life; the continually increasing psychological differentiation of people; the lurking

[12] Relevant literature: Th. Steinbückel, *Existentialismus und christliches Ethos*, Heidelberg 1948; *Christliche Lebenshaltungen in der Krisis der Zeit und des Menschen*, Frankfurt a. M. 1949; *Die Philosophische Grundlegung der katholischen Sittenlehre*, Düsseldorf 1951[4], and *Religion und Moral im Lichte christlicher personaler Existenz*, Frankfurt a. M. 1951; E. Michel, *Der Partner Gottes*, Heidelberg 1946; M. Reding, *Die philosophische Grundlegung der katholischen Moraltheologie*, Munich 1953; F. Tilmann, *Handbuch der katholischen Sittenlehre* 4, Düsseldorf 1951; A. Schüler, *Verantwortung. Vom Sein und Ethos der Person*, Krailling b. M. 1948; see also: "Crise de la Morale," in special issue of *LV* n. 8 (February 1953).

threat to physical existence from war, hunger and economic catastrophe; the constant possibility of radical interference by the state, by economic powers and political parties in the private life of completely obscure individuals; overpopulation; the housing shortage; the severing of established ties; man's loneliness and lack of restraint; the ease with which any imaginable view can be supported and propagated without hindrance: all this has influenced the rise of situation ethics. In former times moral norms were concretely embodied in the life of a society. The individual person was therefore to a great extent excused from having to discover what he ought to do. Problems that earlier were only extreme exceptions are currently almost "normal."[13] In other words, the current awareness of historicity and relativity carried to an extreme in human attitudes lies without doubt at the origin of situation ethics.

Besides this, one may also ask whether a growing immorality and moral indifference have had an effect. Karl Rahner is of the opinion that situation ethics is a form of laxism, a most refined form of half-heartedness, an ingenious attempt to escape obligation imposed by "the law." This may be true in cases of the abuse of situation ethics, but it cannot be considered as situation ethics' origin.

W. Dirks has reacted fiercely against Rahner's manner of finding only, or mainly, laxity and immorality in situationism.[14] It may be true that many take refuge in situation ethics out of laxity, but the authentic situationists (and here Dirks cites T. Steinbückel, Martin Buber, F. Ebner) are inspired by a serious desire to discern God's will here and now and not to be content with the "fulfillment of a law": God may ask more than a general norm requires. Situation-

13 See K. Rahner, *Gefahren im heutigen Katholizismus*, Einsiedeln 1950, Ch. II, I, 1ff.

14 W. Dirks, "Wie erkenne ich was Gott von mir will?" in *Frankfurter Hefte* (April 1951), 229–244; French translation in *VS* (Supplement), 1951, 243–270.

ism is not an invitation to laxity, but a call to a more
generous, non-formalistic living effort. That is why this
tendency is more correctly seen as an authentic moral reaction against disguised forms of legalism and formalism,
pharisaism and exaggerated casuistry.

The Protestant conception of original sin is also connected with the origin of situation ethics. According to this
view, human nature is, through its intrinsically wounded
condition, incapable of acquiring any insight at all into God's
will concerning good and evil. God alone can inform us of
his will by illuminating our conscience through grace. The
Holy Spirit informs the believer of God's will in every
situation. When this view is combined with existential philosophy, the step to a situation ethic is bound to be taken.

Existential philosophy may well be considered the main
cause of situation ethics. Where there is freedom—and man
is that—there can be no talk of a "nature" or general essence
from which one might deduce in advance which human acts
are good and which bad. Man must constantly give himself
determination. For existentialism the impersonal, universal
human being is not the source of values; actual people design
themselves, create their own values on the basis of given
situations.[15] Furthermore, this existentialism is in harmony
with the repugnance with which purely conceptualist thought .
is generally regarded nowadays.

Finally, one can point to Marxism. Although, by reason of
its distorted conception of human freedom, one can hardly
classify this system as a situation ethic, it has nevertheless
promoted awareness of the relativity of abstract universal
norms and can to this degree be considered as a cause of
situation ethics. Even before existentialism, the concept of
"situation" was studied by Marxism. Marx denies that certain
situations should of themselves prevail completely over others;
the needs and wants of a people, the rebellion of a class,

15 S. de Beauvoir, *Ethics of Ambiguity.*

define ends and means. Within a rejected situation a new value will appear, one for which man will make every effort. That which serves this design is good, that which goes against it bad, says Marx. Thus we may, with Simone de Beauvoir,[16] situate Marxism at the cradle of situation ethics.

The Reaction of the Church Authorities to Situation Ethics

There are various papal documents concerning situation ethics.[17] In particular, the instruction of the Holy Office sees in it an ethical system which aims to free itself from "the principles of objective ethics." According to this system it is not the objective order, but the personal judgment of conscience in confrontation with the situation, that will make known what is here and now good or bad. In situation ethics, says the instruction, the final decision of conscience is not the application of an objective general law to a particular case: such a judgment arises exclusively from an "immediate light." The proponents of situation ethics assess the traditional concept of "human nature" as insufficient, they want to return to concrete humanity here and now. This humanity, and thus also the natural law based upon it, they consider changeable. In much of what situation ethics (as supported by Catholics) proposes, the decree sees traces of relativism and modernism. It also calls it "the new morality."

Obviously the fact that situation ethics excludes intervention by an authority, namely the Church, in the upholding

16 *Ibid.*
17 See: the address of Pius XII to the Fedération mondiale des jeunesses féminines catholiques of January 18, 1952, in *AAS* 34 (1952), 413–419; radio discourse of Pius XII on the Christian conscience, March 23, 1952, in *AAS* 34 (1952), 270–278; address of Pius XII to the Fifth International Congress for Psychotherapy and Psychology, on November 13, 1953, in *AAS* 45 (1953), 278–286; Instruction of the Congregation of the Holy Office regarding Situation Ethics, in *AAS* 48 (1956), 114–154.

of moral norms played a part in this Roman reaction; cf., for example, Pius XII's address of March 23, 1952.[18] In his address to the Fédération mondiale des jeunesses féminines catholiques of April 18, 1952, the same pope speaks about "what situation ethics contains by way of correct and positive insights," but adds that we can already discover this good aspect in Thomas's doctrine on Christian prudence, which, however, avoids confusions and deviations.[19]

BROADER PERSPECTIVES

Abstract General Norms and the Concrete Requirements of Reality

From the preceding exposition it will have become evident that one must refrain from labelling situation ethics as a form of laxity and arbitrariness which takes no account of objective norms. Moreover, the Catholic must also be aware of the establishment of value by man himself. Of course, man himself is not the norm. On the other hand, he nevertheless freely chooses his norms, though this is because he sees that they offer themselves to him autonomously as absolute. This means that the insight of my own conscience does not define by its own power the goodness or evil of my concrete act, but that it does so by virtue of objective reality itself, insofar as I am able to appreciate it as such or to accept it in faith. Even in situation ethics there exists a concern to have subjective morality coincide with the objective requirements of reality.

On the other hand, it is clear that the Church must oppose propositions which might propagate relativism. In a relativistic world-view the foundation of Christian faith is radically undermined. Inasmuch as situation ethics denies any value at all to ideational knowledge as an element in the totality of

[18] *AAS* 34 (1952), 270–278.
[19] *AAS* 34 (1952), 413–419.

human knowledge, the Church is rightly opposed to it, because thereby the very meaning of every definition of faith is emptied of content. That these dangers are inherent in extreme situationism is clear.

Nevertheless, in this connection the Church not only has the negative task of closing off paths which obviously lead to error, she must also know how to provide the positive perspective in which the Christian conscience must judge.

With situation ethics the Church sees itself placed before a problem to which not even progressive Catholic theologians have been able to give an adequate solution. In spite of the immense quantity of literature available on the subject, many reject it without distinctions. Only a few Catholic writers have attempted to integrate the core of truth in situationism into Christian ethics, and these attempts have not been uniformly successful.[20] These writers, among whom G. De Brie attains the clearest formulations, all agree that abstract concrete norms are valid in general, but that they do not suffice for a decision on the concrete goodness or evil of human acts, because of "strictly situational" elements which cannot be covered by abstract norms.

The hidden danger in this solution lies in the acceptance of a certain "duality" in ethical norms: the abstract and the concrete. Hence the fundamental problem which confronts both situation ethics and traditional morals is of an episte-

---

20 See J. Fuchs, *Ethique objective et éthique de situation*, in *NRT* 78 (1956), 798–818; *Situationsethik in theologischer Sicht*; in *Schol.* 27 (1952), 161–182; *Situation und Entscheidung*, Frankfurt a. M. 1952, *Morale théologique et morale de situation*, in *NRT* 76 (1954) 1073–1085; K. Rahner, *Christendom en Kerk in onze tijd*, Bruges 1955, pp. 83–106; *Der Einzelne in der Kirche*, in *Schriften zur Theologie* 2, Einsiedeln 1960⁴, pp. 95–114; *Ueber die Frage einer formalen Existentialethik*, ibid., pp. 227–246; *Das Dynamische der Kirche*, Freiburg i. Br. 1958; G. De Brie, *Situationele momenten in een normenethiek*, in *TP* 23 (1961), 3–77; *De bijbelse radicalisering van de Wet*, in *TT* 3 (1963), 139–166, and *De integratie van de positieve wet in de zedlijke en religieuze beleving*, in *TGL* 18 (1962), 689–706; 19 (1963), 5–21 and 171–201.

mological nature: Do our abstract ideas have reality-grasping value in and of themselves, or do they borrow this value from non-ideational contact with the concrete reality to which ideas objectively refer? In the first case there is a certain duality of ethical norms which makes unification difficult and can make moral life "ambiguous." In the second there is only one objective giver of norms, concrete reality itself, which is suggested in an inadequate way by abstract ideas. An abstract idea such as—for example, "human nature" or "humanity" —has in and of itself no value as reality. For humanity is not a part of the real individual human being beside another part which might constitute his individuality; his individuality intrinsically defines his humanity and also differentiates this humanity from all concrete individuals: only when intrinsically individualized is humanity a reality, and only then can it be the source of moral norm-giving.

Thus abstract norms as such cannot be considered real. Nor, moreover, can any invitation proceed from them! Thus abstractness points to man's incapacity to bring reality to exhaustive expression. For in fact it appears in our knowledge only as an element in a more integral knowledge, in which that abstract ideational content acquires the value of an intrinsic reference through concretely existential, non-ideational contact with reality; concrete reality itself lies in the direction which is indicated by the conceptual contents. Abstract general norms are thus perhaps inadequate, but they are nevertheless the real reference to the concrete norm of reality. Thus the abstract norm does not exist of itself, yet in the whole of our appreciation of moral values it does have a real value in the expression of the concretely individual ethical norm, of objective reality itself. In this light, the views of Fuchs, Rahner and De Brie considered earlier must be revised, since one is otherwise forced to present a twofold norm: one norm proceeding from "human nature" as such, and then "strictly situational norms." Considering the current unrest in this domain, I should like in a final point to investigate in more detail the gap, which is experienced especially vividly today, between general norms and concrete reality.

The Current Gap Between Abstract General Norms and the "Opaque" Situations of Life

The problem posed by situation ethics exists in a very concrete way for believers themselves. With many there is at present a certain short-circuiting: from the observable fact that an enormous distance has arisen between human situations and the "objective norms" presented, they conclude that these objective, abstract general norms are untenable. Now I in no sense wish to deny that proposals have sometimes been presented to us from tradition as objective norms which do not in fact stand up to closer investigation. Fresh situations can bring new nuances into the old formulations of norms themselves. Indeed, in many a case it will appear that what was presented as a generally valid norm was in fact no ethical norm, but an "ethical imperative"—which is to say, a moral norm in which calculation was already made for a particular situation, so that the imperative held only "given that particular situation." Formerly, for example, it counted as a "norm" that lending with interest was unjust, and thus sin, because in doing so one appropriates something to which one has no right whatsoever. In actual fact this was not a norm or generally valid ethical requirement but a concrete ethical imperative, held on the grounds of the mediaeval view of monetary value. The generally valid norm: No one may prejudice the rights of another; thus no one may appropriate anything which, all things considered, is not his due (in other words, the demand for recognition of the value of the human person, including his corporeity), became, by virtue of the function of money in the mediaeval economy, the following concrete imperative: You may not demand any interest on a loan. When, on the other hand, money acquired a completely different meaning, as happened after the Middle Ages, then the same objective norm (the distinction between mine and thine) allows lending with interest, because in a modern monetary system the interest is definitely mine.

Often the Church sees the change in situation too late. Hence it continued to maintain the prohibition of "loans with interest" at a time when the change in situation had already long since taken place; in other words, what was in fact an ethical imperative was misused by being presented as a universally valid principle. This, also, causes short-circuiting because, in contrast with absolute norms, ethical imperatives change with changes in situation, and must change if one is to indeed honour the actual norm, which must be safeguarded in all circumstances. In other words: one must concretely realize, here and now, the general duty to live in a humanly worthy manner.

Furthermore, it is not abstract presentations as such, but the concrete inviolability of the fundamental values of the human person, that are the binding norms of moral action. The so-called objective norms are demands of reality; the abstract general norms themselves are only abstract general expressions of this reality, inadequate formulations of the ethical esteem for that which is inviolable in the concrete human person. The norm is not an abstraction, but the concrete personal value itself; that is, this person here and now who must be approached in justice and love. This reality is concretely, existentially determined, and thus escapes our abstract knowledge. But that abstract knowledge is the expression of an experience and inwardly refers, as such, to the concretely determined reality itself. Within the whole of human knowledge, consisting of experience and experience-grasped-in-concepts, the abstractly known content certainly refers objectively to the actual concrete reality that provides me with moral norms. Thus the abstract general norm refers to the ethical regulation of our freedom by concrete reality itself, which in its individual richness escapes the general norm. The abstract norm can therefore only vaguely and generally indicate the content of the one concrete, morally demanding reality and nothing more. Hence I can never read from an abstract norm what I must do here and now, even though these norms give the objective direction in which I must act, for I shall otherwise go against reality and its concrete demands.

There is thus no double moral norm-giving, one by abstract general norms and one by concrete reality, the "situation." There is only moral norm-giving by concrete reality, which is what it is independently of our knowledge and desire; for we are not creators of reality. Nor, equally, can we reproduce this one concretely demanding reality expressly and concretely; all expressed knowledge of concrete reality is achieved conceptually, in ideas which are general by virtue of their abstraction. "Thou shalt not steal" is therefore only a conceptual content which inwardly refers to the inviolability of this person whom I here and now encounter. In other words, the abstract general norm is only of force insofar as it gives an objective perspective of that concretely existential reality which is the actual source of moral norms.

However situations vary, in each one I have to respect the inviolability of the person of my fellow man and of myself: this is what the so-called abstract general norms express. To keep to the same example: in constantly new situations the meaning of "mine" and "thine" will have to be continually sought anew. What earlier generations considered "mine" later generations will possibly, and rightly, consider "yours" (for instance, heavier or lighter fiscal duties). Objective norms have thus a twofold meaning: the actual objective norm is reality itself; the abstract general norms are only called objective by way of reference: they refer explicitly to very general directives of the moral evaluation of fundamental values of human life, without which that life would become absurd, and which one is thus bound in conscience to respect if one wishes to take man seriously. The perspective indicated therein is universally valid because, even if in an abstract and thus general way, it does point to the absolute inviolability of concrete reality itself. But, precisely on account of their abstraction, these general norms or perspectives do not tell us exactly how we must act in this perspective here and now. There is thus a continual gap between the general norm and concrete reality; this limitation is the signature of our human knowledge and of our human moral feeling. The personal judgment of conscience will have to bridge this distance by taking concrete situations into account, thus arriving at a concrete ethical imperative.

Thus, as far as the general structure of our moral action is concerned, there is no difference between former times and today. And yet it is precisely here that the short-circuit is made. Differences are seen between the so-called old morality and "the new morality" where they do not in fact exist, and then, on grounds of the constantly increasing distance between "general norms" and "concrete reality," the norms are cast into doubt. However, there has always been this distance. Personal conscience and responsibility have always had to "fill" that gap. One can never read the ethical goodness or evil of a concrete act solely from general norms. This is not the difference between these and former times. The difference lies in the fundamental alteration of the situations themselves.

In the past the situation of life was a much more transparent datum. To continue the same example: in a primitive, agrarian culture a farmer's fields and pastures were clearly separated from those of his neighbour. The farmer was able to deduce practical consequences from the norm "Thou shalt not steal": for instance, he must not secretly pilot his cow into his neighbour's pasture! The personal judgment of conscience was thus never, or almost never, complicated. But what does "Thou shalt not steal" mean for a manager of a very complex, modern financial organization? What does it mean today for the farmer, now that the price of his agricultural product is determined by a combination of a number of factors, including the political and others which are foreign to his own occupation? Technicalization has rendered situations so "opaque"—that is, has so obscured the grounds on which a moral determination can be made—that personal judgments of conscience and the fixing of responsibility acquire ipso facto a far greater creative significance. The abstract general norm "Thou shalt not steal" preserves its full force as an abstract, inadequate expression of human value in interpersonal relations, but this norm tells me nothing about the particular complex situations themselves! Formerly these situations were so simple, "natural" and transparent that the norm almost coincided with the concrete ethical imperative. What then escaped, by virtue of its concreteness (the concrete situation), from the "abstract norm" was in practice so minimal that no creativeness of conscience was needed: when one knew the norm, the concrete decision of conscience was at the same time fairly evident. In the majority of cases, therefore, Christians could simply rely on what was presented to them as norm.

Things have now completely changed all along the line. Each and every situation has become so culturally complicated that we hardly know what to make of it. The humanly produced structures of our lives are essentially more complex than the former "natural situations" of rural life. In the earlier plan of things it was, for instance, more or less predetermined how children ought to fulfil the command "Honour your father and your mother." The model of family life was so simple, clear and "patterned" beforehand, that the decision of conscience became a cliché and could not (and did not need to) be anything else. The modern situation makes the distance between such an evident norm and concrete family life inconceivably great: parents and children just do not know what to do.

Is the norm therefore outdated? Such a conclusion would display the short-circuit we have mentioned. In fact nothing has happened except this: the situation has become so complicated and obscure that to bridge the gap between abstract norm and concrete reality a much greater inventive capacity and creativity is demanded of our personal responsibility and our own conscience. But it is still within the perspective of the general norm! This call for greater creativity continues to suppose the norm, but the latter, by virtue of the increasing complexity of life, becomes, as it were, still more abstract, seeming to tell us almost nothing. And yet it is precisely this norm that gives the direction in which one must inventively determine the concrete modalities of one's behavior. Through this, personal conscience takes on a much greater burden than in former times; but the moral, religious personality can only gain in depth and richness thereby.

Because of the complexity of the situations in which it has to take up a position, personal conscience needs not only the presentation of moral norms, but also that all these new situations of life should be made clear sociologically, psychologically, and technically. Only thus can new, typological "ethical imperatives" be gradually designed for our time.

Although I cannot develop all this more fully here, it may be noticed how the reaction of some people against "objective norms" is the consequence of an illusion of perspective. These people play the concrete, complicated situation off against the norms, whereas there has in fact always been a distance between the appreciation of concrete reality and the abstract norm, within which space personal conscience has its own inalienable task to fulfill, alone with God. Through the complex structure of modern life, this distance has at present become unsurveyable and maximal; and this is precisely the source of current uncertainty in the ethical sphere, an uncertainty that some unjustly wish to play off against the objective norms. Others, on the contrary, complain that the Church offers no concrete norms. This would seem to mean that they expect the Church to dictate to us our own judgments of conscience—but that is utterly impossible! Thus an objectively frightening domain is freed for the creative conscience: with the norms before us, we have still to begin all the creative work, whereas formerly the labour of personal conscience was practically complete as soon as the norms were given! Subjectively, this also means that personal, creative responsibility must be united with a greater trust in God. Otherwise creativity of conscience leads to anxiety about life, to ethical bewilderment and lethargic insecurity.

Finally, we can say that precisely on account of the increasing distance between the abstract general, material norms and modern, complexly structured society (which, after all, does help determine *my* situation), the importance of objective norms has grown. They do give the direction in which one must push one's search, even though one will have to find the way—one of the many possible ways within the one direction indicated—more creatively with one's own conscience; more creatively than formerly, in any case, because formerly there was usually only one way open within the given norms, while now the same norms leave open a multitude of possibilities. And yet one particular way among the many possibilities might be the only way to bring mankind today to an authentically higher human dignity. Thus the exact choice among the many possibilities is not ethically indifferent or unimportant, but it cannot be defined from the abstract norms themselves. A subjectively justified decision can, when the obscurity of the situation has been clarified, nevertheless appear to the forum of history as having been mistaken. In most cases today, within the direction given by the (abstract) norm, the choice becomes an *ethically creative enterprise.*

Therefore it seems to me that the contention of some people that priests should henceforth remain silent in their preaching as regards "objective norms" is simply indefensible. These norms must be preached because they are the signposts which point out the content of love. They protect the word "love" from becoming a cloak for all sorts of license: they point to the direction in which love must go here and now, if it wishes to remain worthy of being called true, disinterested love. Even when people who act in a subjectively just way fall short with regard to (authentically) objective norms, this is no unimportant or indifferent event (even though their personal salvation is not thereby brought into danger). For suppose (and here I am not making any pronouncement) that the use of nuclear weapons is morally reprehensible, then the fact that someone upholds their use in good faith is, as we say, "subjectively in order," but it is no light matter as far as humanity is concerned! Here is a case in which the chaos-creating significance of an act that is only materially sinful is without doubt obvious, but this holds in essence for every infringement of objective norms. For the latter only express in an abstract manner what are the fundamental values of life for man, without which human life would become absurd and could not be lived in a way worthy of human beings. In centuries past, when the value of social justice had not yet been recognized, people might well have lived in good faith in their injustice. But was this material encroachment upon the "objective norms" therefore less depersonalizing for the workers? Did not humanity suffer under this materially sinful, objective inhumanity? One who studies history from this point of view must come to the bewildering conclusion that humanity has suffered unspeakably under really "subjectively good" actions and that therefore "subjectively good morality" cannot be the final word!

In the light of all this, we must in our present situation lay special emphasis upon the importance of objective norms, as also upon the necessity of a creative conscience and personal responsibility. Any one-sidedness in this matter has its repercussions on authentic human values and, at the same time, on the authenticity of our Christian answer to the present-day grace of the Lord, Jesus Christ. Also in their search for new objective norms—i.e., in the continual recovery of what authentic human dignity involves—Christians ought in the first place to go forth creatively, and not just hesitantly or as imitators.

Table of Original Publications

Index

306